INTERNATIONAL
A BELIEF SYS

International Law as a Belief System considers how we construct international legal discourse and the self-referentiality at the centre of all legal arguments about international law. It explores how the fundamental doctrines (e.g. sources, responsibility, statehood, personality, interpretation, *jus cogens*) constrain legal reasoning by inventing their own origin and dictating the nature of their functioning. In this innovative work, d'Aspremont argues that these processes constitute the mark of a belief system. This book invites international lawyers to temporarily suspend some of their understandings about the fundamental doctrines they adhere to in their professional activities. It aims to provide readers with new tools to reinvent the thinking about international law and combines theory and practice to offer insights that are valuable for both theorists and practitioners.

JEAN D'ASPREMONT is Professor of Public International Law at the University of Manchester, where he founded the Manchester International Law Centre (MILC). He is also Professor of International Law at Sciences Po Law School. He is General Editor of the Cambridge Studies in International and Comparative Law and Director of Oxford International Organisations (OXIO). He was awarded the James Crawford Prize for his work on the International Court of Justice.

CAMBRIDGE STUDIES IN INTERNATIONAL
AND COMPARATIVE LAW: 133

Established in 1946, this series produces high-quality, reflective
and innovative scholarship in the field of public international law.
It publishes works on international law that are of a theoretical, historical,
cross-disciplinary or doctrinal nature. The series also welcomes books
providing insights from private international law, comparative law and
transnational studies which inform international legal thought and
practice more generally.

The series seeks to publish views from diverse legal traditions and
perspectives, and of any geographical origin. In this respect, it invites
studies offering regional perspectives on core *problématiques* of
international law, and in the same vein, it appreciates contrasts and
debates between diverging approaches. Accordingly, books offering new
or less orthodox perspectives are very much welcome. Works of
a generalist character are greatly valued and the series is also open
to studies on specific areas, institutions or problems. Translations of
the most outstanding works published in other languages are also
considered.

After seventy years, *Cambridge Studies in International and Comparative
Law* remains the standard-setter for international legal scholarship and
will continue to define the discipline as it evolves in the years to come.

General Editors

Larissa van den Herik
Professor of Public International Law, Law School Leiden University
Jean d'Aspremont
Professor of Public International Law, University of Manchester and
Sciences Po Law School

A list of books in the series can be found at the end of this volume.

INTERNATIONAL LAW AS A BELIEF SYSTEM

JEAN D'ASPREMONT

University of Manchester
Sciences Po Paris

CAMBRIDGE
UNIVERSITY PRESS

CAMBRIDGE
UNIVERSITY PRESS

University Printing House, Cambridge CB2 8BS, United Kingdom

One Liberty Plaza, 20th Floor, New York, NY 10006, USA

477 Williamstown Road, Port Melbourne, VIC 3207, Australia

314-321, 3rd Floor, Plot 3, Splendor Forum, Jasola District Centre, New Delhi - 110025, India

79 Anson Road, #06-04/06, Singapore 079906

Cambridge University Press is part of the University of Cambridge.

It furthers the University's mission by disseminating knowledge in the pursuit of education, learning and research at the highest international levels of excellence.

www.cambridge.org
Information on this title: www.cambridge.org/9781108434393
DOI: 10.1017/9781108375542

First published 2018
First paperback edition 2018

A catalogue record for this publication is available from the British Library

Library of Congress Cataloging in Publication data
Names: Aspremont, Jean d', author.
Title: International law as a belief system / Jean d'Aspremont.
Description: Cambridge [UK] ; New York : Cambridge University Press, 2017. |
Series: Cambridge studies in international and comparative law ; volume
133 | Includes bibliographical references and index.
Identifiers: LCCN 2017026227 | ISBN 9781108421874 (hardback)
Subjects: LCSH: International law – Psychological aspects. | International
law – Social aspects. | International law – Philosophy. | BISAC: LAW /
International.
Classification: LCC KZ1249 .A87 2017 | DDC 341.01–dc23
LC record available at https://lccn.loc.gov/2017026227

ISBN 978-1-108-42187-4 Hardback
ISBN 978-1-108-43439-3 Paperback

CONTENTS

FOREWORD

A temporary suspension of the belief system known as international law – this is what Jean d'Aspremont calls for in this breathtaking work. Not a refutation or a rejection of these beliefs – that would not be actionable in any event – but an unlearning.

Prefatory to all this, of course, is a recognition that international law is, among other things, a belief system. We will bear down soon enough on Jean d'Aspremont's description of this belief system – what he finds key. But first, let's ask, what is implied in the claim that international law is a belief system at all?

One way of thinking about it is the notion that international law cannot be understood *merely* in terms of its canonical materials. One can stare at Article 38 for as long as one wants or even heed its words and collect as many legal materials as it may reference, and still one will not understand international law. Why not? The simple answer is that even though the assimilation of those materials may enable one to *perform adequately* within this system, one will not appreciate what *fundamental beliefs* make the system work (the relations that enable the legal arguments and interpretations) nor what demarcates the limits of the system (the questions and the claims disallowed).

But let's suppose one can perform adequately within the system as an international lawyer without awareness of the underlying belief system. Why undertake the inquiry proposed by Jean d'Aspremont? I can think of several answers, the most important being offered by Jean himself.

First, the international lawyer has an *instrumental interest* in performing not merely adequately, but well. In this regard, appreciating the web of beliefs that are not fully articulated in the legal materials becomes key. How so? If one does not understand how legal doctrines actually persuade, convince, coerce (and so on), one is left with the law's own stories about how it operates. These tend to be (not surprisingly for such a thoroughly rhetoricised practice) overly self-congratulatory. Law's stories about itself – how it works – in some ways not only inform but also

vii

cloud judgment. To perform well as a lawyer requires, in d'Aspremont's terms, a certain unlearning. One could question this point, of course. It's not clear, for instance, that becoming an art critic will make one a better artist. True enough. But in law, as opposed to art, it would be very surprising if becoming a critic did not make one a better lawyer. The reason might be captured this way: there is *what you say in court during* oral argument and there is *how you think in your office about* what you will say in court in oral argument. If those are one and the same, it will not be a very good oral argument. (At the very least, I would want a different lawyer.) Unlearning is necessary, as is the development of some language to talk about legal doctrine or legal dogmatics that is not itself a thinly veiled academic abstraction or idealisation of those doctrines and dogmatics.

Second, such an unlearning would seem to be an *ethical imperative* for a serious lawyer. How so? Well, in part, the instrumental interest translates into an ethical imperative. As part of a profession where the life and livelihood of other persons (clients, third parties and the community) hang in the balance, performing well becomes an ethical imperative. But there is yet a second ethical imperative – part of the idea of law is that it is and should be a deliberative and reflective enterprise – which means that, among many other things, its self-critical gesture will often be crucial. The contrary idea that law would abjure critical self-examination in favour of mere application or rote reproduction is arguably a failure of law. I say arguably because, of course, critical reflexivity has its own path dependence and pathologies, and besides, one cannot inquire into everything. Nonetheless, bringing to mind the fundamental questions – the beliefs that underpin the law – is itself very much an aspect of what it is to do law. A stark and recent reminder (at least in the United States) of this point was the Bush-era Bybee memorandum, which in its pro forma deployment of banal legal doctrine suitable for tariff regulations to the question of torture showed that law cannot be reduced (without self-injury) to a mere technical discipline.[1] If law is to respect the objects

---

[1] Memorandum from John C. Yoo, Deputy Assistant Attorney General, US Department of Justice Office of Legal Counsel, to Alberto R. Gonzales, Counsel to the President (August 1, 2002), in Karen J. Greenberg and Joshua L. Dratel (eds.), *The Torture Papers: The Road to Abu Ghraib* (Oxford University Press, 2005), p. 172. The Bybee memorandum was severely criticised by Bybee's successor at the Office of Legal Counsel (OLC), a prominent conservative academic legal thinker, for its lack of candor and one-sided selection of legal authority. Jack Goldsmith, *The Terror Presidency: Law and Judgment Inside the Bush Administration* (New York: W.W. Norton, 2007), p. 149. For an excellent discussion of the shortcomings of the memorandum, see David Luban, 'Carhart Memorial Lecture

of its regulative activity, then the identity of those objects (i.e. torture and its victims) must be recognised and, in turn, law must consider to what degree it is itself *à la hauteur*.[2] The Bybee memorandum in all its juridical banality was a shocking reminder of what failure on these scores actually means.

Beyond the instrumental and the ethical, there is an *intellectual interest in understanding* the belief system that underlies international law. In some sense this is much more the vocation of the law professor than the judge or the lawyer. The law professor has made a commitment to seek out understanding (and to impart understanding to his or her students). The refusal to inquire would seem like a betrayal of that calling – a violation of the teacher-student relation (which surely is both more and less than the client-lawyer or the judge-party relation).

Perhaps the most fundamental reason to undertake the inquiry lies in recognising that the paradigmatic sites of *political struggle in law* occurs in its shadows. As d'Aspremont makes clear, the unlearning he charts out for us is not only a descriptive endeavour but, as I would call it, a political one.

The decisive site of struggle where actors fight to determine the modes of legal reasoning of international legal discourse cannot be reduced to the arena where the repositories of fundamental doctrines are promulgated and adopted. Instead, the decisive sites of struggle become those where the modes of legal reasoning and the axiomisation thereof are actually debated and produced.

This is to say that the politics of law are never far from its articulate pronouncements even as their existence, identity and efficacy are nonetheless denied through our own beliefs about law.

So now let's talk about these beliefs underpinning international law as Jean d'Aspremont describes them. There are, he thinks, fundamental doctrines that pertain to international law topic-clusters, such as sources, responsibility, statehood, personality, interpretation and *jus cogens*. Recognisably, these fundamental doctrines play an extremely important role in international law. The question is, how is it that we think about these fundamental doctrines, and how is it that this way of thinking yield a sense of constraint and even systematicity such that the system of international law is reproduced in the minds, arguments, interpretations

Series "That the Laws Be Faithfully Executed": The Perils of the Government Legal Advisor' (2012) 38 *Ohio N. Univ. Law Rev.* 1043.
[2] Robert Cover, 'Violence and the Word' (1986) 95 *Yale Law J.* 160, 1619–21 (recounting the reasons for the release of the criminal defendant in the case of *United States* v. *Tiede*).

and actions of international lawyers? This is the crux of d'Aspremont's inquiry.

In Chapter 2 of this book, the answer, he argues, is that three specific features of international legal discourse is construed as forming a belief system: the idea that fundamental doctrines constitute rules (*ruleness*), the derivation of fundamental doctrines from international instruments (*imaginary genealogy*), and the explanation of the formation and functioning of fundamental doctrines by fundamental doctrines themselves (*self-referentiality*). It is by virtue of such ruleness, imaginary genealogy, and self-referentiality that fundamental doctrines come to invent their own origin as well as dictate their own functioning, thereby generating an experienced sense of constraint among international lawyers. This phenomenon is construed here as the expression of a belief system.

International lawyers thus repeatedly (and largely unknowingly) apprehend and cast fundamental doctrines in these terms. The beliefs, as d'Aspremont argues, are not without effect. *Ruleness* yields law as an object and thus achieves a certain degree of stabilisation, identity, fixity and endurance. The *imaginary genealogy* yields a fictive history, severing what we recognise as international law from its pluralistic and contingent origins. *Self-referentiality* imposes a certain closure and allows the reproduction of law as the self-same. The three combine to produce the sense of systematicity as well as constraint.

What if we, as lawyers, judges or law professors, did not look at international law in such ways? d'Aspremont suggests that we would recognise that international law has been created in much more politicised, pluralistic, planned and contingent ways than we presently imagine. Notice that the four adjectives in that preceding sentence are not clearly on friendly terms with each other. Indeed, they are not – and that is d'Aspremont's point: the ways in which international law is constructed – and thus its resulting identities and meanings – are much more eclectic than our law-like beliefs about international law allow us to recognise. Perhaps, then – and this is exactly d'Aspremont's invitation – we ought to step back and think again?

Pierre Schlag

PREFACE

If international law books come with prefaces, it is usually not by virtue of a demand from the potential readership but because authors relish speaking about themselves and the history of their work. Prefaces are even places commonly meant for authors of international law books to indulge in some well-engineered sentimentalism. This is not surprising. Having courageously fought their way to completion of a decent manuscript and having juggled academic writing with the pressure of a constantly accelerating profession, authors of international law books often finish their work with the feeling of being miserable heroes. In fact, I have regularly come to think that completing a book in the twenty-first century requires the skills of an armchair paratrooper who can intrepidly, dedicatedly and frenetically read, think and write in any moment clear of teaching, administration and management. And yet, whatever the heroic feat of completing a book under such conditions possibly is, it often remains unclear to any such hero what international law books actually contribute to in the distressingly burning world which such books seek to describe, evaluate or manage. If the story of authors of international law books is a story of miserable heroes, we can probably forgive them for the sentimentalism they manifest in their prefaces.

Whatever sentimentalism the rest of this preface may thus betray, this book does not grapple with the sentiments of international lawyers. Rather, it deals with their *beliefs*. It particularly develops the idea that international lawyers – whether as scholars, judges, counsels, militants or teachers – engage with the problems of the world through the deployment of a belief system. According to the heuristics built in this book, being an international lawyer entails the membership to a belief system. This belief system is manifest in the way in which fundamental doctrines – around which international legal discourse is built – operate in international legal thought and practice. Fundamental doctrines of international law, this book argues, create the conditions of their own existence, such self-referentiality guaranteeing a comfort space where international lawyers have to justify neither their fundamental doctrines nor their use thereof when they describe, evaluate or manage the world.

The claim that international law bears the characteristics of a belief system certainly does not amount to belittling international law. Quite the opposite. Belief systems are very serious matters, especially when they are used to describe, evaluate and manage the world. Although the heuristic exercise conducted in the following chapters falls short of any nihilism or utter scepticism, I am aware that my claim could raise the question of a possible rupture with my earlier work on sources, statehood and responsibility. I acknowledge that despite my long interest in unearthing the architecture and politics of international legal argumentation, much of my earlier work engaged with international legal arguments in their own terms and especially in terms of sources and interpretation. In contrast, the following chapters extend an invitation to all international lawyers to 'unlearn' their knowledge and sensibilities regarding the formation and functioning of the fundamental doctrines, which includes a radical break from international lawyers' common representations of their fundamental doctrines in terms of sources and interpretation.

Whether the discussion offered in this book possibly constitutes a discontinuation with my previous work is irrelevant. This is not only because I have always been amused by the descriptions of my earlier work as 'positivist(ic)', for I do not even know what positivism is other than being a convenient strawman in a confrontational and deliberative business. Mainly, questions of continuity or discontinuity are unimportant because I am convinced that consistency of thoughts is overrated in the discipline of international law. Actually, the obsession with consistency of thoughts is something which I have always found very bizarre in a discipline which considers itself intellectual. Thinking must entail a readiness to vandalise one's early thoughts. This does not mean that the suspension of the belief system advocated in this book repudiates anything I have done earlier – it should remain possible to research international legal argumentation from within the belief system. The point made here is rather that it is time to bring an end to the impoverishing social expectation that each international lawyer constantly and invariably abides by the same one-dimensional concept of international law.

The foregoing should suffice to indicate that this book is not meant to belong to (and vindicate) any 'tradition' or 'school' of legal thought. Whilst there is some didactic convenience of segmenting international legal thought in strands, this book turns a blind eye to such conventional subdivisions. This is why it unashamedly borrows from a wide variety of legal scholars, philosophers and social scientists without much interest in the theory or tradition with which they are associated and irrespective of the cross-commensurability of their respective arguments. Instead, I simply use the thoughts of these authors as conceptual tools to design my own thoughts, without seeking to import their respective theories in international legal thought. This purely instrumental approach inevitably transforms and deforms the thoughts of others. This will probably be held against me anyhow. I remain convinced, however, that innovative thinking comes at this price.

Thinking is an experiment. The experimentation that led to the claims developed in this book started a few years ago and benefitted from the decisive support and critical input of some key colleagues and friends. They ought to be mentioned here as they have generously and repeatedly allowed me to bounce half-baked ideas off them whilst also reading parts of the manuscript. In this respect I would like to express my immense gratitude to John Haskell, Akbar Rasulov, Sahib Singh, Justin Desautels-Stein, Geoff Gordon and Yannick Radi. Thanks to their continuous availability and interest, they have offered me a remarkable and permanent sounding board for my ideas throughout this project. I will always be indebted to them. The following chapters explicitly indicate when my exchanges with them have directly informed my reflection. I am hugely indebted to Pierre Schlag, who provided me with extensive feedback on several occasions and who spent hours with me discussing several facets of the argument during a visit at the School of Law of the University of Colorado. Pierre generously accepted to write the Foreword of this book. I am not only appreciative but also humbled that this book is introduced by one of the greatest and most refined legal thinkers of the twenty-first century. I am immensely grateful to Georg Nolte, Heike Krieger and Andreas Zimmermann for inviting me to spend a sabbatical semester in Berlin between September 2016 and February 2017, which provided me with the space and time necessary to finalise this book. I thank Jan Klabbers, Steven Wheatley, Janne Nijman, Catherine Brölmann, Gleider Hernandez, Luíza Leão Soares Pereira, Maruša Veber, Dimitri Van Den Meerssche and Maiko Meguro, who expressed interest in the project and whose repeated feedback and recommendations were very insightful. I thank Rosa Beets, whose research assistance proved enriching, especially regarding the discussion of the fundamental doctrine of statehood. I am very thankful to Richard Clements for his tremendous

assistance at the copy-editing stage. As always, Finola O'Sullivan and
Larissa van den Herik at Cambridge University Press have been wonderful and patient advisors during the maturation of this project.

Thoughts are inevitably refined through debates. I am grateful to the
conveners, participants and funders of the numerous workshops where
parts of the argument developed in this book were presented and debated
over the last two years. I can only mention a few of them here. For
a workshop at the Mississippi College School of Law in May 2015,
I would like to thank John Haskell. For a workshop at the Instituto
Tecnológico Autónomo de México (ITAM) in Mexico City
in November 2015, I would like to thank Alberto Puppo, Jorge Cerdio
and Máximo Langer. For a workshop at the Amsterdam Centre for
International Law (ACIL) in January 2016, I would like to thank Ingo
Venzke, Catherine Brölmann, Roland Pierik and Markos Karavias. For
a workshop at University College Dublin in March 2016, I would like to
thank Richard Collins, John O'Dowd, Gavin Barrett, Imelda Maher and
Claire Hill. For a workshop at Sciences Po Paris in March 2016, I would
like to thank Diego Fernandez Arroyo, Horatia Muir Watt and Mikhaïl
Xifaras. For a workshop at the Faculty of Law of the University of McGill
in March 2016, I would like to thank Cassandra Steer, René Provost,
Frédéric Megret and Ivana Isailovic. For a workshop at Colorado Law
School in April 2016, I would like to thank Michael Zaccaro, Justin
Desautels-Stein, Pierre Schlag, Tiago Guevara and Emilyn Winkelmeyer.
For a workshop at Temple University in April 2016, I would like to thank
Duncan Hollis, Pam Bookman, Jeffrey Dunoff, Meg deGuzman, Jean
Galbraith, Mark Pollack and Brishen Rogers. For a workshop at the VU
Amsterdam in April 2016, I would like to thank Geoff Gordon, Wouter
Werner and Gareth Davies. For a workshop at the Erik Castrén Institute of
International Law and Human Rights at the University of Helsinki
in April 2016, I would like to thank Jan Klabbers, Martti Koskenniemi,
Sahib Singh, Mónica García-Salmones and Walter Rech. For a workshop at
the School of Law of the University of Glasgow in May 2016, I would like to
thank Akbar Rasulov, Christian Tams, James Devaney and Gail Lythgoe.
For a workshop at the School of Law of the University of Durham
in May 2016, I would like to thank Gleider Hernandez, John Linarelli,
Ruth Houghton and David van Rooyen. For a workshop at the Université
Libre de Bruxelles in June 2016, I would like to thank Olivier Corten,
François Dubuisson, Anne Lagerwall and Martyna Fałkowska. For
a workshop at the European University Institute in November 2016,
I would like to thank Dennis Patterson, Nehal Bhuta, Dimitri Van Den

Meerssche, Emmanuel De Groof and Stavros Pantazopoulos. For the possibility of delivering a Thomas Franck Public Lecture at Humboldt University on the topic of this book in February 2017, I would like to thank Georg Nolte, Heike Kriege and Andreas Zimmermann, as well as all the attendees, including Christian Tomuschat. For a workshop at the Ghent Rolin-Jaequemyns International Law Institute at the University of Ghent in February 2017, I would like to thank Tom Ruys. For a presentation at the University of los Andes in Bogota in March 2017, I would like to thank René Fernando Urueña Hernández as well as Vanessa Suelt Cock. For a presentation at the University of Tokyo in March 2017, I would like to thank Koji Teraya, Kazuhiro Nakatani and Maiko Meguro. For a presentation at Waseda University in March 2017, I would like to thank Shuichi Furuya and Yota Negishi. For a presentation at the University of Kyoto in March 2017, I would like to thank Shotaro Hamamoto, Mari Takeuchi and Yohei Okada.

Even for armchair paratroopers such as international lawyers, support and friendship are invaluable. I am thankful to my friends and colleagues at the Manchester International Law Centre and the Amsterdam Centre for International Law for their continuous support. They include my friends and colleagues Iain Scobbie, Yenkong Ngangjoh Hodu, John Haskell, Shavana Musa, Philip Burton, Mariela Apostolaki, André Nollkaemper, Ilias Plakokefalos, Markos Karavias, Ingo Venzke, Janne Nijman, Catherine Brölmann, Kathryn Greenman and Maiko Meguro. As for my previous books, I would like to express my immense gratitude to my friend Alain Brouillet, whose passion for international law books and generosity have allowed me to have at my disposal one of the richest collections of classics of international law rarely privately owned by an international lawyer. I am similarly grateful to Liliane and Christopher Fawcett for providing me with inspiring retreat environments for my reading and writing for several years. Last but not least, I would like to mention – but not name – those most cherished daily supporters without whom even the very little that can be achieved through an international law book would not have been possible. While hiding my passport or lamenting my departure when time to go to the airport came, they have always sarcastically been smiling at the very surreal job all those who can possibly read this preface are engaged in. Thinking about international law and its fundamental doctrines with a bit of distance would not have been possible without their sarcasm and their constant reminders that the real heroes in this world are not international lawyers.

International Law as a Belief System

This book reflects on the way in which international lawyers construct international legal discourse. It particularly zeroes in on the organisation of international legal discourse around some fundamental doctrines that constrain legal reasoning as a result of their inventing their own origin and their regulating their own functioning. It is argued in this book that the articulation of international legal discourse around fundamental doctrines that invent their own origin and regulate their own functioning thereby constraining legal reasoning constitutes the mark of a belief system.

The following chapters constitute an attempt to expose the extent to which international law bears the characteristics of a belief system. The exposition of international law as a belief system is meant to serve critique and should be read as an invitation to international lawyers to temporarily suspend their belief system and unlearn some of their knowledge and sensibilities about the fundamental doctrines they have been trained to reproduce and respond to. Exposing and suspending the international belief system constitute the ambitions of the discussion that follows.

This introduction starts by sketching out the main expository claim developed in the following chapters whereby international law bears the characteristics of a belief system (1). It continues by situating such a descriptive claim in contemporary legal thought, especially in relation to the liberal pattern of legal thought that such a belief system epitomises (2). It then substantiates the ultimate ambition of this book, namely, the temporary suspension of the international belief system with a view to making room for a re-imagining of international law and its fundamental doctrines outside the belief system (3). A few observations on the related inquiries that are left at the periphery of the discussion carried out here are subsequently formulated with a view to preventing any misunderstanding as to the object of this book (4). And finally, this introduction ends with a presentation of the chapters that populate this volume and indicates the way in which the discussion proceeds (5).

A few preliminary caveats are warranted. The claim that international law bears the characteristics of a belief system is exclusively applied to international legal discourse and, more specifically, to the way in which international lawyers build their arguments in relation to the fundamental doctrines of international law. It is true that the exploratory framework around which this book is constructed draws extensively on insights, reflections and tools developed in relation to domestic law and jurisprudence and could potentially be transposed to a whole series of non-international legal discourse. Yet the discussion unfolding in this book remains without prejudice to the question of whether a similar belief system is inherent in legal argumentation as a whole.[1] By the same token, it must be emphasised that this book exclusively grapples with contemporary understandings of the formation and functioning of the fundamental doctrines of international law as they emerged in the second half of the nineteenth century and were consolidated in the twentieth century. Although it is undeniable that such understandings are inherited from international classical legal thought as is discussed below,[2] the following chapters concentrate solely on the modern and contemporary variants of the fundamental doctrines of international law. Finally, it must be highlighted that the image of the formation and functioning of the fundamental doctrines that is produced in the following chapters is not meant to be exclusive of possible alternative outlooks.[3] The account offered here acknowledges that other models can similarly help us to understand

---

[1] Cf. the argument made by Pierre Schlag in relation to US law. See P. Schlag, 'Law as the continuation of god by other means' (1997) *California Law Review* 85.

[2] See Section 2.

[3] For other challenges to current models of cognition of international legal discourse, see Fredrich V. Kratochwil, *Rules, Norms, and Decisions: On the Conditions of Practical and Legal Reasoning in International Relations and Domestic Affairs* (Cambridge: Cambridge University Press, 1989); M. Koskenniemi, *From Apology to Utopia: The Structure of International Legal Argument* (Cambridge: Cambridge University Press, 2005); Philip Allott, 'Language, method and the nature of international law (1971) 45 *British Yearbook of International Law* 79; Fleur Johns, *Non-Legality in International Law: Unruly Law* (Cambridge: Cambridge University Press, 2013); Jutta Brunnée and Stephen J. Toope, *Legitimacy and Legality in International Law* (Cambridge: Cambridge University Press, 2010); I. Scobbie, 'Towards the elimination of international law: some radical scepticism about sceptical radicalism' (1990) 61 *British Yearbook of International Law* 339–62. More recently, see Justin Desautels-Stein, 'Chiastic law in the crystal ball: exploring legal formalism and its alternative futures' (2014) 2 *London Review of International Law* 263–96.

the formation and functioning of the fundamental doctrines of international law and the ways in which international legal discourse is constructed.[4] In this sense, the image produced here amounts to just one of the many possible representations of the formation and functioning of fundamental doctrines without the present account having any kind of rational or empirical superiority.[5]

1 The Expository Claim: International Law as a Belief System

This book makes the claim that international law bears the attributes of a belief system, for the fundamental doctrines (e.g. sources, responsibility, statehood, personality, interpretation, *jus cogens*) around which international legal discourses is articulated invent their origin and dictate their own functioning. According to this expository framework, fundamental doctrines' invention of their origin and regulation of their functioning are made possible by their representation as rules

---

[4] These argumentative patterns can be approached from the perspective of the aesthetics of legal arguments. See e.g. P. Schlag, 'The aesthetics of American law' (2002) 115 *Harvard Law Review* 1047. They can also be approached from the perspective of the episteme. See e.g. Andrea Bianchi, *International Law Theories: An Inquiry into Different Ways of Thinking* (Oxford: Oxford University Press, 2016), pp. 12–13. See also the other structural conditions of legal reasoning identified by Kratochwil, *Rules, Norms, and Decisions*, pp. 38, 232. For a constructivist account of the processes that drive the operation of international legal arguments, see generally Jutta Brunnee and Stephen J. Toope, 'International law and constructivism: elements of an interactional theory of international law' (2000) 39 *Columbia Journal of Transnational Law* 19. For a structuralist account of the constraints on international legal argumentation, see Justin Desautels-Stein, 'The judge and the drone' (2014) 56 *Arizona Law Review* 117. For another famous theory of constraints, see M. Troper, 'Les contraintes de l'argumentation juridique dans la production des normes', in O. Pfersmann and G. Timsti (eds.), *Raisonnement Juridique et Interpretation* (Paris: Publication de la Sorbonne, 2001), pp. 35–48. See also the communitarian of constraints famously identified by Stanley Fish in *Is There a Text in This Class? The Authority of Interpretive Communities* (Cambridge, MA: Harvard University Press, 1980), for whom interpretation is itself a structure of constraints (in particular see p. 356). See also J. Vinuales, 'On legal inquiry', in D. Alland, V. Chetail, O. de Frouville and J. Vinuales (eds.), *Unity and Diversity of International Law: Essays in Honour of Professor Pierre-Marie Dupuy* (Leiden: Martinus Nijhoff, 2014), pp. 45–75. Vinuales construes beliefs, practices, norms, institutions, treaties, laws and instruments as topography. See also R. Collins, *The Institutional Problem in Modern International Law* (Oxford: Hart, 2016). Collins explains and evaluates the self-created deficiency of international law through the common application thereto of some kind of rule of law idealism.

[5] For a similar attempt to describe legal reasoning and generate readers' imaginative empathy for a certain image of legal reasoning without claiming superiority over others, see P. Schlag, 'The aesthetics of American law' (2002) 115 *Harvard Law Review* 1049 at 1054.

derived from some key international instruments (e.g. the Statute of the International Court of Justice, the Montevideo Convention on Rights and Duties of States, the Vienna Convention on the Law of Treaties, the Articles on State Responsibility, the Reparations Advisory Opinion of the International Court of Justice), thereby allowing the formation and functioning of fundamental doctrines to be explained by fundamental doctrines themselves.

According to the expository claim made in the following chapters, three specific features of international legal discourse are construed as forming a belief system: the idea that fundamental doctrines constitute rules (*ruleness*), the derivation of fundamental doctrines from international instruments as a result of a fictive history (*imaginary genealogy*) and the explanation of the formation and functioning of fundamental doctrines by fundamental doctrines themselves (*self-referentiality*). It is by virtue of such ruleness, imaginary genealogy and self-referentiality that fundamental doctrines come to invent their own origin as well as dictate their own functioning, thereby generating an experienced sense of constraint among international lawyers.[6] This phenomenon is construed here as the expression of a belief system.

The following chapters will expound on these features of international legal discourse that are characteristic of a belief system.[7] Yet a few preliminary definitional and methodological observations are warranted at this stage. According to the understanding informing the expository framework developed in this book, a belief system is a set of mutually reinforcing beliefs prevalent in a community or society that is not necessarily formalised.[8] A belief system thus refers to dominant interrelated attitudes of the members

---

[6] Regis Debray, *Transmitting Culture*, trans. Eric Rauth (New York: Columbia University Press, 1997), pp. 19–20: '[S]trictly speaking, there are no "founding key words" or "founding principles" (ill-chosen expressions at best) from which traditions and institutions of transmission originate ... The institutional body supposed to relay these disembodied word-principles has gradually invented its own origin.'

[7] See esp. Chapter 2.

[8] The notion of system of beliefs is sometimes equated with the notion of ideology. See Judith N. Shklar, *Legalism: Law, Morals, and Political Trials* (Cambridge, MA: Harvard University Press, 1986), pp. 1–3. Ideology does not really capture what I have in mind because of the risk of being equated with grand ideologies, that is, an entire system of thoughts and values. This risk is acknowledged by Shklar (*ibid.*, pp. vii – viii; see also p. 4). Cf. S. V. Scott, 'International law as ideology: theorizing the relationship between international law and international politics' (1994) 5 *European Journal of International Law* 313–25. For some general remarks on the links between belief system, symbol system, idea system and ideology, see also Anthony Giddens, *Central Problems in Social Theory: Action, Structure and Contradiction in Social Analysis* (Basingstoke: Macmillan, 1979), pp. 165–97.

of a community or society as to what they regard as true or acceptable or as to make sense of the world. In a belief system, truth or meaning is acquired neither by reason (rationalism) nor by experience (empiricism) but by the deployment of certain transcendental validators that are unjudged and unproved rationally or empirically.[9] This set of validators on the basis of which truth, meaning or sense is constructed is self-explanatory and constitutes what the believers constantly turn to for 'revelation'.[10] The self-explanatory nature of these validators is what allows these validators to acquire a transcendental character and be displaced outside the social praxis where they have been shaped.[11] These validators are simultaneously said to be systemic and to constitute a belief system because of their mutually supportive character and the fact that they explain, justify and vindicate one another.

That law in general is presented as a belief system is not new.[12] Nor is the exposition of international law as a belief system.[13] However, the

---

[9] Cf. P. Schlag, *Laying Dow the Law: Mysticism, Fetishism, and the American Legal Mind* (New York: New York University Press, 1996). See also P. Schlag, 'Law as a continuation of god by other means' (1997) 85 *California Law Review* 427, esp. 437–40.

[10] In the same vein, see P. Bourdieu, 'The force of law: toward a sociology of the juridical field' (1987) 38 *Hastings Law Journal* 805 at 825 and 844. It could be added that belief systems necessarily come with some form of symbolic violence as they impose hierarchies and ways of being and knowing while also restricting the possibility of an alternative world. On the notion of symbolic violence, see P. Bourdieu and L. Wacquant, *An Invitation to Reflexive Sociology* (Chicago: University of Chicago Press, 1992), p. 15. See the remarks of J. D. Schubert, 'Suffering/symbolic violence', in Michael Grenfell (ed.), *Pierre Bourdieu: Key Concepts*, 2nd edn (Durham, NC: Acumen Press, 2012), pp. 179–94, esp. pp. 191–92.

[11] I owe some of these remarks to an exchange with Dimitri Van Den Meerssche.

[12] A. A. Leff, 'Unspeakable ethics, unnatural law' (1979) *Duke Law Journal* 1229, esp. 1231 and 1245–47 (Leff speaks of the Constitution as putting in place a 'god-based system'); P. Schlag, 'Law as the continuation of god by other means' (1997) 85 *California Law Review* 427; John Hart Ely, 'Constitutional interpretivism: its allure and impossibility' (1978) 53 *Indiana Law Journal* 399. The idea of belief has sometimes been referred to in a more general way. See e.g. B. Tamanaha, 'The history and elements of the rule of law' (2012) *Singapore Journal of Legal Studies* 232, for a description or explanation of the way in which legal argumentation works. In contrast, others have preferred to rely on psychological and behavioural frameworks, for instance, by referring to the role of law as 'father substitute' rather than belief system. This is found in the scholarship of legal realists who reject the theological analogy and claim that law is 'paternalised', not 'divinified'. See Jerome Frank, *Law and the Modern Mind* (New York: Transaction Publishers, 2009), pp. 99, 210–18.

[13] Shklar, *Legalism*. See also J. Beckett, 'Countering uncertainty and ending up/down arguments: prolegomena to a response to NAIL' (2005) 16 *European Journal of International Law* 213 at 214 ('Law exists because we believe in it; we do not believe in it because it exists'). See also Bianchi, *International Law Theories*, pp. 8, 11 (who refers to

claim that international law constitutes a belief system that is made here is more specific and has never been fully articulated in international legal thought. In fact, it is unprecedented to present international law as a belief system where fundamental doctrines are held as transcendental validators that are left unjudged and unproved rationally or empirically by virtue of their self-explanatory character and to which international lawyers constantly turn for guidance without such a turn to being considered the result of a few conventional moves repeated cynically or in bad faith.[14]

It should be noted that from a sociological and comparative vantage point, there is nothing surprising that a discipline such as international law and its practice are organised around a belief system. Most professional groups have belief systems that determine their practice and which they are trained to maintain and respond to.[15] Such belief systems coexist with other belief systems of a very different nature. International law is no different in this respect.

The belief system at work in international legal discourse is not a states' belief system. It is the belief system of a community of professionals who constantly turn to some key unjudged fundamental doctrines to construct their legal discourse. The state is hardly mentioned in the following discussion. This is not only because the presupposition that states can have beliefs has always been conceptually very weak.[16] This is also because the very idea of state-centricism in the making of the fundamental doctrines of international law is itself a product of the belief system discussed in the following chapters. Chapter 5 will show in particular that suspending the belief system brings about a radical departure from the state-centricism that occasionally informs the dominant understandings of the making and functioning of fundamental doctrines of international law.

It should similarly be made clear at this preliminary stage of the argument that claiming that international law bears the characteristic

---

the beliefs of international lawyers and the ways such beliefs constitute the necessary background for the exercise of their professional skills).

[14] The foregoing is not to say that there is no consciousness at all about the belief system. See the remarks of Judith N. Shklar, *Legalism*, p. 10. On this point, see Chapter 3.

[15] On the possible awareness of the belief system by international lawyers, see Chapter 3.

[16] For a criticism of such anthropomorphic construction in international legal thought and practice, see J. d'Aspremont, 'The doctrine of fundamental rights of states and anthropomorphic thinking in international law' (2015) 4 *Cambridge Journal of International and Comparative Law* 501. See, generally, T. Adorno and M. Horkheimer, *Dialectic of Enlightenment* (London: Verso, 1997), pp. 6–7.

of a belief system falls short of equating international law to a religious belief system. Belief systems can be very diverse and cannot be reduced to formalised religious systems.[17] Although they similarly rely on some transcendental validators to which the believers turn for truth and revelation,[18] religious belief systems have their complex specificities that cannot easily be transposed to international legal discourse.[19] This is why, in the chapters that follow, the notion of belief system is used in a generic sense and in a way that distinguishes it from religious belief system. This is also the reason why theological vocabularies, despite their well-known descriptive and analytical virtues,[20] as well as their

---

[17] See, generally, Elizabeth A. Minton and Lynn R. Khale (eds.), *Belief Systems, Religion, and Behavioral Economics* (New York: Business Expert Press, 2014).

[18] It is the merit of David Friedrich Strauss to have been one of the first scholars to systematically develop such a critique of the sources of the Christian gospels. See David Friedrich Strauss, *The Life of Jesus Critically Examined*, trans. George Eliot, 4th edn (London [1835]).

[19] Cf. D. Kennedy, 'Images of religion in international legal theory', in Mark Janis (ed.), *Religion and International Law* (Dordrecht: Kluwer Academic Publishers, 1999), p. 153 ('Once our enlightenment narrative has been jostled, the deep and abiding interaction of international law and religion seems unavoidable').

[20] Theological vocabularies are commonly valued for their analytical and descriptive virtues. It is usually claimed that the use of theological vocabularies for analytical and descriptive purposes dates back to Liebniz (this claim is made by Carl Schmitt himself: Carl Schmitt, *Political Theology: Four Chapters on the Concept of Sovereignty*, trans. George Schwab (Chicago: University of Chicago Press, 1985), p. 37). It was, however, Schmitt who – although he himself consciously avoided the use of explicitly theological notions – popularised the idea that law and politics are articulated around secularised theological concepts (see Carl Schmitt, *Political Theology*, esp. pp. 36–38). On this aspect of Schmitt, see Chantal Mouffe, *The Return of the Political* (London: Verso, 1993), pp. 121–22; Marc de Wilde, 'The state of exception: reflections on theologico-political motifs in Benjamin and Schmitt', in Hent de Vries and Lawrence E. Sullivan (eds.), *Political Theologies: Public Religions in a Post-Secular World* (New York: Fordham University Press, 2006), pp. 188–200. For some critical remarks on the use of Carl Schmitt by international lawyers in general, see R. Howse, 'Schmitt, Schmitteanism and contemporary international legal theory', in A. Orford and F. Hoffmann (eds.), *The Oxford Handbook of the Theory of International Law* (Oxford: Oxford University Press, 2016), pp. 212–30. Walter Benjamin also features prominently among those who saw a structural analogy between theological and legal concepts and resorted to theological categories as a descriptive and analytical tool for law. See Walter Benjamin, 'Critique of violence', in *Selected Writings: Volume 1: 1913–1926* (Cambridge, MA: Belknap Press, 1996). See Judith Butler, 'Critique, coercion, and sacred life in Benjamin's 'Critique of Violence'', in de Vries and Sullivan (eds.), *Political Theologies*, pp. 201–19. For a strong rejection of the theological analogy, see Frank, *Law and the Modern Mind*, pp. 200–18.

popularity in international legal scholarship,[21] are avoided in the course of this heuristic exercise.[22]

The notion of fundamental doctrines also warrants a few definitional observations. For the sake of the following chapters, the fundamental doctrines of international law refer to organised clusters of modes of legal reasoning that are constantly deployed by international lawyers when they formulate international legal claims about the existence and extent of the rights and duties of actors subjected to international law and the consequences of breaches thereof.[23] They are distinct from other doctrines that enunciate the standards of behaviour to which international actors recognised by international law are subjected. Fundamental doctrines are diverse. They include clusters of modes of legal reasoning pertaining to sources, statehood, responsibility, interpretation, *jus cogens*, personality and so on. These fundamental

---

[21] International lawyers themselves have relished using the theological analogy for analytical and descriptive purposes. See e.g. James Crawford, 'International law as discipline and profession' (2012) 106 *American Society of International Law Proceedings* 471; J. Beckett, 'The politics of international law – twenty years later: a reply', *EJIL:TALK!*, 19 May 2009, available at www.ejiltalk.org/the-politics-of-international-law-twenty-years-later-a-reply/; Martti Koskenniemi, 'The fate of public international law: between technique and politics' (2007) *Modern Law Review* 1 at 30; A. Carty, *Post-Modern Law: Enlightenment, Revolution and the Death of Man* (Edinburgh: Edinburgh University Press, 1990); Martti Koskenniemi, 'Miserable comforters: international relations as new natural law' (2009) 15 *European Journal of International Relations* 395 at 396; D. Kennedy, 'When renewal repeats: thinking against the box' (2000) 32 *New York University Journal of International Law and Politics* 2, 335 at 375.

[22] In an earlier version of the argument made here, fundamental doctrines were referred to as 'gospels', and their formal repositories were referred to as 'canonical texts'. For a different use of the idea of 'gospel' in relation to the scholarship produced by some of the most authoritative journals in the field, see J. Dugard, 'The future of international law: a human rights perspective – with some comments on the Leiden school of international law' (2007) 20 *Leiden Journal of International Law* 729–39 at 731 ('As academic international lawyers outnumber international law practitioners, unlike the situation with any branch of national law, the opinions of academic lawyers become the law – at least as far as many academic lawyers are concerned. We have the gospels according to the *American Journal of International Law*, the *British Year Book of International Law*, the *Annuaire français*, and the *Zeitschrift* . . . ').

[23] For a useful overview of the various uses of the notion of 'doctrine', see T. Skouteris, *The Notion of Progress in International Law Discourse* (The Hague: TMC Asser Press, 2010), pp. 94–95. He distinguishes three meanings of the term 'legal doctrine', referring to the writing of the most qualified publicists, the programmes and sets of policies proposed by powerful international players and the clusters of international legal rules and analytical categories that allegedly appear in the minds of legal practitioners to operate as analytically distinct normative blocks. For the sake of this study, and as should be clear by now, doctrine is used in this third sense.

doctrines of international law accordingly constitute the seat of international legal discourse, and they correspond, albeit approximately, to what is sometimes called in the literature 'secondary rules',[24] 'sets of conventional disciplinary protocols of reasoning',[25] argumentative 'codes of conduct',[26] 'operative ideals',[27] clusters of 'topois',[28] 'common tropes/argument patterns'[29] or 'rules of legal art'.[30] To some extent they also bear resemblance to what is sometimes called 'legal conventions'.[31] Based on this understanding, fundamental doctrines establish not only the 'starting points'[32] for arguments but also the 'path'[33] for arguments and counter-arguments in international legal discourse. The notion of fundamental doctrines is further spelled out in Chapter 2.

2 The Context: The Belief System of International Law Then and Now

The claim that international law bears the characteristic of a belief system must be situated historically. In this regard, it is submitted here that the characteristics of a belief system born by international legal discourse can be construed as the expression of a liberal paradigm – what has also been

---

[24] See, generally, H. Hart, *The Concept of Law* (Oxford: Clarendon Press, 1994), pp. 94–95, 110–12. For the reasons justifying why this terminology is rejected here, see Chapter 2.

[25] Akbar Rasulov, 'The doctrine of sources in the discourses of the Permanent Court of International Justice', in C. Tams and M. Fitzmaurice (eds.), *Legacies of the Permanent Court of International Justice* (Leiden: Martinus Nijhoff, 2013), pp. 271–72.

[26] Shklar, *Legalism*, p. 1.   [27] *Ibid.*

[28] See Kratochwil, *Rules, Norms, and Decisions*, p. 38. It must be acknowledged that fundamental doctrines, as they are understood here, do not strictly mirror the four main lists of topoi; see Kratochwil, *Rules, Norms, and Decisions*, p. 232. Yet fundamental doctrines share the same structuring effects. It must also be highlighted that fundamental doctrines are not exclusive of other constraints of reasoning being deployed in international legal argumentation.

[29] See Akbar Rasuov, 'Writing about empire: remarks on the logic of a discourse' (2010) 23 *Leiden Journal of International Law* 449 at 460 ('every discursive field operates on the basis of a certain repertoire of common tropes-argument patterns and templates that are used more regularly than others by its participants').

[30] Julius Stone, *Legal System and Lawyers' Reasonings* (Redwood City, CA: Stanford University Press, 1968), p. 23.

[31] R. Dworkin, *Law's Empire* (Cambridge, MA: Belknap Press, 1986), pp. 120–24.

[32] Kratochwil, *Rules, Norms, and Decisions*, pp. 38, 220.

[33] *Ibid.*, p. 241 ('law creation is . . . path- and field-dependent in that dogmatic (systematic) considerations and/or presidential "starting-points" provide the context in which the decision has to be made. Thus, creativity is circumscribed by guidelines that specify what good legal arguing is'). Please note that Kratochwil borrows the idea of 'path' from Josef Esser.

called 'liberal legalism'[34] or, more simply, 'legalism'[35] – directly inherited from the Enlightenment.[36] Said differently, the international belief system exposed here can be construed as a manifestation of the liberal pattern of legal thought that informed classical and, subsequently, modern international legal thought.[37] This means that the invitation made in this book to suspend the belief system that permeates international legal discourse extends the critique of liberal patterns of arguments that was initiated three decades ago in international legal scholarship. The liberal trappings of the belief system exposed here and the kinship of the latter with the liberal paradigm can be explained as follows.

It must first be recalled that the liberal paradigm with which this book engages certainly does not constitute a monolithic idea. At least two dimensions thereof can be distinguished. On the one hand, the liberal paradigm refers to pluralism, a certain cosmopolitan ethos, the defence of individual liberty and some specific configurations of political institutions. On the other hand, the liberal paradigm refers to some form of rationalism and what has been called 'the illusion of providing itself with its own foundations' that is necessary to create the idea of a rational consensus.[38] Both dimensions of the liberal paradigm have permeated international legal thought and practice. Irrespective of the fate of the former dimension of the liberal paradigm in international legal thought,[39] it is argued here that the belief system discussed in this book – and thus fundamental doctrines' self-invention and self-regulation – is more directly inherited from the latter dimension of the liberal paradigm.

[34] F. Hoffman, 'International legalism and international politics', in A. Orford and F. Hoffmann (eds.), *The Oxford Handbook of the Theory of International Law* (Oxford: Oxford University Press, 2016), p. 961.

[35] Shklar, *Legalism*, pp. viii, 1–28.

[36] For a different use of liberalism in international legal thought by reference to a certain configuration of the international society as a collection of liberal democracies, see D. Joyce, 'Liberal internationalism', in A. Orford and F. Hoffmann (eds.), *The Oxford Handbook of the Theory of International Law* (Oxford: Oxford University Press, 2016), pp. 471–87.

[37] I owe several of the thoughts that follow to exchanges with Justin Desautels-Stein, Sahib Singh, and John Haskell.

[38] On this distinction between two dimensions of liberalism, see Chantal Mouffe, *The Return of the Political* (London: Verso, 1993), pp. 123–24 (drawing on Hans Blumenberg, *The Legitimacy of the Modern Age*).

[39] According to Martti Koskenniemi, the liberal cosmopolitan ethos may have possibly lapsed in international legal thought. See M. Koskenniemi, *The Gentle Civilizer of Nations: The Rise and Fall of International Law 1870–1960* (Cambridge: Cambridge University Press, 2001).

Because the belief system exposed here can be more directly traced back to the second dimension of the above-mentioned liberal paradigm, a few observations must be formulated on this specific dimension of the liberal paradigm and the idea of law that it puts in place. In this respect, it must be recalled that from the perspective of the second dimension of liberalism, law comes to be reduced to a 'legal-technical instead of ethico-political matter'[40] whereby rules are formal, objectively and content independently[41] ascertainable and distinct from a programme of governance or a catalogue of moral values.[42] This reduction of law to a legal-technical matter is made possible by the creation of an illusion of rational consensus around law that is meant to isolate law from power, morality, antagonism and the plurality of interests.[43] This illusion of a rational consensus – and thus the isolation of law from disruptive questions and the reduction of law to a legal-technical matter – is possible by virtue of law's providing itself with its own foundations.

Unsurprisingly, this reduction of law to a legal-technical matter distinct from the plurality of interest, power, morality and antagonism made its way into international legal thought.[44] In particular, such a transposition to international law was made possible by virtue of, among others things, an analogy between the state and the individual of the liberal

---

[40] M. Koskenniemi, *From Apology to Utopia: The Structure of International Legal Argument* (Cambridge: Cambridge University Press, 2006), p. 82.

[41] It is content independent because ascertainment is generated in a way that does not hinge on the substance of the institution whose membership to the legal order is tested. On the notion of content independence, see Noam Gur, 'Are legal rules content-independent reasons?' (2001) 5 *Problema: Anuario de Filosofía y Teoría del Derecho* 275. For some classical discussion, see H. L. A. Hart, *Essays on Bentham* (Oxford: Clarendon Press, 1982), pp. 243–68; and J. Raz, *The Morality of Freedom* (Oxford: Clarendon Press, 1986), pp. 35–37. See also Fabio P. Schecaira, *Legal Scholarship as a Source* (New York: Springer, 2013), pp. 26–27.

[42] R. M. Unger, *Knowledge and Politics* (New York: Free Press, 1975), pp. 76–81; Koskenniemi, *From Apology to Utopia*, p. 71; M. Koskenniemi, 'The politics of international law (1990) 1 *European Journal of International Law* 4 at 4–5; T. O'Hagan, *The End of Law?* (Oxford: Blackwell, 1984), p. 183; Paul W. Kahn, *The Cultural Study of Law: Reconstructing Legal Scholarship* (Chicago: University of Chicago Press, 1999), pp. 16–18; Shklar, *Legalism*, pp. 8–9, 16–23; Olivier Corten, *Le Discours du Droit International: Pour un Positivisme Critique* (Paris: Pedone, 2009), pp. 45–67.

[43] Mouffe, *The Return of the Political*, pp. 121, 140. See also T. Adorno and M. Horkheimer, *Dialectic of Enlightenment* (London: Verso, 1997), p. 12.

[44] On the distinction between primitive international legal thought, classical international legal thought and modern international legal thought, see D. Kennedy, 'Primitive legal scholarship' (1986) 27 *Harvard International Law Journal* 1. On the transposition of the liberal paradigm to international law, see also the remarks of Judith N. Shklar, *Legalism*, pp. 123–43.

doctrine of politics.[45] This move gave rise to what has been called 'classical international legal thought'.[46] The rise of modern international law in the nineteenth and twentieth centuries that accompanied the professionalisation of the discipline[47] perpetuated the above-mentioned liberal structure of legal thought[48] and the demands for more international law to domesticate politics.[49] In that sense, irrespective of the fate of the first dimension of the liberal paradigm, modern international legal thought has remained very much pervaded by the liberal modes of legal reasoning according to the second dimension of the liberal paradigm mentioned earlier.[50]

[45] After Hobbes and Spinoza paved the way for a human analogy, Pufendorf ascribed an intellect to the state and created anthropomorphic vocabularies and images about the main institution of international law, that is, the state. Such anthropomorphism was later taken over by Vattel – not without adjustment – and subsequently translated itself in the classical positivist doctrine of fundamental rights of states, which contributed to the consolidation of modern international law in the nineteenth century. On this point, see Michael Nutkiewicz, 'Samuel Pufendorf: obligation as the basis of the state' (1983) 21 *Journal of the History of Philosophy* 15–29; Fiammetta Palladini, 'Pufendorf disciple of Hobbes: the nature of man and the state of nature – the doctrine of socialitas' (2008) 34 *History of European Ideas* 26–60. For a criticism of the analogy, see Edwin De Witt Dickinson, 'The analogy between natural persons and international persons in the law of nations' (1917) 26 *Yale Law Journal* 564–91. See the discussion of this analogy in J. d'Aspremont, 'The doctrine of fundamental rights of states and anthropomorphic thinking in international law' (2015) 4 *Cambridge Journal of International and Comparative Law* 501; or T. Carty, *The Decay of International Law? A Reappraisal of the Limits of Imagination in International Affairs* (Manchester: Manchester University Press, 1986), pp. 44–46.

[46] Koskenniemi, *From Apology to Utopia*, p. 106.

[47] See S. Neff, *Justice among Nations* (Cambridge: Harvard University Press, 2014), pp. 300–10. See also J. d'Aspremont, 'The professionalization of international law', in J. d'Aspremont, T. Gazzini, A. Nollkaemper and W. Werner (eds.), *International Law as a Profession* (Cambridge: Cambridge University Press, 2016), p. 19.

[48] D. Kennedy, 'The disciplines of international law and policy' (1999) 12 *Leiden Journal of International Law* 9; D. Kennedy, 'Tom Franck and the Manhattan School' (2003) 35 *New York University Journal of International Law and Policy* 397–435; Koskenniemi, *From Apology to Utopia*, p. 158; M. Koskenniemi, 'The politics of international law' (1990) 1 *European Journal of International Law* 4 at 5–7. E. Jouannet, 'A critical introduction', in M. Koskenniemi (ed.), *The Politics of International Law* (Oxford: Hart, 2011), p. 15; Corten, *Le Discours du droit international*, pp. 45–67.

[49] For Jochen von Bernstorff, the idea of 'more international law is more progress' culminated in the late nineteenth century and the beginning of the twentieth century. See J. von Bernstorff, 'International legal scholarship as a cooling medium in international law and politics' (2014) 25 *European Journal of International Law* 977, esp. 984–86.

[50] For a good illustration, see J. L. Brierly, 'The basis of obligations in international law', in H. Lauterpacht and C. H. M. Waldock (eds.), *The Basis of Obligation in International Law and Other Papers by the Late James Leslie Brierly* (Oxford: Clarendon Press, 1959), pp. 21–36.

In the light of the foregoing, it should be possible to understand how fundamental doctrines' inventions of their own origins and regulation of their functioning – which are understood here as the marks of a belief system – simultaneously constitute a manifestation of the liberal structure of legal thought. Indeed, the international belief system exposed here projects an image of fundamental doctrines and the modes of legal reasoning they prescribe as being isolated from disruptive questions such as the plurality of interest, power, morality and antagonism. In the same vein, the international belief system ensures the imposition of sets of constraints on legal discourse – i.e. fundamental doctrines – and justifies such constraints by the very modes of legal reasoning that are put in place, thereby creating an impression of a rational consensus.[51] This simultaneously allows fundamental doctrines and their modes of legal reasoning to be considered distinct from any programme of governance, those fundamental doctrines having allegedly no other agenda than ensuring the possibility of legal reasoning. The feeling of distinctiveness of fundamental doctrines from regulatory enterprises is further reinforced by the proceduralisation of the making of the fundamental doctrines that are held to be the outcome of a law-making process thanks to their ruleness.[52] Ultimately, the belief system discussed in this book allows all thoughts about international law to be thought in advance, just like the Enlightenment makes thoughts and ideas calculable and predictable.[53]

Liberal patterns of international legal discourse – and especially those inherited from the second dimension of the liberal paradigm – have been scrutinised extensively in the scholarship of the last three decades.[54] In that sense, we have been here before.[55] Yet the

---

[51] See Chapter 3.   [52] See Chapter 3, Section 1.

[53] Adorno and Horkheimer, *Dialectic of Enlightenment*, pp. 7, 12.

[54] See the seminal work of Martti Koskenniemi that revealed the ascending and descending patterns of international legal argumentation which he traced back to the liberal political project: M. Koskenniemi, *From Apology to Utopia: The Structure of International Legal Argument* (Cambridge: Cambridge University Press, 2006). See also M. Koskenniemi, 'The Politics of International Law' (1990) 1 *European Journal of International Law* 4. See also D. Kennedy, *International Legal Structures* (Baden-Baden: Nomos, 1987). More recently, see also F. Hoffman, 'International legalism and international politics', in A. Orford and F. Hoffmann (eds.), *The Oxford Handbook of the Theory of International Law* (Oxford: Oxford University Press, 2016), pp. 954–84. Cf. China Miéville, *Between Equal Rights: A Marxist Theory of International Law* (Chicago: Pluto Press, 2005), esp. pp. 314–18.

[55] This is part of the legacy of critical thinking. For a discussion of this legacy and the challenge of liberalism, see Bianchi, *International Law Theories*, pp. 135–62.

following discussion is predicated on the idea that fundamental doctrines' invention of their origin and regulation of their functioning constitute a liberal pattern of legal reasoning that eluded the intense scrutiny of international lawyers. At first glance, given the intense scrutiny of the liberal pattern of legal thought in contemporary scholarship, it may be surprising that not much attention has been paid to the characteristics of the belief system born by international law and the liberal pattern they manifest. Yet such an oversight can be explained as follows. First, belief systems are self-obfuscating,[56] and they can even elude the attention of the most critical and self-reflective international lawyers.[57] Second, despite an overall growing interest in international legal theory and critical inquiries in contemporary studies, international lawyers have recently ceased to be concerned with the hidden patterns of their modes of legal reasoning. Indeed, as I have argued elsewhere, after the early denial and perplexity of the first encounters with critical thinking, international lawyers came to feel that they had domesticated critical challenges to their liberal modes of argumentation and had completed the extraction of the hidden patterns of their modes of legal reasoning.[58] It could even be extrapolated that the success of critical thinking has reinforced the belief system because, confronted with the realisation of the impossibility to displace politics though law, international lawyers have returned to their transcendentally acquired validators. A third, and maybe simpler, reason for the contemporary dwindling attention to liberal patterns of international legal thought and practice, and especially for fundamental doctrines' self-invention and self-regulation, lies with the fact that international lawyers are more interested today in a wide array of scholarly inquiries of a completely different nature. Nowadays, what international lawyers devote their efforts to, besides common doctrinal investigations, rather pertains to the empirical study of the conditions under which international law is formed and bears effects on its addressees through the systematic use

---

[56] See Chapter 3.
[57] On the question of awareness of the belief system, see Chapter 2, Section 3. See also the remarks of Shklar, *Legalism*, p. 10.
[58] About this return to the old vocabularies, see J. d'Aspremont, 'Martti Koskenniemi, the mainstream, and self-reflectivity' (2016) 29 *Leiden Journal of International Law*. On the domestication of critique, see, generally, Pierre Schlag, '"Le hors de texte, c'est moi": the politics of form and the domestication of deconstruction' (1989–1990) 11 *Cardozo Law Review* 1631–74; Pierre Schlag, 'A brief survey of deconstruction' (2005) 27 *Cardozo Law Review* 741–52.

of qualitative or quantitative methods,[59] inquiries into the means to ensure accountability in the exercises of power that cannot be apprehended by traditional legal categories,[60] possibilities of a new modelling of authority at the international level and the structure of global governance,[61] the continuous expansion of the regulatory powers of international law to address the new crises of the world,[62] the renewal of the Enlightenment's international rule of

---

[59] See Gregory Shaffer and Tom Ginsburg, 'The empirical turn in international legal scholarship' (2012) 106 *American Journal of International Law* 1. For an illustration, see Pierre-Hugues Verdier and Erik Voeten, 'How does customary international law change? The case of state immunity' (2015) 59 *International Studies Quarterly* 209–22. See also Jakob Holtermann and Mikael Madsen, 'Toleration, synthesis or replacement? The "empirical turn" and its consequences for the science of international law' (2016) 29 *Leiden Journal of International Law* 1001. The turn to empirical studies of international law is not completely unprecedented. See e.g. the work of the New Haven School and in particular that of Myres McDougal, 'Law and power' (1952) 46 *American Journal of International Law* 102. See also the work of the legal process school, as illustrated by Abram Chayes and Antonia Handler Chayes, *The New Sovereignty: Compliance with International. Regulatory Agreements* (Cambridge, MA: Harvard University Press, 1995). For a claim about the virtuosity of empirical sensitivity, see J. Vinuales, 'On legal inquiry', in D. Alland, V. Chetail, O. de Frouville and J. Vinuales (eds.), *Unity and Diversity of International Law: Essays in Honour of Professor Pierre-Marie Dupuy* (Leiden: Martinus Nijhoff, 2014), pp. 72–75.

[60] See e.g. the studies on global administrative law by B. Kingsbury, N. Krisch and R. Steward, 'The emergence of global administrative law' (2005) 68 *Law and Contemporary Problems* 3–4, 15–61, 29; C. Harlow, 'Global administrative law: the quest for principles and values' (2006) 17 *European Journal of International Law* 1, 187; See also the studies on the exercise of international public authority by A. von Bogdandy, P. Dann and M. Goldmann, 'Developing the publicness of public international law: towards a legal framework for global governance activities' (2008) 9 *German Law Journal* 1375; M. Goldmann, 'Inside relative normativity: from sources to standard instruments for the exercise of international public authority' (2008) 9 *German Law Journal* 1865. On this agenda of international lawyers, see the remarks of D. Kennedy, 'The mystery of global governance' (2008) 34 *Ohio Northern University Law Review* 827.

[61] N. Krisch, *Beyond Constitutionalism: The Pluralistic Structure of Postnational Law* (Oxford: Oxford University Press, 2010); N. Krisch, 'Subsidiarity in global governance' (2016) 79 *Law and Contemporary Problems* 1; see also E. Benvenisti, *The Law of Global Governance* (The Hague: Brill, 2014); E. Benvenisti and G. W. Downs, 'The empire's new clothes: political economy and the fragmentation of international law' (2007) 60 *Stanford Law Review* 595. N. Krisch, 'Authority, solid and liquid, in postnational governance', in Roger Cotterrell and Maksymilian Del Mar (eds.), *Authority in Transnational Legal Theory: Theorising across Disciplines* (London: Elgar, 2016), pp. 25–48. For a general overview of contemporary approaches to international lawmaking, see Ingo Venzke, 'Contemporary theories of international law-making', in C. Brölmann and Y. Radi (eds.), *Research Handbook on the Theory and Practice of International Law-Making* (2014), pp. 66–84.

[62] For an illustration, see the literature on cyber operations and *ius ad bellum*. See the examples provided in Jean d'Aspremont, 'Cyber operations and international law: an interventionist legal thought' (2016) 21 *Journal of Conflict & Security Law* 575.

law project,[63] the production of sociological insights about the functioning of international law,[64] expert ruling and expert knowledge[65], to name only a few of the areas of interest of contemporary international legal scholars. In shifting their attention to these new objects of investigation, and irrespective of their newly acquired theoretical,[66] historical[67] and multi-disciplinary[68] appetites, international lawyers have ceased being interested in the possible liberal patterns of international legal discourse. This is even more so at a time the world continues to be torn by war and violence, forced

[63] See e.g. André Nollkaemper, *National Courts and the International Rule of Law* (Oxford: Oxford University Press, 2012). See also Machiko Kanetake and André Nollkaemper (eds.), *The Rule of Law at the National and International Levels: Contestations and Deference* (Oxford: Hart, 2016); J. Alvarez, 'International organizations and the rule of law' (2016) Institute for International Law and Justice Working Paper 2016/4, available at www.iilj.org/wp-content/uploads/2016/07/Alvarez-International-Organizations-and-the-Rule-of-Law-IILJ-WP-2016_4-GAL.pdf (accessed 5 March 2017). See also the renewal of the rule of law project through constitutionalist thinking about international law. See e.g. Erika de Wet, 'The constitutionalisation of public international law', in Michel Rosenfeld and Andras Sajo (eds.), *The Oxford Handbook of Comparative Constitutional Law* (Oxford: Oxford University Press, 2012), p. 1209; Erika de Wet, 'The international constitutional order' (2006) 55 *International and Comparative Law Quarterly* 51–76; A. Peters, 'The merits of global constitutionalism' (2009) 16 *Indiana Journal of Global Legal Studies* 397; A. Peters, 'Are we moving towards constitutionalisation of the world community', in A. Cassese (ed.), *Realising Utopia: The Future of International Law* (Oxford: Oxford University Press, 2012), pp. 118–135; A. Peters, 'Compensatory constitutionalism: the function and potential of fundamental international norms and structures' (2006) 19 *Leiden Journal of International Law* 579.
[64] Moshe Hirsch, *Invitation to the Sociology of International Law* (Oxford: Oxford University Press, 2015). See also J. d'Aspremont, T. Gazzini, A. Nollkaemper and W. Werner, *International Law as Profession* (Cambridge: Cambridge University Press, 2017).
[65] See e.g. David Kennedy, *A World of Struggle: How Power, Law, and Expertise Shape Global Political Economy* (Princeton, NJ: Princeton University Press, 2016); M. Koskenniemi, 'The politics of international law: 20 years later' (2009) 20 *European Journal of International Law* 7.
[66] See some recent and unprecedented collections of essays on the theory of international law, including Alexander Orakhelashvili, *Research Handbook on the Theory and History of International Law* (Cheltenham: Elgar, 2013); A. Orford and F. Hoffmann (eds.), *The Oxford Handbook of the Theory of International Law* (Oxford: Oxford University Press, 2016); J. d'Aspremont and S. Singh (eds.), *Concepts for International Law* (Cheltenham: Edward Elgar, 2018) (forthcoming).
[67] On the turn to history in contemporary international legal scholarship, see M. Craven, 'Theorizing the turn to history in international law', in A. Orford and F. Hoffmann (eds.), *The Oxford Handbook of the Theory of International Law* (Oxford: Oxford University Press, 2016), pp. 21–37; see also G. Galindo, 'Martti Koskenniemi and the historiographical turn in international law' (2005) 16 *European Journal of International Law* 539. See also remarks in Section 4.
[68] See e.g. Jeffrey L. Dunoff and Mark A. Pollack (eds.), *Interdisciplinary Perspectives on International Law and International Relations: The State of the Art* (Cambridge: Cambridge University Press, 2013).

migrations of populations, disruptions of the climate and severe inequalities in terms of distributive justice. The following discussion is premised on the idea that laying bare the belief system that permeates international lawyers' understandings of the formation and functioning of fundamental doctrines – itself an offspring of the liberal paradigm inherited from the Enlightenment – constitutes a much-needed undertaking. It is the object of Section 3 to spell out what can be achieved by the expository claim developed in this book and what the ultimate ambition of this book is.

3 The Ambition: A Temporary Suspension of the Belief System

As explained earlier, this book first attempts to make international lawyers sensitive to a new image of international law presented as a belief system. In doing so, this book perpetuates the scrutiny of liberal patterns of legal thought and the disclosure of some of the politics behind them. Thus, the discussion that follows is heuristic[69] and seeks to project a specific image of international law and its fundamental doctrine with a view to raising awareness about under-explored dimensions of international legal discourse. Therefore, the expository claim made in this book is not meant to take any grand descriptive position as to the kind of rationality at work in international legal discourse. Instead, this heuristic undertaking is at the service of a more fundamental ambition, namely, a temporary suspension of the belief system exposed here.[70] It is the object of this section to spell out what such a suspension of the belief system at work in international legal thought and practice entails.

Suspending the belief system, as envisaged here, cannot be reduced to a mere posture of openness and amenability to external perspectives. What is ambitioned here is a more fundamental disruption of some of the 'routines' of international lawyers[71] and, in particular, a falsification of

---

[69] For a useful definition of the heuristic method of inquiry in international legal studies, see Cédric Dupont and Thomas Schultz, 'Towards a new heuristic model: investment arbitration as a political system' (2016) 7 *Journal of International Dispute Settlement* (2016) 3 at 3–4.

[70] For a similar use of the notion of 'suspension of belief', see Paul W. Kahn, *The Cultural Study of Law: Reconstructing Legal Scholarship* (Chicago: University of Chicago Press, 1999), p. 2.

[71] For a rather pejorative use of the notion of routine in relation to legal thought, see P. Schlag: 'Normative legal thought is part of a routine: our routine. It is the highly repetitive, cognitively entrenched, institutionally sanctioned, and politically encoded routine of the legal academy – a routine that silently produces our thoughts and keeps our work channelled within the same old cognitive and rhetorical matrices. Like most routines, it

the transcendental character of the fundamental doctrines to which international lawyers turn to generate truth, meaning or sense in international legal discourse. In other words, suspending the belief system requires that such doctrines are no longer looked at via the very categories they have put in place, principally sources and interpretation.[72]

The invitation extended in this book for a suspension of the belief system serves critique in two different ways. The first critical gain of the suspension of the belief system that permeates the common understanding of the formation and functioning of the fundamental doctrines lies in the discontinuation by international lawyers of their knowledge and sensibilities about the fundamental doctrines they have been trained to mechanically reproduce and respond to.[73] Indeed, this book is meant to offer international lawyers the possibility to *unlearn* the explanations provided by fundamental doctrines about their own formation and functioning.[74] Said differently, suspending the belief system means interrupting the 'miscognition' (*méconnaissance*)[75] that is generated by the belief system at work in

has been so well internalized that we repeat it automatically, without thinking' (P. Schalg, 'Normative and nowhere to go' (1990) 43 *Stanford Law Review* 167 at 180–81).

[72] For a similar ambition with respect to the study of law in general, see Paul W. Kahn, *The Cultural Study of Law: Reconstructing Legal Scholarship* (Chicago: University of Chicago Press, 1999).

[73] This is an idea that I had the chance to fine-tune thanks to the input of Akbar Rasulov.

[74] In relation to myths, this corresponds to what François Ost has called the 'unwriting' (*désécriture*). See François Ost, *Raconter la loi: aux sources de l'imaginaire juridique* (Paris: Les Éditions Odile Jacob, 2004), pp. 263–64.

[75] The term 'miscognition' was famously coined by Bourdieu: 'But above all, knowledge by itself exercises an effect – one which appears to me to be liberating – every time the mechanisms whose laws of operation it establishes owe part of their effectiveness to miscognition'; see Pierre Bourdieu, 'A lecture on the lecture', in Pierre Bourdieu, *In Other Words: Essays towards a Reflexive Sociology*, trans. Matthew Adamson (Redwood City, CA: Stanford University Press, 1990), pp. 177, 183. Bourdieu also contended that 'the magical ambition of transforming the social world without knowing the mechanisms that drive it exposes itself to the risk of replacing the "inert violence" of the mechanisms that its pretentious ignorance has destroyed with another and sometimes even more inhuman violence.' *Ibid.*, p. 189. See also the definition of miscognition by Richard Terdiman in his introduction to the translation of P. Bourdieu, 'The force of law: toward a sociology of the juridical field' (1987) 38 *Hasting Law Journal* 805 at 813: miscognition (*méconnaissance*) 'is the term by which Bourdieu designates induced misunderstanding, the process by which power relations come to be perceived not for what they objectively are, but in a form which renders them legitimate in the eyes of those subject to the power. This induced misunderstanding is obtained not by conspiratorial but by structural means. It implies the inherent advantage of the holders of power through their capacity to control not only the actions of those they dominate, but also the language through which those subjected comprehend their domination. Such miscognition is structurally

international law.[76] More concretely, such a suspension of the belief system allows the disclosure of some of the most significant interventions by powerful actors that punctuate the formation and functioning of the fundamental doctrines that are too often obfuscated.[77] Some of these interventions are examined in Chapter 4. What can be unlearned by virtue of the suspension of the international belief system is also further discussed in Chapter 5. The reformist empowerment promoted by the unlearning of the fundamental doctrines accompanying such a suspension of the belief system is discussed in the Epilogue (Chapter 6) of this book.

The second critical dimension of the heuristic exercise attempted here is found in its contestation of mainstream historical accounts whereby the making of the fundamental doctrines of international law – and that of the modes of legal reasoning they put in place – is articulated around the adoption of some key international instruments.[78] The heuristic attempted here, even if it seeks to neither examine the causes of the emergence of the belief system in its present form[79] nor to explain or challenge the present authority of the fundamental doctrines by looking at their past,[80] involves a historicising exercise.[81] Indeed, it leads to a

---

necessary for the reproduction of the social order, which would become intolerably conflicted without it.'

[76] Cf. the understanding of postmodernism by P. Schlag, 'Normative and nowhere to go' (1990) 43 *Stanford Law Review* 167 at 176, n. 23 ('It is precisely this disciplinary hubris that postmodernism is out to deflate. Postmodernism is out to intensify the critical reflexivity that is already present in and marks the relative evolutionary achievements of rationalist and modernist thought. Postmodernism is simply more serious in pushing the bounds of critical thought. And as these bounds are pushed, much of what previously appeared to be very "serious" thought, very "serious" work, very "important" work, no longer seems that way anymore'). This footnote was drawn to my attention by Akbar Rasulov.

[77] Cf. the attempt by T. Schultz to move away from doctrinal understandings of international arbitration. See T. Schultz, *Transnational Legality: Stateless Law and International Arbitration* (Oxford: Oxford University Press, 2014), p. 6 ('International arbitration, and more generally international dispute settlement, is commonly represented as a technical field, as a subject-matter that is all about procedural technicalities and black letter intricacies. This must stop').

[78] For a criticism of such a linear account of the history of international law, see David Koller, '. . . and New York and The Hague and Tokyo and Geneva and Nuremberg and . . . : the geographies of international law' (2012) 23 *European Journal of International Law* 97.

[79] For similar methodological choices, see Koskenniemi, *From Apology to Utopia*, pp. 72–73.

[80] This was a dominant approach to the history of international law until twenty years ago. See the remarks of George Rodrigo Bandeira Galindo, 'Force field: on history and theory of international law' (2012) 20 *Journal of the Max Planck Institute for European Legal History* 86, esp. 87.

[81] For a useful overview of various ways in which theory and history engage with one another, see Galindo, 'Force field', 86–103.

questioning of the common linear history of the fundamental doctrines of international law whereby the design of modes of legal reasoning originates in the adoption of some key international instruments from which they are supposedly derived.[82]

It is important to emphasise that while this book invites international lawyers to suspend their belief system, it acknowledges that a total abandonment of such a belief system – i.e. the project of apostasy – is neither possible nor desirable. Even the most distant and critical observer would continue to espouse some of the cognitive biases created by the fundamental doctrines of international law.[83] What is more, there can probably be no argumentative practice built outside any belief system whatsoever: getting rid of the current belief system without substituting a new belief system probably would entail riddance of international law as an argumentative practice.[84] In this sense, any endeavour to terminate

[82] This is a point I owe to exchanges with Nehal Bhuta. It should be noted that the counter-historical claim that accompanies the argument made in this book is itself a political intervention (see, generally, Anne Orford, 'International law and the limits of history', in W. Werner, A. Galan and M. de Hoon (eds.), *The Law of International Lawyers: Reading Martti Koskenniemi* (Cambridge: Cambridge University Press, 2017), p. 265.

[83] On the inescapability of tradition, see A. McIntyre, *Whose Justice? Which Rationality?* (London: Duckworth, 1988), pp. 352–53, 367. François Ost has made a similar point in relation to the 'unwriting' of myths. See François Ost, *Raconter la loi: aux sources de l'imaginaire juridique* (Paris: Les Éditions Odile Jacob, 2004), p. 264 ('Des désécritures qui, notons-le cependant, si elles ont retourné et subverti le mythe, ne continuent pas moins à s'inscrire dans le champ des possibles narratifs qu'il autorise'). See also E. Laclau, *Emancipation(s)* (London: Verso, 2007), p. 103 ('[T]he movement of modernity to postmodernity … will not necessarily involve the collapse of all the objects and values contained within the horizon of modernity but, instead, will involve their reformulation from a different perspective').

[84] This has been very elegantly and insightfully explained by Pierre Schlag speaking about the mysticism of law. He writes: 'Law is constructed precisely through this kind of collective, projected objectification; get rid of the objectification, or, to put it another way, get rid of the illusion of objectification, and you get rid of law.' See Schlag, 'Law as the continuation of god by other means' (1997) 85 *California Law Review* 427 at 439. See also P. Schlag, *Laying Down the Law* (New York: New York University Press, 1996), p. 6 ('We are the ones who live in a culture in which it is no longer possible to believe in the law and not yet possible not to believe in the law'). See Schlag, 'Law as the continuation of god by other means' (1997) 85 *California Law Review* 427 at 440 ('It is no more possible to continue doing law in an intellectually respectable way once the metaphysic is gone, than to continue worship once god is dead. Law is like God – here. And once you say that God is just a bunch of conventions, he loses a great deal of his appeal. Correspondingly, worship comes to lack a certain seriousness. The same goes for law'). This also echoes Carl Schmitt's warning against the suppression of the 'mystically produced' nature of sovereignty and community which, according to him, would but obstruct the possibility of both enabling political transparency and holding decision makers morally responsible. See Carl Schmitt, *Political Theology: Four*

the belief system at work behind the common understanding of the formation and functioning of the fundamental doctrines of international law could well be a sterile enterprise.[85] Because the belief system at work in international law simultaneously is what allows communication as well as reform, a radical denial of the belief system looks not only unfeasible but also undesirable. This is why the call for a suspension of the current belief system contemplated here falls short of any termination thereof. The Epilogue (Chapter 6) will return to the impossibility and undesirability of an abandonment of the belief system informing international lawyers' understanding of the formation and functioning of the fundamental doctrines of international law.

It is equally important to highlight that allowing international lawyers to suspend the belief system at work behind the fundamental doctrines of international law does not amount to a call for repudiation of the fundamental doctrines themselves. Actually, calling for a suspension of the belief system of international lawyers does not in itself imply that one needs to invalidate the fundamental doctrines or the legal arguments made on their basis.[86] In addition, the insights sought here do not necessitate suspension of the belief system to a point where such doctrines are permanently invalidated. Reforming the fundamental doctrines of international law is simply another project that is alien to what is endeavoured in this book.[87]

Chapters on the Concept of Sovereignty, trans. George Schwab (Chicago: University of Chicago Press, 1985), pp. 36–40. See also Stanley Fish, *Is There a Text in This Class? The Authority of Interpretive Communities* (Cambridge, MA: Harvard University Press, 1980), p. 276. On the idea that international lawyers cannot be outside a situation, see the remarks of Bianchi, *International Law Theories*, pp. 3–4.

[85] Paul W. Kahn, *The Cultural Study of Law: Reconstructing Legal Scholarship* (Chicago: University of Chicago Press, 1999), p. 3.

[86] This book is thus not the quest to show the 'impossibility of our discipline'. This is how James Crawford introduced the work of Martti Koskenniemi at the annual meeting of the American Society of International Law. See J. Crawford, 'Introductory remarks' (1994) 88 *Proceedings of the American Society of International Law* 22 at 22.

[87] It is in that sense that the inquiry carried out in this book has much in common with Paul W. Khan's cultural study of law ('We must accept the proposition that there is nothing natural about the legal order, that it is a constructed social world that could be constructed differently. Nevertheless, we must put off the impulse to re-create that world on our own blueprint. We must first bring the legal world to light, by raising to self-conscious examination of the social and psychological meanings of a world understood as the rule of law. Who are we and what does our world look like when we find ourselves in this culture of law's rule? Both the mainstream and the radical scholar are too much of this world to ask this question. We need a form of scholarship that gives up the project of

What is sought here is a reflexive distance from the fundamental doctrines, not their abandonment.[88]

4 The Periphery: Legitimacy, Mysticism and Systematicity

The idea that international law constitutes a belief system ties in with a great variety of theoretical controversies that this book does not seek to address in any way. This is why a few observations are formulated here with a view to avoiding any misunderstanding as to the breadth of the ambitions of this book.

It must first be emphasised that the following discussion shies away from addressing the need – probably exacerbated by the findings that this book seeks to produce – to revisit the legitimacy of the belief system and that of the fundamental doctrines. It is acknowledged that by temporarily suspending the belief system and ceasing to think about the fundamental doctrines in their own terms, the unlearning contemplated here inevitably creates an 'unknown' in terms of legitimacy.[89] Indeed, by virtue of the unlearning envisaged here, the legitimacy of the belief system as well as that of the fundamental doctrines can no longer be addressed in the very terms of these doctrines and must, accordingly, be reinvented.[90] By the same token, as the modes of legal reasoning prescribed by the fundamental doctrines come to be portrayed here as the outcome of a series of interventions that can no longer be construed in terms of law-making or interpretation, the question of the legitimacy of these interventions becomes more pressing. Yet this possible need for new tools, frameworks, perspectives and vocabularies in terms of legitimacy is not discussed here. It should be repeated, however, that even if the question of the legitimacy of the belief system and that of the

reform, not because it is satisfied with things as they are, but because it wants better to understand who and what we are'). See Paul W. Kahn, *The Cultural Study of Law: Reconstructing Legal Scholarship* (Chicago: University of Chicago Press, 1999), p. 30. See also J. von Bernstorff, 'International legal scholarship as a cooling medium in international law and politics' (2014) 25 *European Journal of International Law* 977 ('who develops the idea that scholarship should operate as a "cooling" regulator for the overheated discursive operations of the political, economic, and legal subsystems of World Society').

[88] See also Chapter 6, Epilogue.
[89] Cf. A. Orford, 'The destiny of international law' (2004) 17 *Leiden Journal of International Law* 441 at 476; cf. the notion of a 'culture of formalism' from Koskenniemi, *The Gentle Civilizer of Nations*, p. 500. See also the remarks of Justin Desautels-Stein, 'Chiastic law in the crystal ball: exploring legal formalism and its alternative futures' (2014) 2 *London Review of International Law* 263.
[90] This is a point I owe to an exchange with René Provost.

fundamental doctrines is left aside, such a restriction of the scope of inquiry should not be construed as a form of complacency or as an attempt to legitimise the exercise of power and the interventions that have shaped the belief system of international law or its fundamental doctrines and their consequences in terms of distributive justice. After all, this book is primarily about suspending the product of such interventions.

It is equally important to note that the following discussion leaves aside the idea that studying the belief system at work in international law constitutes a venture into mysticism as well as the corresponding idea that the project of 'unlearning' the belief system boils down to nothing more than a demystifying enterprise.[91] This remark is important because belief systems can work in tandem with a few foundational myths,[92] and it cannot be excluded that the same holds for the international belief system.[93] At least, this is a perspective that has been

---

[91] For some critical remarks on the idea that works of critical theory are designed to demystify, see Akbar Rasulov, 'Writing about empire: remarks on the logic of a discourse' (2010) 23 *Leiden Journal of International Law* 449 esp. 450. Derrida argued that mysticism – which is how he construes fabricated genealogy – is what gives law a deconstructible structure, thereby allowing the possibility of deconstruction. J. Derrida, 'Force of law – the "mystical foundation of authority"', in Gil Anidjar (ed.), *Acts of Religion: Jacques Derrida* (New York: Routledge, 2002), pp. 230–98. He writes at pp. 242–43 that the mystical character of law means that 'law is essential deconstructible, whether because it is founded, that is to say constructed, upon interpretable and transformable textual strata ... or because its ultimate foundation is by definition unfounded. The fact that law is deconstructible is not bad news. One may even find in this the political chance of all historical progress ... it is this deconstructible structure of law ... that also ensures the possibility of deconstruction.'

[92] It is no coincidence that on other occasions I described the structure of the fundamental doctrines of international law as mystical. See J. d'Aspremont, 'Jus cogens: a social construct without pedigree' (2015) 46 *Netherlands Yearbook of International Law* 85; and 'Editors' choice 2015', *European Journal of International Law* (2016). See also Strauss, *The Life of Jesus Critically Examined*, who compared the fabricated sources of the gospels to some form of mysticism. See also P. Fitzpatrick, *The Mythology of Modern Law* (London: Routledge, 1992); and O. Corten, *Le discours du droit international*, pp. 153–76.

[93] In the same vein, belief systems can be part of an overarching cultural apparatus (this is a point to which Jan Klabbers and Sahib Singh drew my attention. In this respect, see also the remarks of Mario Prost, *The Concept of Unity in Public International Law* (Oxford: Hart, 2012), pp. 139–40). For the sake of the discussion that follows, the perspective of the study of culture is deemed too all-embracing to allow the following discussion to capture the way in which fundamental doctrines are presented, discussed, interpreted and argued by international lawyers. It is true that, like belief systems, culture generates capacity for the members of the community or society concerned to create the categories of their own experience (see Lawrence Rosen, *Law as Culture: An Invitation* (Princeton, NJ: Princeton University Press, 2006), p. 4). Yet the attitudes that are constitutive of culture are not limited to beliefs but also encapsulate myths and other self-referential modes of actions (Paul W. Kahn, *The Cultural Study of Law: Reconstructing Legal Scholarship* (Chicago:

espoused by others. For instance, as is well known, Montaigne – on which Derrida famously relied extensively to make a similar contention[94] – explained the authority of law through its mystic character.[95] It is also well known that legal realists at the beginning of the twentieth century used similar analytical categories to describe the way lawyers are attached to their legal concepts. Felix Cohen, for instance, spoke of legal concepts as 'supernatural entities which do not have a verifiable existence except to the eyes of faith'.[96] The scholarship of Pierre Schlag shows a similar use of mysticism to describe some liberal patterns of legal thought.[97] International lawyers themselves have resorted to the use of myth to explain certain moves in international legal discourse[98] or in historical narratives.[99]

University of Chicago Press, 1999), p. 1, for whom culture also 'has it founding myths, necessary beliefs, and its reasons that are internal to its own norms'). On the concept of legal culture, see also H. Patrick Glenn, *Legal Traditions of the World* (Oxford: Oxford University Press, 2007). This is why approaching the common understanding of the formation and functioning of fundamental doctrines as a study of culture would not provide an expository lens that is precise enough for what is attempted here.

[94] Derrida, 'Force of law – the "mystical foundation of authority"', pp. 230–98. On p. 240, he writes: 'The authority of laws rests on the credit that is granted them. One believes in it; that is their only foundation. This act of faith is not an ontological or rational foundation.' Derrida also claims that such myths are deeply prejudiced in favour of what he called a 'white mythology'. See J. Derrida and F. C. T. Moore, 'Metaphor in the text of philosophy' (1974) 6 *New Literary History* 5.

[95] Montaigne, *De l'expérience*, essai 3, chap. 13.

[96] Felix Cohen, 'Transcendental nonsense and the functional approach' (1935) 35 *Columbia Law Review* 809 at 821 and 823.

[97] P. Schlag, 'The empty circles of liberal justification' (1997) 96 *Michigan Law Review* 1.

[98] See Andrea Bianchi, 'Human rights and the magic of jus cogens' (2008) 19 *European Journal of International Law* 491; R. Collins, *The Institutional Problem in Modern International Law* (Oxford: Hart, 2016), chap. 6. On the myth that international law can be identified by looking at the sources, see M. Reisman, 'International lawmaking: a process of communication' (1981) 75 *American Society of International Law Proceedings* 101. On the myths of international adjudication, see Ingo Venzke, 'The role of international courts as interpreters and developers of the law: working out the jurisgenerative practice of interpretation' (2011) 34 *Loyola of Los Angeles International and Comparative Law Review* 99.

[99] On the particular idea of the myth of Westphalia, see Andreas Osiander, 'Sovereignty, international relations, and the Westphalian myth' (2001) 55 *International Organization* 251; Pärtel Piirimäe, 'The Westphalian myth and the idea of external sovereignty', in Skinner Kalmo (ed.), *Sovereignty in Fragments: The Past, Present and Future of a Contested Concept* (Cambridge: Cambridge University Press, 2010), pp. 64–80; B. Teschke, *The Myth of 1648: Class, Geopolitics, and the Making of Modern International Relations* (London: Verso, 2009). See, more generally, D. Kennedy, 'International law and the nineteenth century: history of an illusion' (1997) 17 *Quinnipiac Law Review* 99 at 121. See also M. Koskenniemi, *The Gentle Civilizer of Nations: The Rise and Fall of International Law 1870–1960* (Cambridge: Cambridge University Press, 2001), pp. 95 and 143.

There are a few sensible arguments that could justify resort to the notion of myth – rather than that of belief system – to discuss the way in which fundamental doctrines operate in international legal thought and practice.[100] For instance, the international belief system and mysticism share a reliance on self-referentiality and the invention of their own sources.[101] Furthermore, the derivation of fundamental doctrines from a certain key authoritative text is meant to ensure a form of permanence of the modes of legal reasoning prescribed by the doctrine that is also found in myths.[102] The composite character of fundamental doctrines and their functioning as clusters of modes of legal reasoning[103] are similarly reminiscent of the structure of myths.[104] In the same vein, fundamental doctrines are mutually dependent,[105] just like myths.[106] It must also be acknowledged that common understandings of fundamental doctrines allow a certain amnesia, as international lawyers tend to be oblivious to the process of their making[107] and presuppose that they have always been there.[108] The mysticism at work in international lawyers' understanding of the formation and functioning of fundamental doctrines is reinforced by the extent to which fundamental doctrines seem to fulfil international lawyers' needs for both knowledge and ordering[109] or their eagerness to gain some representation of existing conditions or the origin of

---

[100] This could also be seen as the manifestation of some romanticisation of law. On this idea, see Pierre Schlag, 'Normativity and the politics of form' (1991) 139 *University of Pennsylvania Law Review* 4, 802 at 804. This idea is not explored here.

[101] On that aspect of myths in relation to law, see François Ost, *Raconter la loi: aux sources de l'imaginaire juridique* (Paris: Les Éditions Jacob Odile Jacob, 2004), pp. 257–60.

[102] Claude Lévi-Strauss, 'Chapitre XI: La structure des mythes', in *Anthropologie Structural* (Paris: Plon, 1958).

[103] See Chapter 2, Section 1.

[104] See the idea of 'mythèmes' and that of 'paquet de relations' developed by Claude Lévi-Strauss, in 'Chapitre XI: La structure des mythes'. See the earlier version published in English (1958). See also Jean Pouillon, 'L'analyse des myths' (1966) 6 *L'Homme* 100.

[105] See Chapter 3.

[106] See Peter Fitzpatrick, *The Mythology of Modern Law* (London: Routledge, 1992), p. 146.

[107] On the relation between mythology and amnesia, see Fitzpatrick, *Mythology*, p. x.

[108] François Ost (ed.), *Le Temps du Droit* (Paris: Les Éditions Odile Jacob, 1999), pp. 58–60.

[109] Lévi-Strauss, 'La structure des mythes', pp. 8–12. This aspect of myth has famously led Andrea Bianchi to use mysticism as a framework to describe the way international lawyers construe *jus cogens*. See Andrea Bianchi, 'Human rights and the magic of jus cogens' (2008) 19 *European Journal of International Law* 491 esp. 507–8.

their formal modes of legal reasoning.[110] Eventually, belief systems may share with myths the suppression of time.[111]

Even if, for the above-mentioned reasons, international lawyers' understanding of the formation and functioning of the fundamental doctrines could be approached from the perspective of a study of myths, the possible mysticism that accompanies the international belief system is disregarded, and the sole perspective of the belief system is preferred. It is suggested here that in some significant respects fundamental doctrines of international law, even if they invent their own origin and dictate their functioning, differ from myths. As is illustrated by the discussion on the fundamental doctrine of responsibility below,[112] the origin of the fundamental doctrines can be traced, at least roughly. What is more, the function of fundamental doctrines cannot be conflated with the eschatological function of myths.[113] For these reasons, it does not seem helpful for the sake of this inquiry to approach the operation of fundamental doctrines as a form of mysticism.

Finally, a remark is necessary about the relationship between the belief system at work in international legal thought and practice and the idea that international law constitutes a system.[114] Systemic thinking about international law is probably a heritage of German public law

---

[110] For instance, as far as psychological processes are concerned, it could be argued that the genealogical link between the international texts and the fundamental doctrines of international law is nothing more than the manifestation of a rather mundane need felt by international lawyers to gain some representation of existing conditions or the origin of their formal modes of legal reasoning. In this respect, see the remarks of Strauss, *The Life of Jesus Critically Examined*, p. 62. It could even be said that the mythical roots of the fundamental doctrines of international law and the false causality traditionally established between them and the international instruments from which they are derived helped international lawyers push the metaphysical or the morality away. It seems no coincidence that from a chronological perspective, the consolidation of such mythical genealogy corresponds with the rise of legal positivism as the dominant school of thought in international law and the retreat of natural law. On the rise of international legal positivism, see Mónica García-Salmones Rovira, *The Project of Positivism in International Law* (Oxford: Oxford University Press, 2013).

[111] See Anthony Giddens, *Central Problems in Social Theory: Action, Structure and Contradiction in Social Analysis* (Basingstoke: Macmillan, 1979), p. 21.

[112] See Chapter 4, Section 1.   [113] See Chapter 2, Section 1.

[114] For some critical remarks on the idea of international legal system, see R. Collins, *The Institutional Problem in Modern International Law* (Oxford: Hart, 2016), chap. 3; E. Benvenisti, 'Comments on the systemic vision of national courts as part of an international rule of law' (2012) 4 *Jerusalem Review of Legal Studies* 42 at 43. See J. d'Aspremont, 'The International Court of Justice and the paradox of system-design' (2016) 7 *Journal of International Dispute Settlement* 1.

scholarship.[115] As a brainchild of German public law scholarship, systemic thinking quickly became central in European thinking about international law. It has been argued that systemic thinking about law was introduced in the Anglo-American tradition of international law by Germans and German-speaking émigrés such as Francis Lieber, Lassa Oppenheim, Hersch Lauterpacht, Georg Schwarzenberger and Hans Kelsen.[116] Although the idea of an international legal system came to be severely challenged,[117] especially in more recent North American legal thought,[118] systemic thinking permeates almost all traditions.[119] Indeed, most international lawyers like to think of international law as a system.[120] The popularity of such a representation is probably informed by a great variety of parameters.[121] For instance, a systemic representation of international law makes the object of study in such a field look more noble and

---

[115] Martti Koskenniemi, 'Georg Friedrish von Martens (1756–1821) and the origins of modern international law' (2008) 15 *Constellations* 2. See also E. Benvenisti, 'The conception of international law as a legal system' (2008) *Tel Aviv University Law Faculty Papers* 2008/83, 2.

[116] E. Benvenisti, 'The conception of international law as a legal system' (2008) *Tel Aviv University Law Faculty Papers* 2008/83, 3.

[117] Nowadays it is common to think of international law as an argumentative practice or to take refuge in a culture of non-order called 'pluralism' which makes no claim on the systematisation of international law. See Neil Walker, 'Beyond boundary disputes and basic grids: mapping the global disorder of normative orders' (2008) 6 *I.CONnect* 373 at 391 ('Rather than proposing an alternative order of orders, pluralism proposes a kind of "nonorder" of orders, in which no general steering mechanism is available to frame the relations between orders; instead, any such relational complex (with the attendant virtues of countervailing power) emerges serendipitously out of the undirected interaction of the parts').

[118] This is not without paradox given that US scholarship was one of the birthplaces of the idea of an international legal system. In this respect, Duncan Kennedy has argued that until the Second World War, the United States was a massive importer of European legal thought. After that, he argues, the United States stopped importing or even relating to legal developments abroad, except to try to influence them in various imperial ventures. See Duncan Kennedy, 'The hermeneutic of suspicion in contemporary American legal thought' (2014) 25 *Law and Critique* 91 at 92.

[119] It cannot be contested that it is particularly dominant in continental Europe. There may be only the English tradition where the idea of international law as a system has had a more limited foray because of the traditional antipathy of the latter towards sophisticated taxonomies and dichotomies and its ability to work disorders at a low level of abstraction.

[120] Philippe Weckel speaks of an 'obsession'. See P. Weckel, 'Ouverture de la réflexion sur le droit international à la science des systèmes', in D. Alland, V. Chetail, O. de Frouville and J. Vinuales (eds.), *Unity and Diversity of International Law: Essays in Honour of Professor Pierre-Marie Dupuy* (Leiden: Martinus Nijhoff, 2014), p. 130.

[121] For other possible drivers, see E. Benvenisti, 'Comments on the systemic vision of national courts as part of an international rule of law' (2012) 4 *Jerusalem Review of*

sophisticated. It also enhances the image of international lawyers themselves, as a systemic portrayal of international law makes practitioners look like masterful geeks rather than unrefined sophists.[122] The image of a system simultaneously throws a rather technical veil on doctrinal controversies, seemingly keeping them alien to the supposedly 'dirty' normative and political choices of the law-appliers and law-interpreters. Systemic thinking about international law thus eventually reveals an infinite world of possibilities for international law and international lawyers.

The popularity of the idea of an international legal system is not self-evident. Indeed, it is uncontested that the notion of system remains an operation of the mind. The international legal system is not 'out there' and ready to be discovered. Rather, it is created by the systemic descriptive frameworks deployed by international lawyers.[123] It is because the international legal system does not exist as such but is always constructed that the question arises as to whether the idea of an international legal system is informed by the belief system this book seeks to expose. In other words, one may wonder whether the inclination of international lawyers to think of international law in systemic terms is not a product of the belief system at work in international legal thought and practice.

My contention here is that the ruleness, imaginary genealogy and self-referentiality at the heart of the belief system, while allowing fundamental doctrines to be turned into transcendentally acquired validators that generate a sense of constraint, simultaneously contribute to the representation of international law as a legal system for two reasons. First, the ruleness, imaginary genealogy and self-referentiality create inter-dependence between the fundamental doctrines, thereby projecting an image of those fundamental doctrines as being the interconnected components of a composite order.[124] Second, the belief system is also

Legal Studies 42 at 43–44 (where he refers to the room it provides for both continuity and change as well as the denial of politics).

[122] Pierre Schlag, 'Normativity and the politics of form' (1991) 139 *University of Pennsylvania Law Review* 801 at 845 : 'Not surprisingly, those theories that are the most popular within the legal academy are those that project the most attractive self-image.'

[123] See Charles de Visscher, *Théories et Réalités en Droit International Public*, 4th edn (Paris: Pedone, 1970), p. 171: 'l'homme de droit, à la recherche d'une legitimation, reconstitue (les forces politiques) ex post facto pour les intégrer dans un ordre qu'il tient pour souhaitable.'

[124] This is the understanding of system that one sees in ILC, 'Fragmentation of international law: problems caused by the diversification and expansion of international law, report of the study group of the International Law Commission, finalized by Martti Koskenniemi', 13 April 2006, UN Doc. A/CN.4/L.682, paras. 65–101. See also B. Simma, 'Self-contained

what provides a foundation to the mechanisms of (in)validation that govern the formation, termination and interpretation of standards of behaviours as well as the consequences of a breach thereof and that are held, in most common understandings, to constitute the main components of the international legal system. The idea of an international legal system and the belief system at work in international legal thought and practice are thus closely intertwined, as the belief system is instrumental to the sense of systematicity of international lawyers. It can even be contended that the idea of an international legal system is the very product of the belief system exposed in this book. This being said, the idea of an international legal system is not further explored here. Although it is facilitated, if not generated, by the belief system itself, the idea of an international legal system is unhelpful in allowing one to capture the extent to which fundamental doctrines are the transcendental validators that international lawyers turn to in articulating their legal discourse.

5 The Contents: The Following Chapters

The claim made in this book that international law constitutes a belief system and the attempt to pursue a suspension of that belief system proceed as follows. The two chapters that follow introduce the various components of the belief system at work behind the fundamental doctrines. Chapter 2 elaborates on the object of the belief system and its conditions of realisation, namely, ruleness, imaginary genealogy and self-referentiality. The chapter shows that it is only as long as these three conditions are met that fundamental doctrines will generate a sense of constraint. Chapter 3 focuses more specifically on the self-referentiality that allows fundamental doctrines to be explained in their own terms and generate a sense of constraint. The attention turns more specifically to the role of the fundamental doctrine of sources to explain the formation of all fundamental doctrines (what is called 'sources-based self-referentiality') as well as the role of the fundamental doctrine of interpretation to explain the functioning of all fundamental doctrines (what is called 'interpretation-based self-referentiality'). Chapter 4

regimes' (1985) 16 *Netherlands Yearbook of International Law* 112; B. Simma and D. Pulkowski, 'Of planets and the universe: self-contained regimes and international law' (2006) 17 *European Journal of International Law* 483; A. Lindroos and M. Mehling, 'Dispelling the chimera of "self-contained regimes" international law and the WTO' (2005) 16 *European Journal of International Law* 857.

discusses some of the concrete manifestations of the international belief system by pointing out the manner in which the fundamental doctrines of responsibility, statehood, customary law and *jus cogens* are commonly understood and deployed. In particular, the chapter examines and illustrates the design process of fundamental doctrines, the choice of international instruments from which to derive fundamental doctrines, the derivation of fundamental doctrines from international instruments and the transcendental comfort provided by the belief system. Chapter 5 introduces the idea of a suspension of the international belief system and elaborates on the consequences of the unlearning of sources- and interpretation-based self-referentiality. The final chapter is an epilogue that expounds on the value of unlearning, its reformist potential as well as the risk of apostasy.

2

Structure of the International Belief System

This chapter substantiates the expository claim made in this book that international law constitutes a belief system where fundamental doctrines generate a sense of constraint. This chapter specifically argues that the fundamental doctrines turn into transcendental validators of international legal discourse and generate an experienced sense of constraint as long as three interdependent conditions are met: ruleness, imaginary genealogy and self-referentiality. The *ruleness* refers here to the need to represent fundamental doctrines as sets of rules. The *imaginary genealogy* is the derivation of fundamental doctrines from some key authoritative instruments. And *self-referentiality* is the potential for fundamental doctrines to explain their own formation and functioning. It is only once fundamental doctrines are construed as rules derived from international instruments whose formation and functioning can be explained by fundamental doctrines themselves that those doctrines can generate a sense of constraint.

This chapter starts by spelling out the very object of the international belief system, namely, fundamental doctrines (1). It continues by elucidating the above-mentioned necessary conditions for fundamental doctrines to become transcendental validators of international legal discourse and generate a sense of constraint, namely, ruleness, imaginary genealogy and self-referentiality (2). Finally, it expounds on how fundamental doctrines generate an experienced sense of constraint (3).

1   Object of the Belief System: Fundamental Doctrines as Clusters of Modes of Legal Reasoning

Fundamental doctrines constitute the very object of the belief system exposed here. In fact, it is towards the fundamental doctrines that international lawyers experience a sense of constraint. Fundamental doctrines boil down to clusters of modes of legal reasoning that international lawyers ought to rely on when they formulate international legal claims about the existence and extent of the rights and duties of actors subjected to international law and the consequences of breaches thereof.[1] Their prescriptive character holds for anyone involved in international legal discourse, whether they are scholars, legal advisers, practitioners, activists, teachers or judges.[2] Given such an understanding, fundamental doctrines of international law are diverse and include clusters of modes of legal reasoning pertaining to sources, personality, responsibility, statehood, interpretation, *jus cogens* and so on. They are distinct from other doctrines that enunciate the standards of behaviour to which international actors recognised by international law are subjected.

The main characteristic of fundamental doctrines is to put in place argumentative templates around which modes of legal reasoning are axiomatically organised and where only a limited number of combinatory possibilities can be accepted to build a legal argument. Such axiomisation is what determines the world of possible and impossible combinations of modes of legal reasoning within the argumentative template put in place by fundamental doctrines.[3] This axiomisation can vary in degree. The organisation of the modes of legal reasoning can be more or less sophisticated. These variations are well illustrated, for instance, by the contrasts between the fundamental doctrine of customary law[4] and that of responsibility.[5] The axiomisation conducted by fundamental doctrines can also evolve in time and become more or less rigid. This is exemplified by the fundamental doctrine

---

[1] On the prescriptive character of legal thought in general, see also Pierre Schlag, 'Normativity and the politics of form' (1991) 139 *University of Pennsylvania Law Review* 801 at 839. He also writes at p. 807: 'We are free, but we must choose – which is to say that we are not free at all. On the contrary, we (you and I) have been constituted as the kind of beings, the kind of thinkers who compulsively treat every intellectual, social, or legal event as calling for a choice. We must choose.'

[2] On the variations of argumentative constraints between the various professions of international law, see J. d'Aspremont, T. Gazzini, A. Nollkaemper and W. Werner (eds.), *International Law as a Profession* (Cambridge: Cambridge University Press, 2017).

[3] It could be said that the fundamental doctrines simultaneously provide a vernacular through which the violence of the field is both articulated and clouded. See D. Kennedy, *A World of Struggle: How Power, Law, and Expertise Shape Global Political Economy* (Princeton, NJ: Princeton University Press, 2016), p. 72. This is a point that does not need to be explored here. On violence and international legal argumentation in general, see I. Feichtner, 'Critical scholarship and responsible practice of international law: how can the two be reconciled?' (2016) 29 *Leiden Journal of International Law* 4, 979.

[4] See Chapter 4, Section 3.   [5] See Chapter 4, Section 1.

of custom.[6] Eventually, it should be noted that the axiomisation carried out by fundamental doctrines is not solely restrictive; it restricts as much as it permits in that it constitutes an argumentative space where legal claims and counterclaims can be made.

It is important to realise that fundamental doctrines inevitably come with a certain degree of indeterminacy and malleability, and this is usually not reined in by the regular attempts by codifying bodies to put them in writing.[7] The same holds for the occasional comprehensive judicial pronouncements and the authoritative academic literature, which have restated or refined some of them but have failed to curb their indeterminacy or malleability.[8] The written captures and restatements, themselves in need of interpretation, further fuel the fluctuations in the contents of fundamental doctrines and the modes of legal reasoning they organise.[9] The content of fundamental doctrines can also be the object of severe contestation by the very professionals who resort to them. Indeed, there are some inevitable and permanent squabbles about the content of the modes of legal reasoning that fundamental doctrines put in place and the way in which they are organised.[10] Contestation of the content of a particular fundamental doctrine should not necessarily be construed as a challenge of its role as a fundamental

---

[6] See Chapter 4, Section 3. See also J. d'Aspremont, 'The decay of modern customary international law in spite of scholarly heroism', in G. Capaldo (ed.), *Global Community: Yearbook of International Law and Jurisprudence* (Oxford: Oxford University Press, 2015).

[7] On the challenges of distinguishing between codification and progressive developments, see J. Crawford, 'The progressive development of international law: history, theory and practice', in D. Alland, V. Chetail, O. de Frouville and J. Vinuales (eds.), *Unity and Diversity of International Law: Essays in Honour of Professor Pierre-Marie Dupuy*, pp. 3–22.

[8] In relation to customary international law, see e.g. *North Sea Continental Shelf (West Germany v Denmark, West Germany v Netherlands)*, ICJ Rep. 1969, 3; in relation to *jus cogens*, see *Armed Activities on the Territory of the Congo (Democratic Republic of the Congo v Rwanda)* (Jurisdiction and Admissibility), ICJ Rep. 2006, 1, paras. 64 and 125. See the remarks in Chapter 6.

[9] J. Vinuales, 'On legal inquiry', in D. Alland, V. Chetail, O. de Frouville and J. Vinuales (eds.), *Unity and Diversity of International Law: Essays in Honour of Professor Pierre-Marie Dupuy*, pp. 45–75 (for Vinuales, such indeterminacy can be explained by variations of what he calls 'conceptual charts').

[10] In the same sense, see A. A. Leff, 'Unspeakable ethics, unnatural law' (1979) *Duke Law Journal* 1229 at 1247 (speaking about the Constitution functioning as God): 'There will be, as with all divine pronouncements, a continuous controversy over what God says, but whatever the practical importance of the power to determine those questions, they are theoretically unthreatening. It is only when Constitution ceases to be seen as fulfilling God's normative role, ceases, that is, to be outside the normative system it totally constitutes, or when, as is impossible with a real God, it is seen to have "gaps" that a crisis comes to exist.'

doctrine. On the contrary, as illustrated by the doctrine of statehood (discussed below),[11] contestation is generally an expression that the doctrine concerned is held as fundamental and taken as the seat of international legal arguments on a particular issue.

The above-mentioned contingency and possible contestation of the content of fundamental doctrines, when taken in combination with complex epistemic dynamics and hierarchies,[12] explain why an erudite command of such fundamental doctrines, even when accompanied by a very orthodox deployment of the modes of legal reasoning they put in place, is no guarantee of success – that is, acceptance – of the legal discourse concerned. This means that international lawyers have no assurance whatsoever that their arguments will be held valid by others despite their obedient reliance on (and mastery of) the main organised clusters of modes of legal reasoning of international law.[13] It remains that, while offering no assurance of the success of a legal argument, abiding by the modes of legal reasoning prescribed by the fundamental doctrines of international law remains a prerequisite in any attempt to make an international legal argument. Only a legal discourse constructed around the modes of legal reasoning prescribed by those fundamental doctrines has a chance to be heard and accepted by other professionals.[14]

The foregoing should suffice to show that fundamental doctrines are distinct from the standards of behaviour that are actually argued and applied by international lawyers when they build international legal

---

[11] See Chapter 4, Section 2.

[12] I have discussed some of these dynamics and structures elsewhere. J. d'Aspremont, *Epistemic Forces in International Law: Foundational Doctrines and Techniques of International Legal Argumentation* (Cheltenham: Edward Elgar, 2015). See also Nikolas Rajkovic, 'Rules, lawyering, and the politics of legality: critical sociology and international law's rule' (2014) 27 *Leiden Journal of International Law* 331. See also Andrea Bianchi, *International Law Theories: An Inquiry into Different Ways of Thinking* (Oxford: Oxford University Press, 2016), pp. 9–11.

[13] Pierre Schlag, 'Normativity and the politics of form' (1991) 139 *University of Pennsylvania Law Review* 801 at 930 ('At the borderlands of consciousness, there is a sense in which normative legal thinkers know that their prescriptions and recommendations are not going anywhere. At the borderlands of consciousness, legal thinkers know that within the tens of thousands of pages of volumes 1 to 103 of the *Harvard Law Review* – for instance – there is an abundance of prescriptions and recommendations that have gone nowhere and done nothing but serve as the occasion for repeating argument structures and forms we now look back upon with an odd mixture of amusement, disdain, and humbling self-recognition').

[14] For some additional insights on the validation of international legal arguments, see J. d'Aspremont, 'Wording in international law' (2012) 25 *Leiden Journal of International Law* 575.

discourse.[15] Instead, fundamental doctrines refer to the organised clusters of modes of legal reasoning that regulate how legal discourse about those standards of behaviour is articulated. In this sense, fundamental doctrines correspond to what is commonly called 'secondary rules'. Yet the notion of secondary rules is consciously rejected here, despite constituting a popular descriptive and analytical notion in international legal scholarship.[16] The rationale of such a rejection is that the very idea of *rules* is an integral part of the belief system that this book seeks to expose. In fact, the idea that fundamental doctrines constitute a set of (secondary) rules is what allows their derivation from some key international instruments and the reduction of their formation and functioning to the making and interpretation of those texts.[17] Thus the resort to the notion of secondary rules to describe fundamental doctrines would defeat the very suspension of the belief system contemplated by this book.

Based on the understanding put forward here, fundamental doctrines must be similarly distinguished from legal fictions. Indeed, if one takes the traditional understanding of legal fictions as being consciously temporary and meant to be corrected or exhausted by legal reasoning,[18] the difference between fundamental doctrines and legal fictions becomes conspicuous. Indeed, fundamental doctrines are not meant to be temporary but are rather deployed as permanent organised clusters of modes of legal reasoning. Their permanence is absolutely crucial to what they can achieve, for any one relying on fundamental doctrines believes that they will ensure the continuous validity of their argument in the future. Even if one takes the Kelsenian approach to legal fictions by virtue of which legal fictions can permanently found the international legal order,[19] fundamental doctrines, as they are understood here, remain

---

[15] This is probably what distinguishes the account made here from the interactional account proposed by Jutta Brunnée and Stephen J. Toope in their study, *Legitimacy and Legality in International Law* (Cambridge: Cambridge University Press, 2010).

[16] I previously used this notion as well. See J. d'Aspremont, *Formalism and the Sources of International Law* (Oxford: Oxford University Press, 2011). I later came to reject it. See J. d'Aspremont, 'The idea of "rules" in the sources of international law' (2014) 84 *British Yearbook of International Law* 103. See also the departure from that notion carefully advocated by A. Nollkaemper and D. Jacobs, 'Shared responsibility in international law: a conceptual framework' (2013) 34 *Michigan Journal of International Law* 408.

[17] See Chapter 3, Section 1.

[18] This corresponds to the traditional definition of Hans Vaihinger, *La Philosophie du comme si* (1911).

[19] On the divergences between Kelsen and Vaihinger regarding legal fictions, see Christophe Bouriau, *Les fictions du droit: Kelsen, lecteur de Vaihinger* (Lyon: Ens Éditions, 2013).

distinct. They are not meant to provide foundations to the international legal order but, more modestly, to organise international legal discourse. This does not exclude that fictions play a role in the making of fundamental doctrines.[20]

2   Conditions of the International Belief System: Ruleness, Imaginary Genealogy and Self-Referentiality

The object of the belief system, namely, fundamental doctrines, comes to generate an experienced sense of constraint only to the extent that they are represented as sets of rules derived from a few international instruments whose formation and functioning can be explained in the very terms of the fundamental doctrines. Thus three conditions must be fulfilled for the fundamental doctrines to generate a sense of constraint: ruleness (2.1), imaginary genealogy (2.2) and self-referentiality (2.3). These three conditions are cumulative. These three conditions of realisation of the belief system are examined in turn in this section.

A few preliminary remarks are warranted as to the cumulative character of the three conditions of the international belief system. First, ruleness, imaginary genealogy and self-referentiality must all be realised for the fundamental doctrines to generate a sense of constraint. These features of international legal discourse are mutually reinforcing. As will be explained below, ruleness and the imaginary genealogy make self-referentiality possible.[21] Indeed, self-referentiality is contingent on the fact that fundamental doctrines are rules derived from international instruments and on the reduction of the formation and functioning of fundamental doctrines to the making and interpretation of the instruments from which they are derived. In turn, self-referentiality, once it is realised by virtue of ruleness and imaginary genealogy, reinforces the representation of fundamental doctrines as rules derived from international instruments. In fact, because fundamental doctrines explain their own formation and functioning, they must be rules derived from international instruments. Second, the three conditions of the belief system do not need to be realised in a certain order or according to a certain sequence. This means that the following account of the three conditions of the international belief system does not express any chronological

---

[20] François Ost, *Le Temps du Droit* (Paris: Les Éditions Odile Jacob, 1999), p. 60.
[21] The connection between ruleness and self-referentiality is not new. See P. Schlag, *Laying Down the Law* (New York: New York University Press, 1996), p. 11.

causality. All the processes described below are simultaneous and inter-meshed, without any of them taking place before the other. Third, the idea that international legal discourse is articulated around mutually reinforcing components is obviously not new.[22] Yet, in contrast with other accounts of relations of mutual dependence of the components of international legal discourse, ruleness, imaginary genealogy and self-referentiality do not simultaneously constitute antithetical and mutually exclusive notions. This is why it can be said that the expository frame-work promoted here is alien to any structuralist analytical model.[23] Whatever such differences, the point here is that the three conditions discussed herein are cumulative and must all be met for the fundamental doctrines to generate a sense of constraint and the belief system to be in place.

2.1 Fundamental Doctrines as Rules: Ruleness

The representation of fundamental doctrines as rules is one of the elementary conditions of the realisation of the belief system. This specific representation of the fundamental doctrines is what is called here the *ruleness* of fundamental doctrines. It specifically refers to the reduction of the fundamental doctrines to sets of rules, thereby pro-viding these doctrines with some sort of tangibility, identity and endurance. By virtue of this ruleness, rules become the cognisable units through which fundamental doctrines are represented, appre-hended, experienced and explained. It will be shown later that the reduction of fundamental doctrines to sets of rules simultaneously

---

[22] See how opposing notions such as concreteness and normativity depend on one another in the account of international legal argumentation famously provided by M. Koskenniemi, *From Apology to Utopia*.

[23] On the structuralist foundations of M. Koskenniemi's account of international legal argumentation, see Sahib Singh, 'International legal positivism and new approaches to international law', in J. Kammerhofer and J. d'Aspremont (eds.), *International Legal Positivism in a Postmodern World* (Cambridge: Cambridge University Press, 2014), pp. 291–316; Justin Desautels-Stein, 'International legal structuralism: a primer' (2016) 8 *International Theory* 201; E. Jouannet provides a similar but more nuanced account. See E. Jouannet, 'A critical introduction', in M. Koskenniemi, *The Politics of International Law* (Oxford: Hart, 2011), pp. 2, 7–12. For a very insightful overview of the merits of structuralism for international legal thought, see Justin Desautels-Stein, 'International legal structuralism: a primer'; and Justin Desautels-Stein, 'Structuralist legal histories' (2015) 78 *Law and Contemporary Problems* 37. See also John Morss, 'Structuralism and interpretation in the theory of international law: cracking the code?', available at http://ssrn.com/abstract=2781388 (accessed on 8 March 2017).

gives self-referentiality a particular calibre and breadth, for only the instruments that are the repository of such rules are in need of justification. Ruleness is a prerequisite of the other conditions of realisation of the belief system, namely, imaginary genealogy and self-referentiality.[24]

Representations of fundamental doctrines as sets of rules are rife in international legal thought and practice. It is very common, for instance, to represent the doctrines of sources,[25]

---

[24] This is not to say that the only rationale of ruleness is self-referentiality. There may be other reasons for the dominance of ruleness in legal thought in general. See F. Schauer, *Thinking Like a Lawyer: A New Introduction to Legal Reasoning* (Cambridge, MA: Harvard University Press, 2009), p.13; Christian Reus-Smit, 'Introduction', in Christian Reus-Smit (ed.), *The Politics of International Law* (Cambridge: Cambridge University Press, 2004), p. 5; Gerry Simpson, 'On the magic mountain: teaching public international law' (1999) 10 *European Journal of International Law* 70 at 75. Fuad Zarbiyev, *Le Discours Interprétatif en Droit International Contemporain: Un Essai Critique* (Brussels: Bruylant, 2015), pp. 23–35. On the imperialistic dimension of ruleness, see China Miéville, *Between Equal Rights: A Marxist Theory of International Law* (London: Pluto Press, 2005), pp. 66–74, 318–19.

[25] J. Brierly, 'The basis of obligation in international law', in H. Lauterpacht and C. H. M. Waldock (eds.), *The Basis of Obligation in International Law and Other Papers by the Late James Leslie Brierly* (Oxford: Clarendon Press, 1959) pp. 1, 10; P. Guggenheim, *Traite de Droit International Public* (Paris: Georg & Cie, 1953), pp. 6–8; P. Weil, 'Le droit international en quête de son identité – Cours général de droit international public' (1992) 237 *Recueil des Cours* 131; A. D'Amato, 'The concept of special custom in international law' (1969) 63 *American Journal of International Law* 211; T. Nardin, *Law, Morality, and the Relations of States* (Princeton, NJ: Princeton University Press, 1983), p. 172 (arguing, however, that there is no rule on customary international law). It is noteworthy that Michael Wood uses quotation marks when he refers to the rules for the formation of customary international law: see M. Wood, 'What is public international law? The need for clarity about sources' (2011) 1 *Asian Journal of International Law* 205 at 213. Malcolm Shaw speaks about 'provisions operating with the legal system on a technical level': see M. Shaw, *International Law*, 5th edn (Cambridge: Cambridge University Press, 2003), p. 66. Hugh Thirlway, for his part, speaks about the 'law of sources': see H. Thirlway, *The Sources of International Law* (Oxford: Oxford University Press, 2014). The same idea of ruleness also imbues those commonly heard statements that Article 38 is declaratory of general international law. See A. Pellet, 'Article 38', in A. Zimmermann, C. Tomuschat, K. Oellers-Frahm and C. Tams (eds.), *The Statute of the International Court of Justice: A Commentary*, 2nd edn (Oxford: Oxford University Press, 2012), p. 750; G. Abi-Saab, 'Les sources du droit international: essai de deconstruction', in M. Rama-Montaldo (ed.), *International Law in an Evolving World: Liber Amicorum in Tribute to Professor Eduardo Jiménez de Aréchaga*, vol. 1 (Montevideo: Fundacici de Cultura Universitaria, 1994), pp. 29–49. The same holds with those works that attempt to transpose Hart's *Concept of Law* to sources of international law and especially to theory of customary international law; see G.J.H. Van Hoof, *Rethinking the Sources of International Law* (Alphen aan den Rijn, Netherlands: Kluwer Law, 1983); G. M. Danilenko, *Law-Making in the International Community* (Leiden: Martinus Nijhoff, 1993), pp. 16ff; G. M. Danilenko, 'The theory of international customary law' (1988) 31 *German Yearbook of International Law* 9; H. Meijers, 'How is international law made?' (1979) 9 *Netherlands Yearbook of International Law* 3.

interpretation,[26] responsibility,[27] *jus cogens*[28], and statehood[29] as rules. It is noteworthy that ruleness is a pattern of legal thought that has hardly been discussed in the literature,[30] even less so in relation to its contribution to the common understanding of the formation and functioning of fundamental doctrines in international legal thought and practice. This is not surprising. As already mentioned, one of the characteristics of the belief system is that it is self-obfuscating and thus hides the conditions of its realisation.

2.2 Fundamental Doctrines as Derived from a Formal Respository: Imaginary Genealogy

Because they are seen as rules, fundamental doctrines must be given a repository where they are formally nested. For international lawyers, the

---

[26] For an overview of this dominant understanding, see Fuad Zarbiyev, *Le Discours Interprétatif en Droit International Contemporain: Un Essai Critique* (Lyon: Bruylant, 2015), pp. 23–28.

[27] See e.g. *Case Concerning Application of the Convention on the Prevention and Punishment of the Crime of Genocide (Bosnia Herzegovina v Serbia and Montenegro)*, ICJ Rep. 2007, 202, paras. 385, 398, 420. See J. Crawford and T. Grant, 'Responsibility of states for injuries to foreigners', in J. P. Grant and J. Craig Barker (eds.), *The Harvard Research in International Law: Contemporary Analysis and Appraisal* (Buffalo: Hein, 2007), p. 77.

[28] See e.g. *Restatement of the Foreign Relations Law of the United States, Revised* (1985), para. 102; M. Ragazzi, *The Concept of International Obligations Erga Omnes* (Oxford: Clarendon Press, 1997), p. 53. Jordan Paust, 'The reality of jus cogens' (1981) 7 *Connecticut Journal of International Law* 81 at 82; D'Amato, *The Concept of Custom in International Law* (Ithaca, NY: Cornell University Press, 1971), pp. 111, 132; T. Meron, 'The Geneva Conventions as customary law' (1987) 81 *American Journal of International Law* 348 at 350; U. Linderfalk, 'The creation of jus cogens: making sense of Article 53 of the Vienna Convention' (2011) 71 *Zeitschrift für ausländisches öffentliches Recht und Völkerrecht* 2, 359; U. Linderfalk, 'The source of jus cogens obligations: how legal positivism copes with peremptory international law' (2013) 82 *Nordic Journal of International Law* 369; M. Byers, 'Conceptualising the relationship between jus cogens and erga omnes' (1997) 66 *Nordic Journal of International Law* 220; P.-M. Dupuy, 'L'unité de l'ordre juridique international: cours général de droit international public' (2002) 297 *Collected Course* 9 at 275–76; J. Verhoeven 'Considérations sur ce qui est commun: cours général de droit international public' (2008) 334 *Collected Courses* 9 at 231; J. Sztucki, *Jus Cogens and the Vienna Convention on the Law of Treaties: A Critical Appraisal* (Wien: Springer-Verlag, 1974), p. 75; B. Conforti, 'Cours général de droit international public' (1988) 212 *Collected Courses* 9 at 129.

[29] C. Ryngaert and S. Sobrie, 'Recognition of states: international law or realpolitik? The practice of recognition in the wake of Kosovo, South Ossetia, and Abkhazia' (2011) 24 *Leiden Journal of International Law* 467.

[30] See J. d'Aspremont, 'The idea of "rules" in the sources of international law' (2014) 84 *British Yearbook of International Law* 103.

rules forming the fundamental doctrines can simply not be left floating without being anchored in a formal repository. To provide fundamental doctrines with such a formal repository, a kinship with formal instruments must be created. Providing kinship with a formal repository is the function of what is called here *imaginary genealogy* in the belief system.[31] Imaginary genealogy is a fictive history that ensures that a genealogical link unites the rules constituting the fundamental doctrines with some key authoritative texts, thereby giving the former a formal nest. Imaginary genealogy thus is what allows the derivation of the rules of a given fundamental doctrine from an international instrument. In other words, the imaginary genealogy mediates between the fundamental doctrines and the modes of legal reasoning they put in place, on the one hand, and the international instruments from which the doctrine derives, on the other hand. As a result of the imaginary genealogy, the distinction between the fundamental doctrines and the international instruments that host them is transcended.

Concretely, the imaginary genealogy that realises the derivation of fundamental doctrines from an international instrument entails an association between a fundamental doctrine and a key artefact such as an international legal instrument or a landmark case. This association is a form of genealogy. This genealogy is imaginary[32] not by virtue of any falsity by comparison to some sort of universal reality[33] but because the derivation of the fundamental doctrines from an international

---

[31] It should be stressed that the term 'genealogy' is not used here in a Foucauldian sense. On the Foucauldian use of genealogy, see Michel Foucault, *Surveiller et Punir* (Paris: Gallimard, 1975), pp. 30–32. See also David Garland, 'What is a "history of the present"? On Foucault's genealogies and their critical preconditions' (2014) 16 *Punishment and Society* 365 at 369–71; Ellen K. Feder, 'Power/knowledge', in D. Taylor (ed.), *Michel Foucault: Key Concepts* (London: Routledge, 2014), pp. 55–68. See also N. Berman, 'In the wake of empire' (1999) 14 *American University International Law Review* 1521. For a recent use of the notion of genealogy in that sense, see Ingo Venzke, 'Cracking the frame? On the prospects of change in a world of struggle' (2016) 27 *European Journal of International Law* 831. The use of genealogy here also defers from the idea of 'doctrinal genealogy' as is understood by Akbar Rasulov, 'The life and times of the modern law of reservations: the doctrinal genealogy of General Comment No. 24' (2009) 14 *Austrian Review of International and European Law* 103, esp. 131–35.

[32] Cf. Phillp Allott, 'The idealist's dilemma' (International Law Association British Branch Conference, 23–24 May 2014), p. 5 ('The whole of the law is a vast work of fiction, a masterpiece of the human imagination, creating its own entirely artificial reality. Lawyers - even practising lawyers - are creative writers, re-inventing the story of the law every day').

[33] This is a crucial nuance that I owe to exchanges with Ingo Venzke and Pierre Schlag. On this type of artificiality or falsity, see Pierre Schlag, 'Law as the continuation of god by other means' (1997) 85 *California Law Review* 427.

instrument is a product of the collective consciousness of international lawyers.[34] For instance, as will be discussed in Chapter 4, the genealogy that unites the 1933 Montevideo Convention on Rights and Duties of States and the doctrine of statehood is fabricated. The same chapter will also discuss the derivation of the two-element doctrine of customary law from Article 38 of the Statute of the Permanent Court of International Justice by virtue of a imaginary genealogy.

It is important to highlight that those instruments from which funda-mental doctrines are derived by virtue of imaginary genealogy are not chosen arbitrarily. Although it cannot be excluded that other parameters play a role,[35] what makes an international instrument a candidate for the status of repository of a given fundamental doctrine is that the instru-ment concerned comes with some formal trappings that can potentially be recognised by fundamental doctrines themselves. Indeed, the main repositories of fundamental doctrines most of the time have some formal status, whether it is their formally binding character upon states (e.g. an interstate treaty), their design and adoption by a body entrusted with codifying power and allegedly drawing on customary international law (e.g. the International Law Commission (ILC)) or their judicial nature (e. g. a judgment or an advisory opinion of the International Court of Justice (ICJ)).[36] In this sense, the main international instruments from which fundamental doctrines are derived are either of a legislative nature – such as the Statute of the International Court of Justice or the Vienna Convention on the Law of Treaties – of a semi-legislative character – such as the Articles on State Responsibility[37] – or of a judicial nature. As will be further demonstrated in Chapters 3 and 4, this is no coincidence

---

[34] This is a thought that originated in exchanges with Akbar Rasulov. On the notion of legal consciousness in general, see Duncan Kennedy, *The Rise and Fall of Classical Legal Thought* (New York: Beard Books, 2006), pp. xiv–xvii, 5–7.

[35] For Giorgio Gaja, the frequency of the references to the *Articles on State Responsibility* may be explained by the quality of the text and the absence of any alternative statement of the law that judicial or arbitral bodies can invoke. See G. Gaja, 'Interpreting articles adopted by the International Law Commission' (2016) 85 *British Yearbook of International Law* 10 at 11.

[36] The authority of the international instruments from which fundamental doctrines are derived and the authority of fundamental doctrines ought to be distinguished, although they are inevitably intertwined. The authority of fundamental doctrines is discussed in Chapter 4.

[37] It should be noted that the derivation of fundamental doctrines from formal instruments that have a quasi-legislative nature is not specific to international law. See N. Jansen, *The Making of Legal Authority: Non-Legislative Codifications in Historical and Comparative Perspective* (Oxford: Oxford University Press, 2010).

because such instruments can potentially be explained by the fundamental doctrines themselves and contribute to the self-referentiality of the belief system.

Chapter 4 will specifically discuss the repositories from which four fundamental doctrines are derived by virtue of imaginary genealogy: the Statute of the International Court of Justice, the Montevideo Convention on Rights and Duties of States, the Vienna Convention on the Law of Treaties and the Articles on State Responsibility. It will be shown how these instruments have been elected as the international instruments from which four fundamental doctrines have been derived by virtue of imaginary genealogy, sometimes supplemented by auxiliary texts.[38] It goes without saying that such a list is not exhaustive, as other international instruments play this role in relation to other fundamental doctrines. For instance, when it comes to legal reasoning on the use of force, the United Nations Charter performs the function of repository from which the doctrine is derived.

As mentioned earlier, landmark judicial pronouncements can also play the role of repositories from which fundamental doctrines are derived through imaginary genealogy. It suffices to refer here to the 1924 judgment of the Permanent Court of International Justice in the *Mavrommatis Palestine Concessions* case[39] regarding the modes of legal reasoning pertaining to diplomatic protection, the famous *Reparations for Injuries* advisory opinion of the International Court of Justice that put in place some central modes of legal reasoning in relation to international organisations,[40] and its judgment in *Barcelona Traction*,[41] which hosts the fundamental doctrine

---

[38] On how the Opinions of the Badinter Commission came to supplement the 1933 Montevideo Convention on Rights and Duties of States as the repository of the fundamental doctrine of statehood, see Chapter 4, Section 1.

[39] See *Mavrommatis Palestine Concessions Case (Greece v United Kingdom)*, PCIJ Rep. 1924, series A, no. 2. See Article 1 of the Draft Articles on Diplomatic Protection with Commentaries, UN Doc. A/61/10, in *Yearbook of the International Law Commission 2006*, vol. II, part 2.

[40] See *Reparation for Injuries Suffered in the Service of the United Nations* (Advisory Opinion) ICJ Rep. 1949, 174. On the idea that the *Reparation for Injuries* case constitutes the repository for several of the fundamental doctrines of the law of international organisations, see Jean d'Aspremont, 'The law of international organizations and the art of reconciliation: from dichotomies to dialectics' (2014) 11 *International Organizations Law Review* 428. See also D. Bederman, 'The souls of international organizations: legal personality and the lighthouse at cape spartel' (1995–96) 36 *Virginia Journal of International Law* 275 at 279.

[41] See *Barcelona Traction, Light and Power Company, Limited (Belgium v Spain)* (New Application, 1962) ICJ Rep. 1970, 1. For some critical remarks, see C. Tams and A.

pertaining to universal legal standing (*erga omnes*) that accompanies certain types of international obligations. It is important to note that these judicial pronoucements are not discussed here because the fundamental doctrines they 'host' are not examined in the following chapters. This does not mean, however, that judicial pronouncements will be totally ignored in the exploration of the international belief system carried out in the remaining chapters. Actually, the fact that the main repository of a given fundamental doctrine is found in a formal international instrument – be it a treaty or the final outcome of an international codification process – does not demote judicial pronouncements to irrelevance. As will be demonstrated by the following discussion on responsibility, custom and *jus cogens*, judicial pronouncements about these fundamental doctrines and their repository often buttress one another in a way that reinforces the derivation of a fundamental doctrine from an international instrument.[42]

It should be acknowledged that some fundamental doctrines may come with a less tangible repository, in which case imaginary genealogy seems to play a very limited role. In other words, there may be fundamental doctrines that are more loosely derived from an international instrument or for which there seem to be no repository whatsoever.[43] Such an impression may, for instance, surface in relation to some fundamental doctrines in the law of international organisations.[44] I submit, however, that even fundamental doctrines with a less obvious textual underpinning always remain anchored in some form of repository. In such situations, the repository may not be an international instrument, a judicial pronouncement or the product of a codification process. It can, less visibly, be a seminal piece of

---

Tzanakopoulos, '*Barcelona Traction* at 40: the ICJ as an agent of legal development' (2010) 23 *Leiden Journal of International Law* 781.

[42] See Chapter 4. On the dialogue between the International Court of Justice and the International Law Commission, see, generally, Stephen M. Schwebel, 'The inter-active influence of the International Court of Justice and the International Law Commission', in Calixto A. Armas Barea et al. (eds.), *Liber Amicorum 'In Memoriam' of José María Ruda* (The Hague: Kluwer, 2000), pp. 479–505.

[43] I owe this remark to exchanges with Jan Klabbers.

[44] If functionalism is construed as a fundamental doctrine of the law of international organisations, it may be accompanied by the impression of having no formal repository. On functionalism, see J. Klabbers, 'The emergence of functionalism in international institutional law: colonial inspirations' (2014) 25 *European Journal of International Law* 645. For an overview of some of the fundamental doctrines of the law of international organisations, see J. d'Aspremont, 'The law of international organisations and the art of reconciliation: from dichotomies to dialectics' (2014) 11 *International Organizations Law Review* 428.

scholarship.[45] Thus, seminal pieces of literature or famous textbooks may sometimes perform the role of repository. It is noteworthy that the anchorage in such repositories is often witnessed in relation to fundamental doctrines that have not yet been the object of any codification, judicial pronouncement or restatement.[46]

Be that as it may, by virtue of the imaginary genealogy, the international instruments from which fundamental doctrines are derived come to provide universality and permanence to those doctrines. Indeed, these international instruments where fundamental doctrines are nested bring about universality understood as a 'depersonification'[47] of the making and functioning of fundamental doctrines. The multitude of individual and collective interventions in the design of the fundamental doctrines disappears behind these instruments and is left unrecognised.[48] It will be shown in Chapter 5 that suspending the belief system, as is contemplated in this book, contributes to interrupting the obfuscation of the interventions in the design of fundamental doctrines provided by the repositories of these doctrines. What is more, the imaginary genealogy and the derivation of fundamental doctrines from these instruments give assurances that fundamental doctrines will continue to dictate the same modes of legal reasoning tomorrow. In other words, the imaginary genealogy offers all those involved in international legal discourse guarantees that their present use of the modes of legal reasoning prescribed by fundamental doctrines will still be intelligible and recognised in the future.[49]

---

[45] See e.g. M. Virally, 'La notion de fonction dans la théorie de l'organisation internationale', in Charles E. Rousseau (ed.), *Mélanges offerts à Charles Rousseau: La Communauté internationale* (Paris: Pedone, 1974), pp. 277–300.

[46] Before the codification of the law of responsibility, some key pieces of scholarship played the role of formal repositories. See e.g. Dionisio Anzilotti, 'La responsabilité internationale des États à raison des dommages soufferts par les étrangers' (1906) *Revue générale de droit international public* 5 at 5–29, 285–309. On the development of the fundamental doctrine of responsibility, see Chapter 4, Section 1. Before the 1933 Montevideo Convention became the formal repository for modes of legal reasoning on statehood and recognition in the 1950s and 1960s, some influential scholarly pieces functioned as formal repository. See H. Lauterpacht, *Recognition in International Law* (Cambridge: Cambridge University Press, 1947).

[47] The term was suggested to me by Tiago Guevara.

[48] See Pierre Bourdieu, 'The force of law: toward a sociology of the juridical field' (1987) 38 *Hastings Law Journal* 805 at 844 ('law can exercise its specific power only to the extent that it attains recognition, that is, to the extent that the element of arbitrariness at the heart of its functioning . . . remains unrecognized').

[49] This is a consequence that Bourdieu traces back to formalisation. For the sake of the argument made here, I contend that it is the universalisation operated by the formal

It is noteworthy that the imaginary genealogy simultaneously gives rise to a historical narrative whereby the modes of legal reasoning put in place by a fundamental doctrine are considered to have been created and agreed upon by virtue of the adoption of the international instrument that serves as its formal repository.[50] The imaginary genealogy is thus accompanied by a specific historical account of the origin of the fundamental doctrine concerned and of the modes of legal reasoning the latter puts in place.[51]

Taken together, the ruleness whereby fundamental doctrines are represented as rules and the imaginary genealogy whereby fundamental doctrines are derived from key international instruments clear the way for the self-referentiality necessary for the experience of a sense of constraint . Chapters 3 and 4 show how ruleness and the derivation of fundamental doctrines from international instruments by virtue of imaginary genealogy allow fundamental doctrines to be explained in their own terms.

2.3   Fundamental Doctrines as Self-Explanatory Frameworks: Self-Referentiality

Fundamental doctrines only come to generate a sense of constraint to the extent that they are represented as sets of rules derived from a few international instruments whose formation and functioning can be explained in the very terms of the fundamental doctrines. This means that besides ruleness and imaginary genealogy, a third condition must be met: *self-referentiality.* Self-referentiality refers to the potential of fundamental doctrines to invent and dictate their own formation and functioning.[52] Self-referentiality allows closure of the belief system.

---

repository that provides such a guarantee. Cf. Pierre Bourdieu, 'The force of law: toward a sociology of the juridical field' (1987) 38 *Hastings Law Journal* 805 at 845.

[50] In this sense, the imaginary genealogy is part of a process of 'inventing a tradition'. On the notion of invention of tradition, see Eric Hobsbawn, 'Introduction: inventing traditions', in E. Hobsbawn and T. Ranger (eds.), *The Invention of Tradition* (Cambridge: Cambridge University Press, 1983), pp. 1–14.

[51] Cf. the efforts of Samuel Moyn to disclose the imaginary genealogy that unites Christian human rights and international human rights and by virtue of which human rights seem to have always been there. See Samuel Moyn, *Christian Human Rights* (Philadelphia: University of Pennsylvania Press, 2015), p. 5 ('Christian human rights were injected into tradition by pretending they had always been there, and on the basis of minor antecedents now treated as fonts of enduring commitments').

[52] This is what has sometimes been called 'self-transcendence' ('auto-transcendence'). See F. Ost, *Du Sinaï au Champ-de-Mars: L'autre et le même au fondement du droit* (Brussels: Lessius, 1999), 20ff. For an in-depth discussion of the very concept of self-referentiality,

It is argued here that in the international belief system, self-referentiality – and thus the explanation of fundamental doctrines in their own terms – is implemented through the doctrine that regulates the making of rules in international law, that is, the *doctrine of sources*, as well as the doctrine that governs the application and interpretation of rules in international law, that is, the *doctrine of interpretation*. In other words, once fundamental doctrines are equated to rules derived from international instruments, their making and functioning become the object of the specific doctrines that explain the formation and functioning of rules in international law, namely, the doctrine of sources and the doctrine of interpretation. This means that the international belief system bestows a very critical function to sources and interpretation, as the latter allow fundamental doctrines to invent their own origin and dictate their functioning. The doctrine of sources explains the formation of fundamental doctrines – that is, how they are made – whereas the doctrine of interpretation explains the functioning of those doctrines – that is, how they should be applied and interpreted. Said differently, the formation of fundamental doctrines becomes a question of sources of international law governed by the fundamental doctrine of sources, and the functioning of fundamental doctrines becomes a question of interpretation governed by the fundamental doctrine of interpretation.

The foregoing confirms the mutually reinforcing character of all the conditions of the realisation of the international belief system. It is only once the fundamental doctrines are construed as rules derived from international instruments that their formation and functioning can be turned into questions governed by the fundamental doctrines that pertain specifically to the making and the interpretation of international instruments. Indeed, the fundamental doctrines of sources and interpretation can only explain the formation and functioning of fundamental doctrines as long as those doctrines are given a format that can be apprehended by such doctrines, namely, rules derived from formal international instruments that can potentially be the object of sources and interpretation. At the same time, once self-referentiality is realised, it comes to reinforce the representation of fundamental doctrines as rules derived from international instruments. Indeed, if the formation of fundamental doctrines is a question of sources and their functioning is a question of interpretation, the fundamental doctrines, in the eyes of

see Niklas Luhmann, *Social Systems*, trans. John Bednarz, with Dirk Baecker) (Redwood City, CA: Stanford University Press, 1995).

international lawyers, can only be rules derived from international instruments.

With ruleness, imaginary genealogy and self-referentiality, the belief system that permeates the common understanding of the formation and functioning of fundamental doctrines is fully in place. The following section will elaborate on how the international belief system takes effect once all the above-mentioned conditions – ruleness, imaginary genealogy and self-referentiality – have been met. In doing so, it will elucidate how self-referentiality is conducive to the experience of a sense of constraint towards fundamental doctrines.

3   The International Belief System in Place: An Experienced Sense of Constraint

Beliefs generally arise through experience. That experience, in turn, creates commitment towards the object that has been experienced.[53] In the specific case of international law, by virtue of ruleness, imaginary genealogy and self-referentiality, the fundamental doctrines become transcendental validators of international legal discourse towards which international lawyers come to experience a sense of constraint.

The experience through which international lawyers come to feel committed to fundamental doctrines once the belief system is in place must now be further explicated. According to the argument made here, this experience is one where international lawyers experience the presence of the very instruments from which fundamental doctrines are derived by virtue of imaginary genealogy. They more specifically experience that these instruments dictate to them the way in which they must articulate their legal discourse. In other words, international lawyers hear international instruments speak to them and enunciate the fundamental doctrines.[54] Having heard these international instruments speak the fundamental doctrines,[55] international lawyers come to think of fundamental doctrines as truth that calls for no empirical or rational

---

[53] Oliver Wendell Holmes, 'Natural law' (1918) *Harvard Law Review* 40 at 41 ('one's experience thus makes certain preferences dogmatic for oneself').

[54] A. A. Leff, 'Unspeakable ethics, unnatural law' (1979) *Duke Law Journal* 1229 at 1245.

[55] On the idea that international lawyers feel the repositories of a handful of doctrines, see A. Bianchi, 'The game of interpretation in international law: the players, the cards, and why the game is worth the candle', in Andrea Bianchi, Daniel Peat and Matthew Windsor (eds.), *Interpretation in International Law* (Oxford: Oxford University Press, 2015), p. 55.

demonstration.[56] By virtue of such an experience, they come to feel committed to such truth.[57] The belief system thus arises out of an experience of a sense of constraint by virtue of which fundamental doctrines have been irrefutably and transcendentally enunciated.[58]

Such experience is only possible to the extent that sufficient space is provided to that end. 'Space' refers here to the possibility of a justification that international lawyers can confidently rely on and explicitly invoke to shelter their beliefs from any evidentiary demand coming from outside the belief system. This justificatory space is where the sense of constraint towards fundamental doctrines can thrive unjudged and ungrounded. The function of providing the necessary justificatory space to international lawyers' and immunising them from any evidentiary demand coming from outside the belief system is performed by self-referentiality.[59] Indeed, self-referentiality, that is, the explanation of the formation and functioning of fundamental doctrines in the very terms of the doctrines of sources and interpretation, is what creates the necessary space for the experience of a sense of constraint towards the fundamental doctrines and stifles any evidentiary demand from outside the belief system.[60]

---

[56] Oliver Wendell Holmes, 'Natural law' 40 at 41 ('What we most love and revere generally is determined by early associations').

[57] This commitment towards fundamental doctrines simultaneously creates an internal morality in the profession, for any transgression of fundamental doctrines is perceived as a sin, the consequence of which being a loss of argumentative persuasiveness. See the remarks of Judith N. Shklar, *Legalism*, p. 45. Cf. the idea of fidelity: see Lon L. Fuller, 'Positivism and fidelity to law: a reply to Professor Hart' (1958) 71 *Harvard Law Review* 630; W. Bradley Wendel, *Lawyers and Fidelity to Law* (Princeton, NJ: Princeton University Press, 2010). See also G. Postema, 'Law's rule, reflexivity, mutual accountability, and the rule of law', in Xiaobo Zhai and Michael Quinn (eds.), *Bentham's Theory of Law and Public Opinion* (Cambridge: Cambridge University Press, 2014).

[58] Julius Stone, *Legal System and Lawyers' Reasonings* (Redwood City, CA: Stanford University Press, 1968), p. 24 ('Lawyers, like other men, tend to regard what they most value as self-evidently right, and therefore as not in need of explanation, much less justification'). See also P. Schlag, *Laying Down the Law* (New York: New York University Press, 1996), p. 9.

[59] That self-referentiality is used to evade evidentiary questions is something found in myths, too. See François Ost, *Raconter la Loi: Aux Sources de l'Imaginaire Juridique*, pp. 77–81.

[60] Cf. Pierre Bourdieu, 'The force of law: toward a sociology of the juridical field' (1987) 38 *Hastings Law Journal* 805 at 849 ('the explicit statement of principles makes possible explicit verification of consensus concerning the principles of consensus or disagreement themselves').

It is important to note, at this stage, that this need for a justificatory space protecting the participants in the belief system from any evidentiary demand from the outside world arises irrespective of whether international lawyers have or not some minimal awareness of the belief system. Whether international lawyers have at least some minimal awareness of the belief system is controversial.[61] It is true that full awareness of the belief system seems unlikely because the belief system obfuscates its origin and functioning and miscognises those who have been socialised to it.[62] Yet the fact that miscognition is part of the belief system does not exclude some awareness thereof. This being said, the debate on the possible awareness by international lawyers of the belief system – and the reasons why they decide to believe[63] – is not crucial for the claim developed in this book. Indeed, whether they are conscious of their beliefs or not, international lawyers will not allow their sense of constraint and beliefs to rest unexplained and unjustified in the eyes

---

[61] For Anthony Giddens, all actors have some degree of discursive consciousness of the social system to whose constitution they contribute. From Giddens' perspective, we can assume that international lawyers know a great deal about the conditions of reproduction of the belief system of which they are a member. See Anthony Giddens, *Central Problems in Social Theory: Action, Structure and Contradiction in Social Analysis* (Basingstoke: Macmillan, 1979), p. 5. See also the remarks of Shklar, *Legalism*, p. 10 (for whom there is a bit of awareness). See also Martti Koskenniemi, 'Between commitment and cynicism: outline for a theory of international law as practice', in *The Politics of International Law* (Cambridge: Cambridge University Press, 2011), pp. 274–75 (for him, there always is some self-reflective distance and awareness of risk). Cf. Philip Allott, 'The idealist's dilemma', p. 5 ('The international world is a world of ultimate bad faith – world in which humanity lies to itself about itself'). See also Philip Allott, 'The true function of law in the international community' (1998) 5 *Indiana Journal of Global Studies* 391 ('human beings have the interesting characteristic that we have consciousness, which means that we can be aware of our law abidingness, and that we can use it purposively for the unlimited further self-evolution of the human species).

[62] As Bourdieu explained, miscognitions are accurate recognitions of culturally literate agents. It is thus socialisation that leads to miscognition. See P. Bourdieu, *Practical Reason*, trans.(R. Johnson (London: Polity Press, 1998), p. 103. In that sense, even those non-aware international lawyers should not be blamed for indulging in the belief system and being miscognised by it. See also the remarks of J. D. Schubert, 'Suffering/symbolic violence', in Michael Grenfell (ed.), *Pierre Bourdieu: Key Concepts*, 2nd edn (London: Routledge, 2012), p. 192. On the notion of miscognition, see Chapter 1, Section 3. See, generally, Pierre Bourdieu, 'A lecture on the lecture', in Pierre Bourdieu, *In Other Words: Essays towards a Reflexive Sociology*, trans. Matthew Adamson (Redwood City, CA: Stanford University Press, 1990), pp. 177, 183.

[63] For some critical remarks on this question, see J. Beckett, 'Countering uncertainty and ending up/down arguments: prolegomena to a response to NAIL' (2005) 16 *European Journal of International Law* 213.

of those external to the belief system. Should they have some degree of awareness of the belief system, they will not want to acknowledge that they experience the fundamental doctrines speaking to them for fear of exposing themselves to the charges of arbitrariness, naive objectivism or dogmatism.[64] Should they have no degree of awareness of any of the manifestations of the belief system whatsoever, they similarly not satisfy themselves with a mere explanation of *argumentative acquis*.[65] Either way, international lawyers cannot tolerate that their sense of constraint looks like it is either unexplained or metaphysically, supernaturally or psychologically constituted. They want a justification for their sense of constraint towards the fundamental doctrines that looks sufficiently plausible, modern and somewhat 'scientific'.[66] This is where the above-mentioned self-referentiality that is

---

[64] Oliver Wendell Holmes, 'Natural law', 40 at 41; A. A. Leff, 'Unspeakable ethics, unnatural law' (1979) *Duke Law Journal* 1229 at 1247: 'To put it as bluntly as possible, if we go to find what law ought to govern us, and if what we find is not an authoritative Holy Writ but just ourselves, just people, making that law, how can we be governed by what we have found?'.

[65] It does not seem controversial to claim that international lawyers have some '*horror vacui*'. See A. Bianchi, 'The game of interpretation in international law: the players, the cards, and why the game is worth the candle', p. 55.

[66] This quest for a cover that allows international lawyers to avoid any metaphysical or supernatural explanation for their dogmatism is itself an expression of the liberal paradigm that was described in Chapter 1. Indeed, the association of international law – and especially of international legal scholarship – with the idea of legal science conveys an image of scholarship as being rooted in rigorous and systematic methods of investigation that only professionals can possibly master and that are distinct from morals and politics. Very popular in the nineteenth century and the early twentieth century, the idea of a 'science of international law' particularly came to equate professionalisation of international legal scholarship with the use of a set of objective methods of inquiry of an inductive nature distinct from the study of political phenomena and geared towards the extraction of standards of behaviour to be applied to facts also objectively ascertained. International law professionals, by claiming that the foundations of their mode of argumentation are scientific, seek to vest their authority in perceived objectivity, in an alleged opposition to morals or politics. Obviously, the scientification of international law has been subject to intense criticism. For instance, it has demonstrated that scientification brought about other forms of politics. In the same vein, and more fundamentally, the very claim that international legal scholarship constitutes a science has been seriously discredited in the second half of the twentieth century. Yet, even if international lawyers may now refrain from using such vocabulary, they still espouse the attitude that comes with it. The use of self-referentiality as is discussed in this chapter is a good illustration of that attitude. For some classical exposition of international law as a science, see L. Oppenheim, 'The science of international law: its task and method' (1908) 2 *American Journal of International Law* 313; R. Ago, 'Science juridique et droit international' (1956) 90 *Collected Courses of the Hague Academy of International Law* 851; F. Castberg, 'La Méthodologie du droit international public' (1934) 43 *Collected Courses of the Hague*

realised through ruleness and imaginary genealogy and that was discussed in the preceding section comes into play and allows fundamental doctrines to invent their own creation and dictate their own functioning, thereby shielding the believers from the demands of the outside world. This is why it can be said that awareness of the belief system by the believers does not constitute an obstacle to its operation.

The above-mentioned function of self-referentiality in the belief system calls for additional clarification. It must be stressed here that in the international belief system self-referentiality is not in itself the cause of the sense of constraint or of the experience thereof. In other words, it is not because the fundamental doctrines are derived from key international instruments that international lawyers feel obligated towards them. International lawyers' sense of obligation comes from their own experience. The function of self-referentiality is thus not the generation of commitment but the creation of a justificatory space where international lawyers can indulge in their sense of constraint without having to acknowledge the lack of foundation or the metaphysical, supernatural and psychological origins thereof and without being frustrated by evidentiary demands from outside the belief system.[67]

It is noteworthy that the experience of a sense of constraint towards the fundamental doctrines does not come naturally. It is acquired by training

Acadamy of International Law; see also A. Somek, 'Legal science as a source of law: a late reply by Puchta to Kantorowicz', University of Iowa Legal Studies Research Paper Series, no. 13-7; on the notion of legal science in general, see, generally, J. Reitz, 'The importance of and need for legal science', University of Iowa Legal Studies Research Paper 2012. For a criticism of this idea in relation to international law, see M. Koskenniemi, 'Letter to the editors of the symposium' (1999) 93 American Journal of International Law 351; J. Crawford, 'International law as discipline and profession' (2012) American Society of International Law Proceedings 1.

[67] It is probably not difficult to understand that self-referentiality simultaneously facilitates a pragmatist mind-set that is averse to theoretical inquiries, something that was rather common in the second half of the twentieth century. The most famous and archetypical example of such pragmatism is Iain Brownlie: see I. Brownlie, 'International law at the fiftieth anniversary of the United Nations: general course on public international law' (1995) 255 Collected Courses of the Hague Academy of International Law 9 at 30 (for whom theory provides no real benefit). For some additional reflections on the reasons behind the anti-theoretical stance of mainstream legal scholarship, see J. Klabbers, 'Constitutionalism and the making of international law' (2008) 5 NoFo 84 at 95. The famous British aversion to theory is sometimes traced back to Lauterpacht. See A. Carty, 'Why theory: the implications for international law teaching', in P. Allott et al. (eds.), Theory and International Law: An Introduction (London: Institute of International and Comparative Law, 1991), p. 77. For a contestation of this contention, see I. Scobbie, 'The theorist as judge: Hersch Lauterpacht's concept of the international judicial function' (1997) 2 European Journal of International Law 264.

and through knowledge of the experiences of others. First, such an experience originates in a predisposition that is ingrained in international lawyers as early as the start of their education.[68] Such an experience is perpetuated as they continue to engage in international legal argumentation. Second, this sense of obligation comes from knowledge of the experiences of others.[69] Indeed, their own experience of a sense of constraint is generally reinforced by the memory of a corresponding sense of constraint that is cultivated and taught by peers and teachers. Sometimes it may be that the collective memory of a sense of constraint towards the fundamental doctrines surpasses the actual experience of individual international lawyers when it comes to generate commitment towards the fundamental doctrines.[70]

The foregoing does obviously not suffice to explain how the individual international lawyer, as a legal self, is prepared to be seduced and believe in fundamental doctrines.[71] Indeed, complex psychological, social and institutional dynamics[72] are at work in the process of

---

[68] In that sense, the experience of a sense of constraint can be said to be a central focus of the process of socialisation of international lawyers as international lawyers, this process being geared towards the training to experience the feeling of constraint towards the fundamental doctrine as well as the teaching of the memory of that sense of constraint in earlier works. On the process of socialisation of international lawyers as international lawyers, see Jean d'Aspremont, *Epistemic Forces in International Law: Foundational Doctrines and Techniques of International Legal Argumentation* (London: Elgar, 2015). See also P. Schlag, *Laying Down the Law* (New York: New York University Press, 1996), p. 9. For a similar idea, see Andrea Bianchi, *International Law Theories: An Inquiry into Different Ways of Thinking* (Oxford: Oxford University Press, 2016), pp. 10–11.

[69] This is a thought that originated in an exchange with Justin Desautels-Stein. On how tradition and training are conducive to the transfer of modes of legal reasoning, see J. d'Aspremont, *Epistemic Forces in International Law: Foundational Doctrines and Techniques of International Legal Argumentation*, pp. 9–22. See also A. Orford, 'The destiny of international law' (2004) 17 *Leiden Journal of International Law* 441 at 464–75.

[70] Regis Debray, *Transmitting Culture*, trans. Eric Rauth (New York: Columbia University Press, 1997), p. 19: 'So yes, the generation of Jesus' apostles has long vanished, in subjection to biological law, but not their belief. It was transmitted to Paul of Tarsus, for instance, someone who did not meet the living Jesus during his ministry yet saw him with his own eyes risen from the dead on the road to Damascus. The converted Paul found ways to convert others, who in their turn forged the chain from age to age, city to city. The articulation of Christian faith turns on solid pivots: on relics, sacred images, and holy scriptures that are directed less toward propagating the memory of past words and deeds than the impersonal interpretation that the distant alleged witnesses, Matthew, Mark, Luke, and John, are supposed to have given them in their lifetime. Doctrine refers to an admirable propagation of Christianity, adding further cause for believing in it.'

[71] I owe this description of the question of the reception to exchanges with Pierre Schlag.

[72] This was part of the ambition of an earlier study. See J. d'Aspremont, 'Wording in international law' (2012) 25 *Leiden Journal of International Law* 575. See also Nikolas

experience of a sense of constraint.[73] This book is not the place to unravel such processes further.[74] It should simply be highlighted here that this aspect of the belief system of international law has not been completely ignored by international lawyers, although they have been resorting to diverging descriptive notions in this regard. It is, for instance, common to invoke faith to explain how international legal lawyers adulate some legal arguments and constantly deploy them without much self-reflectivity.[75] Mention also has been made of international lawyers' 'sentimental attachment to the field's constitutive rhetoric and traditions'.[76] The debate on how to best describe the

---

Rajkovic, 'Rules, lawyering, and the politics of legality: critical sociology and international law's rule', p. 331.

[73] For an example of a reliance on behavioural studies and psychology in studies of international legal argumentation, see Anne van Aaken, 'Behavioral international law and economics' (2014) 55 *Harvard International Law Journal* 421. See also the resort to psychoanalysis in the work of Nathaniel Berman that is well reflected in the title of the French translation of his work: see N. Berman, *Passions et Ambivalences* (Paris: Pedone, 2008). It is noteworthy that legal theorists do not hesitate to embark on psychological inquiries of the structure of legal argumentation. For a venture into the psychological dynamics of international legal argumentations, see G. Simpson, 'The sentimental life of international law' (2015) 3 *London Review of International Law* 3. For a psychological account of how lawyers engage in what he calls the hermeneutic of suspicion, see Duncan Kennedy, 'The hermeneutic of suspicion in contemporary American legal thought' (2014) 25 *Law and Critique* 91 esp. 124–36.

[74] It is not even sure that deployment of descriptive and analytical tools very alien to those which international lawyers are familiar with would not allow us to trace the whole process whereby such fundamental doctrines have acquired authority. In the same vein, see Nils Jansen, *The Making of Legal Authority: Non-legislative Codifications in Historical and Comparative Perspective* (Oxford: Oxford University Press, 2010), p 95.

[75] Justin Desautels-Stein, 'Chiastic law in the crystal ball: exploring legal formalism and its alternative futures' (2014) 2 *London Review of International Law* 263. In general legal theory and sociology of law, faith has long been used as an explanatory concept. See e.g. Richard Terdiman, 'Introduction to Pierre Bourdieu', in 'The force of law: toward a sociology of the juridical field' (1987) 38 *Hastings Law Journal* 805 at 810. See also Pierre Schlag, 'Law as the continuation of god by other means' (1997) 85 *California Law Review* 427 at 438. See also John Gardner, *Law as a Leap of Faith*, (Oxford: Oxford University Press, 2012).

[76] This is what he has called a 'commitment', which he sees as being constantly counterbalanced by a bout of cynicism. See Martti Koskenniemi, 'Between commitment and cynicism: outline for a theory of international law as practice', in *The Politics of International Law* (Cambridge: Cambridge University Press, 2011), p. 272. See also James Crawford and Martti Koskenniemi, 'Introduction', in J. Crawford and M. Koskenniemi (eds.), *Cambridge Companion to International Law* (Cambridge: Cambridge University Press, 2012), p. 14. In the same vein, see Umut Ozsu, 'The question of form: methodological notes on dialectics and international law' (2010) 23 *Leiden Journal of International Law* 687 at 688. Cf. Gerry Simpson, 'On the magic mountain:

seduction at work in the belief system of international law ought not to be taken on here.[77]

This chapter has shown that as long as fundamental doctrines as rules (ruleness) derived from a few international instruments (imaginary genealogy) invent their own origin and dictate their own functioning (self-referentiality), international lawyers come to experience a sense of constraint towards fundamental doctrines. So works the belief system behind the fundamental doctrines of international law.

teaching public international law' (1999) 10 *European Journal of International Law* 70 at 75 (who sees teachers making students oscillate between enthusiasm and cynicism).

[77] It should be made clear that the experience of a sense of constraint towards the fundamental doctrines is distinct from the authority of international law as a whole. Regarding the latter, see, generally, Basak Çali, *The Authority of International Law: Obedience, Respect, and Rebuttal* (Oxford: Oxford University Press, 2015).

3

Self-Referentiality of the International Belief System

Chapter 2 introduced the structure of the belief system at work behind the fundamental doctrines of international law and the conditions that ought to be fulfilled for fundamental doctrines to generate an experienced sense of constraint. Three conditions were mentioned, namely, ruleness, imaginary genealogy and self-referentiality. On this occasion, the discussion shed light on the critical function performed by self-referentiality, that is, the explanation of the formation and functioning of fundamental doctrines in their own terms. It was contended that self-referentiality guarantees a justificatory space where the sense of constraint of international lawyers towards fundamental doctrines can play out without interference from justificatory demands from outside the belief system. It remains to expound on how self-referentiality is specifically and concretely implemented in the belief system. This is the object of this chapter.

Based on the self-referentiality of the belief system discussed in Chapter 2, this chapter shows that the formation of fundamental doctrines is commonly reduced to a question of sources of international law governed by the fundamental doctrine of sources (1). In the same vein, this chapter demonstrates that the functioning of the fundamental doctrines is usually turned to a question of interpretation governed by the fundamental doctrine of interpretation (2). This chapter accordingly formulates a few remarks on each of these two types of self-referentiality, namely, sources-based self-referentiality (1) and interpretation-based self-referentiality (2).

1 Explaining the Formation of the Fundamental Doctrines through Sources

At the level of the formation of fundamental doctrines, ruleness of fundamental doctrines and their derivation from an international instrument allow them to be considered the product of a rule-making process.

Given that it is one of the functions of the doctrine of sources to identify the processes that can validly lead to the creation of legal rules, ruleness of fundamental doctrines and imaginary genealogy reduce the making thereof to the adoption of formal instruments recognised by the doctrine of sources. In the international belief system, the formation of fundamental doctrines is more specifically reduced to the adoption of international instruments or a custom-making process. It is accordingly very common to represent the fundamental doctrines of international law – e.g. responsibility, *jus cogens*, statehood, succession – as rules of a conventional or customary character.[1]

Such a contribution of the doctrine of sources to self-referentiality at the level of the formation of the fundamental doctrines calls for a few observations. First, it should be recalled that, in contemporary legal discourse, the doctrine of sources *itself* presents all the common trappings of a fundamental doctrine as it is understood here.[2] Indeed, sources of international law are generally construed as putting into place the modes of legal

---

[1] For some illustrations of statements of the customary character of the articles on state responsibility, see e.g. *Case Concerning Application of the Convention on the Prevention and Punishment of the Crime of Genocide (Bosnia Herzegovina v. Serbia and Montenegro)*, ICJ Rep. 2007, 202, paras. 385, 398 and 420. On the idea that the doctrine of statehood, as is expressed in the Montevideo Convention on Rights and Duties of States, constitutes a customary rule, see C. Ryngaert and S. Sobrie, 'Recognition of states: international law or realpolitik? The practice of recognition in the wake of Kosovo, South Ossetia, and Abkhazia' (2011) 24 *Leiden Journal of International Law* 467. On the idea that the doctrine of *jus cogens* constitutes a rule of customary law, see Restatement of the Foreign Relations Law of the United States, Revised (1985), para. 102; M. Ragazzi, *The Concept of International Obligations Erga Omnes* (Oxford: Clarendon Press, 1997), p. 53; Jordan Paust, 'The reality of jus cogens' (1981) 7 *Connecticut Journal of International Law* 81 at 82; D'Amato, *The Concept of Custom in International Law* (London: Cornell University Press, 1971), pp. 111 and 132; T. Meron, 'The Geneva Conventions as customary law' (1987) 81 *American Journal of International Law* 348 at 350; U. Linderfalk, 'The creation of jus cogens – making sense of Article 53 of the Vienna Convention' (2011) 71 *Zeitschrift für ausländisches öffentliches Recht und Völkerrecht* 2, 359; U. Linderfalk, 'The source of jus cogens obligations – how legal positivism copes with peremptory international law' (2013) 82 *Nordic Journal of International Law* 369; M. Byers, 'Conceptualising the relationship between jus cogens and erga omnes' (1997) 66 *Nordic Journal of International Law* 220; P.-M. Dupuy, 'L'unité de l'ordre juridique international: cours général de droit international public' (2002) 297 *Collected Courses of the Hague Academy of International Law* 9 at 275–76; J. Verhoeven 'Considérations sur ce qui est commun: cours général de droit international public' (2008) 334 *Collected Courses of the Hague Academy of International Law* 9 at 231; J. Sztucki, *Jus Cogens and the Vienna Convention on the Law of Treaties: A Critical Appraisal* (Wien: Springer-Verlag, 1974), p. 75; B. Conforti, 'Cours général de droit international public' (1988) 212 *Collected Courses of the Hague Academy of International Law* 9 at 129.

[2] See Chapter 2, Section 1.

reasoning pertaining to the identification of international legal rules as well as the identification of the processes through which legal rules are validly made.[3] As with any fundamental doctrine, the sources determine the world of possible and impossible combinations of modes of legal reasoning in relation to the identification of the rules of international law and the processes whereby those rules are made. By the same token, the doctrine of sources and the modes of legal reasoning it puts in place are associated with Article 38 of the Statute of the International Court of Justice, to which they are genealogically linked.[4] This is very well illustrated by customary international law, whose two-element variant is commonly considered to be a prescription of Article 38, as will be discussed later.[5] Last but not least, sources, like other fundamental doctrines, are construed as rules. The ruleness of the sources, although it corresponds to representations found for other doctrines, is not self-evident. In fact, jurisprudential problems associated with the ruleness of sources are aplenty and cannot be easily dismissed as arcane hair-splitting controversies.[6] Yet such issues never frustrated international lawyers' espousal of the idea of the ruleness of sources. In this respect, one probably does not need to carry out extensive research to grasp the preponderance of a rule-based understanding of the

---

[3] On these two aspects of the doctrine of sources, see Jean d'Aspremont and Samantha Besson, 'Introduction', in Samantha Besson and Jean d'Aspremont (eds.), *Oxford Handbook on the Sources of International Law* (Oxford: Oxford University Press, 2017) pp. 1–39.

[4] On Article 38 as the formal repository for anything that pertains to sources, see D. Hollis, 'Why state consent still matters – non-state actors, treaties, and the changing sources of international law' (2005) 23 *Berkeley Journal of International Law* 137 at 141. See also Sienho Yee, 'Article 38 of the ICJ Statute and applicable law: selected issues in recent cases' (2016) 7 *Journal of International Dispute Settlement* 472.

[5] See Chapter 4, Section 3.

[6] For an overview of these problems, see J. d'Aspremont, 'The idea of "rules" in the sources of international law' (2014) 84 *British Yearbook of International Law* 103. See also Cass R. Sunstein, *Leal Reasoning and Political Conflict* (Oxford: Oxford University Press, 1996), pp. 130–35. Even the ruleness of the 'rule of recognition' is contested. See F. Schauer, *Playing by the Rules* (Oxford: Clarendon Press, 1991), p. 199; see also F. Schauer, 'Amending the presuppositions of a constitution', in S. Levinson (ed.), *Responding to Imperfection* (Princeton, NJ: Princeton University Press, 1995), pp. 145, 150–51: 'In referring to the ultimate rule of recognition as a rule, Hart has probably misled us. There is no reason to suppose that the ultimate source of law need be anything that looks at all like a rule, whether simple or complex, or even a collection of rules ... The ultimate source of law, therefore, is better described as the practice by which it is determined that some things are to count as law and some things are not.' See also F. Schauer, 'Is the rule of recognition a rule?' (2012) 3 *Transnational Legal Theory* 2, 173. See also A. W. B. Simpson, 'The common law and legal theory', in A. W. B. Simpson (ed.), *Oxford Essays in Jurisprudence*, Second Series (Oxford: Clarendon Press, 1973), p. 77.

sources of international law. General as well as specialised literature on sources of international law is dominated by the idea that sources of international law constitute a set of rules properly so-called[7], customary law being the prime candidate to formally nest such rules.[8] The idea of ruleness of sources is similarly widespread in connection with the modes of legal reasoning associated with customary international law. Among others, the International Law Association's 2000 London Statement of Principles Applicable to the Formation of (General) Customary International Law

[7] A few examples can be provided here. J. Brierly, 'The basis of obligation in international law', in H. Lauterpacht and C. H. M. Waldock (eds.), *The Basis of Obligation in International Law and Other Papers by the Late James Leslie Brierly* (Oxford: Clarendon Press, 1959), pp. 1, 10; P. Guggenheim, *Traite de Droit International Public* (Paris: Georg & Cie, 1953), pp. 6–8; P. Weil, 'Le droit international en quête de son identité: cours général de droit international public' (1992) 237 *Recueil des cours* 131; A. D'Amato, 'The concept of special custom in international law' (1969) 63 *American Journal of International Law* 211; T. Nardin, *Law, Morality and the Relations of States* (Princeton, NJ: Princeton University Press, 1983), p. 172 (arguing, however, that there is no rule on customary international law). It is noteworthy that Michael Wood uses quotation marks when he refers to the rules for the formation of customary international law; see M. Wood, 'What is public international law? The need for clarity about sources' (2011) 1 *Asian Journal of International Law* 205 at 213. Malcolm Shaw speaks about 'provisions operating with the legal system on a technical level'. See M. Shaw, *International Law*, 5th edn (Cambridge: Cambridge University Press, 2003), p. 66. Hugh Thirlway, for his part, speaks about the 'law of sources'; see H. Thirlway, *The Sources of International Law* (Oxford: Oxford University Press, 2014). The same idea of ruleness also imbues those commonly heard statements that Article 38 is declaratory of general international law: see A. Pellet, 'Article 38', in A. Zimmermann, C. Tomuschat, K. Oellers-Frahm and C. Tams (eds.), *The Statute of the International Court of Justice: A Commentary*, 2nd edn (Oxford: Oxford University Press, 2012), p. 750; G. Abi-Saab, 'Les sources du droit international: essai de deconstruction', in M. Rama-Montaldo (ed.), *International Law in an Evolving World: Liber Amicorum in Tribute to Professor Eduardo Jiménez de Aréchaga*, vol. 1 (Montevideo: Fundacici de Cultura Universitaria, 1994), pp. 29–49. The same holds with works that attempt to transpose Hart's *concept of law* to sources of international law, and especially to theory of customary international law; see G. J. H. Van Hoof, *Rethinking the Sources of International Law* (Deventer: Kluwer Law, 1983); G. M. Danilenko, *Law-Making in the International Community* (Leiden: Martinus Nijhoff, 1993), pp. 16 et seq.; G. M. Danilenko, 'The theory of international customary law' (1988) 31 *German Yearbook of International Law* 9; H. Meijers, 'How is international law made?' (1979) 9 *Netherlands Yearbook of International Law* 3.

[8] See e.g. D. J. Bederman, *Custom as a Source of Law* (Cambridge: Cambridge University Press, 2010), p. 137 ('Finally, and (perhaps) most influentially, CIL norms dictate the construction and application of "meta-norms" of public international law. These include what H. L. A. Hart would call secondary rules of recognition for other international law sources, as with principles of treaty formation, interpretation, and termination. Likewise, the substance of international law of state responsibility and the procedures under which states make claim for redress of international wrongs are dictated by custom.').

adopted a rule-based approach to custom.[9] The same holds for the work of the International Law Commission's (ILC) Special Rapporteur on the identification of customary international law, which, despite its self-restraint, takes a similar rule-based conception of the sources of international law.[10] The ruleness of sources equally dominates the understanding of international treaties. With respect to treaties, this idea is probably the specific prolongation of the law of treaties being itself cast in the form of formal conventional rules.[11] The ruleness of the sources similarly expresses itself in international lawyers' extensive reliance on Hart's rule of recognition to describe the sources of international law.[12]

---

[9] International Law Association, 'Final report of the committee on formation of customary (general) international law', *International Law Association London Conference* (2000), para. 6.

[10] International Law Commission, 'First report on the formation and evidence of customary international law by the Special Rapporteur, Sir Michael Wood', 17 May 2013, A/CN.4/663, para. 38: 'It is perhaps unnecessary, at least at this stage, to enter upon the question of the nature of the rules governing the formation and identification of rules of customary international law, for example, whether such rules are themselves part of customary international law. But as in any legal system, there must in public international law be rules for identifying the sources of the law. These can be found for present purposes by examining in particular how States and courts set about the task of identifying the law.'

[11] This approach was not followed for the international law of state responsibility. See J. Crawford, S. Olleson and J. Peel, 'The ILC's articles on responsibility of states for internationally wrongful acts: completion of the second reading' (2001) 12 *European Journal of International Law* 963; J. Crawford and S. Olleson, 'The continuing debate on a un convention on state responsibility' (2005) 54 *International and Comparative Law Quarterly* 959.

[12] International lawyers generously refer to Hart. To cite only a few examples, see the general courses of P.-M. Dupuy, 'L'unité de l'ordre juridique international: cours général de droit international public' (2002) 297 *Recueil des cours* 9; P. Weil, 'Le droit international en quête de son identité – cours général de droit international public' (1992) 237 *Recueil des cours* 9; O. Schachter, 'International law in theory and practice: general course in public international law' (1982-V) 178 *Recueil des cours* 1. For a significant exception, see Ian Brownlie, who discards Hart as too abstract and adopts a much more pragmatic conception of international law, drawing on the assumption that those in charge usually do not even understand law as a unitary concept. For Brownlie, there is no such thing as a 'neat ultimate rule of recognition which provides an intellectual basis for a system of rules but a complex state of political fact': I. Brownlie 'International law at the fiftieth anniversary of the United Nations: general course on public international law', (1995) 255 *Recueil des cours* 9 at 24. In a way that seems to indicate that he construed Hart's theory as a theory of obedience and not a theory of law ascertainment, Brownlie also formulates the objection that the population may decide to abide by other rules of recognition: *ibid.* at 25. For another rejection of Hart and the defense of a Kelsenian understanding of international law, see J. Kammerhofer, 'Uncertainty in the formal sources of international law: customary international law and some of its problems' (2004) 15 *European Journal of International Law* 523, esp. 543–47. His views are further

As far as the ruleness of sources is concerned, it can be surmised that international lawyers' representation of the doctrine of sources as rules has probably been reinforced by the fact that Article 38 of the Statute of the International Court of Justice actually functions like a rule for this specific judicial institution. In fact, Article 38 formally limits the law applicable by the Court, thereby creating an internal rule for this adjudicatory body.[13] This has been confirmed by the Court itself on several occasions.[14] It would be of no avail to discuss whether Article 38 constitutes, within the framework of the Statute, a rule for the Court.[15] What matters here is to highlight that this specific internal effect of Article 38 has led many international lawyers to generalise the rule-based normativity of Article 38 and to transpose it to the sources of international law beyond the specific framework of the Statute of the International Court of Justice. Correspondingly, other tribunals frequently refer to Article 38[16] and thus can generate the impression that the doctrine of sources supposedly found in Article 38 is composed of rules. Whatever these reinforcing parameters, the idea that sources of international law constitute rules is well entrenched in contemporary discourse, thereby further vindicating their understanding as a fundamental doctrine of international law. It is because the doctrine of sources is itself a fundamental doctrine that the explanation of the

---

elaborated in J. Kammerhofer, *Uncertainty in International Law: A Kelsenian Perspective* (London: Routledge, 2010), esp. pp. 205 et seq. and 224 et seq.

[13] A. Pellet, 'Article 38', p. 759; P.-M. Dupuy, 'La pratique de l'article 38 du Statut de la Cour internationale de Justice dans le cadre des plaidoiries écrites et orales', in *Collection of Essays by Legal Advisers of States, Legal Advisers of International Organizations and Practitioners in the Field of International Law* (New York: United Nations, 1999), pp. 377, 379; P. Weil, 'Le droit international en quête de son identité – Cours général de droit international public' (1992) 237 *Recueil des cours* 1, 139. For an overview of the challenges and insufficiencies of Article 38, see D. Hollis, 'Why state consent still matters – non-state actors, treaties, and the changing sources of international law' (2005) 23 *Berkeley Journal of International Law* 137 at 142–44.

[14] *Continental Shelf (Tunisia v. Libyan Arab Jamahiriya)*, ICJ Rep 1982, 18, para. 23; *Military and Paramilitary Activities in and against Nicaragua (Nicaragua v. United States of America)*, ICJ Rep 1986, 14, para. 187; *Frontier Dispute (Burkina Faso v. Mali)*, ICJ Rep 1986, 554, para. 42; *Gulf of Maine (Canada v. United States of America)*, ICJ Rep 1999, 120, para. 93; *Maritime Delimitation in the Area Between Greenland and Jan Mayen (Denmark v. Norway)*, ICJ Rep 1993, 38, para. 52; *Jurisdictional Immunities of the States (Italy v. Germany)*, ICJ Rep 2012, 99, para. 55.

[15] This has sometimes been challenged. See Joe Verhoeven, who argues that Article 38 only gives 'indications' to the Court, Joe Verhoeven, 'Considérations sur ce qui est commun: cours general de droit international public' (2002) 334 *Recueil des cours* 109.

[16] For some examples, see A. Pellet, 'Article 38', pp. 746–47.

formation of all fundamental doctrines through sources entails self-referentiality, that is, an explanation of fundamental doctrines in their own terms.

A second remark is warranted on the contribution of sources to self-referentiality. Although the rise of the doctrine of sources is an off-spring of the legalistic and liberal project of the Enlightenment,[17] the critical contribution of this doctrine to the self-referentiality at the heart of the international belief system is a modern invention.[18] Indeed, it took until the twentieth century to fully achieve the centrality of the doctrine of sources given the resilience of both subject-based approaches to international law[19] as well as (naturalist) scholastic-inspired approaches.[20] In fact, although some groundwork for the central explanatory role of sources was realised by legal scholars of the nineteenth century,[21] it is to

---

[17] See Chapter 1, Section 2. This does not mean the doctrine of sources was totally absent from the early thinking about international law. Indeed, theories of substantive validity of rules, as those found on scholastic theories, allowed for an autonomous concept of sources. Yet the dualism – by virtue of which immanent considerations would trump any formal aspects of validity – at the heart of such theories of substantive validity inevitably demoted sources to a very secondary mechanism. See, generally, A. Pagden and J. Lawrence (eds.), *Vitoria: Political Writings* (Cambridge: Cambridge University Press, 1991); A. Gentili, *On the Law of War*, trans. J. C. Rolfe (Oxford: Clarendon Press, 1933). On Gentili, see, generally, B. Kingsbury and B. Straumann (eds.), *The Roman Foundations of the Law of Nations* (Oxford: Oxford University Press, 2011).

[18] On the idea that sources are not inherent in law and that the legal system can be constructed differently, see Pierre LePaulle, 'Reflections on the sources of law', in Ralph. A. Newman (ed.), *Essays in Jurisprudence in Honor of Roscoe Pound* (Indianapolis: Bobbs-Merrill, 1962), p. 87, esp. pp. 88–89.

[19] According to this approach, a correlation was established between states as the makers of international law and those rules that could qualify as rules of international law. See e.g. J. Bentham, *An Introduction to the Principles of Morals and Legislation* (London: Kessinger, Whitefish, 2005, first published 1781), p. 326. For some comments on that era of international legal thought, see Philip Allott, 'The true function of law in the international community' (1998) 5 *Global Legal Studies Journal* 391 at 404.

[20] For some illustrations, see S. Pufendorf, *On the Law of Nature and of Nations*, trans. C. H. Oldfather and W. A. Oldfather. (Oxford: Clarendon Press, 1934, first published 1672). See the comments by E. Jouannet, *Emer de Vattel et l'émergence doctrinale du droit international classique* (Paris: Pedone, 1998), pp. 361 et seq. See also C. Wolff, *Law of Nations Treated according to a Scientific Method*, trans. J. H. Drake. (Oxford: Clarendon Press, 1934). On the emancipation from the naturalist models of substantive validity, see the account provided by P. Guggenheim, 'Les origines de la notion autonome du droit des gens', in J. H. W. Verzijl, *Symbolae Verzijl: présentées au professeur J. H. W. Verzijl a l'occasion de son LXX-ieme anniversaire* (The Hague: Martinus Nijhoff, 1958), pp. 177–89.

[21] In particular, under the influence of Vattel and Martens, natural law and reason became demoted to a secondary parameter, thereby creating the possibility for a theory of sources. It is said that they elevated the will of the state to the only validator of legal rules. The idea

twentieth-century international lawyers[22] that is owed the design of sophisticated formal law-ascertaining criteria as they are known today.[23]
Interestingly, this modern sophistication of the law-ascertainment criteria
has remained accompanied by an extreme theoretical paucity. The
architects of the doctrines of sources all remained very aloof from the
debates about its theoretical foundations.[24] Very few scholars ventured

that the voluntarists of the nineteenth century paved the way for the emergence of a
theory of sources is certainly not without paradox. Indeed, voluntarism is not structurally
different from substantive validity. If the will of the state is the validator of rules, there is
no autonomous pedigree by virtue of which the rule is identified and validated. In both
substantive validity and voluntarism, there is simply no neutralisation of the indeterminacy – and the politics – of the will that ought to be determined, whether such a will is that
of the state or God or is simply reason. In that sense, these voluntarist scholars of the
nineteenth century were still one step away from inventing the theory of sources as
exclusive validator. However, by moving away from the will of God, nature or reason,
these scholars prepared the ground for one of the sophisticated conceptual engineering
that led to the design of the theory of sources in the twentieth century. For critical remarks
on the image of nineteenth-century international lawyers which we have inherited, see,
generally, D. Kennedy, 'International law and the nineteenth century: history of an
illusion' (1996) 65 Nordic Journal of International Law 385.

[22] It must be noted that, in their great majority, twentieth-century scholars did not shed the
idea of their predecessors according to which international law rests on the consent of
states. At least, they agreed that the will of the state is the most obvious material source of
law remained unchallenged. See D. Anzilotti, 'Il diritto internazionale nei giudizi interni',
reprinted in D. Anzilotti, Scritti di Diritto Internazionale Pubblico (Padua: CEDAM,
1956–7), p. 318; T. J. Lawrence, The Principles of International Law, 7th edn (London:
Macmillan, 1923), pp. 1–14; L. Oppenheim, 'The science of international law: its task and
method' (1908) 2 American Journal of International Law 313; L. Oppenheim,
International Law: A Treatise, 1st edn (London: Longmans, Green and Co., 1905), esp.
p. 92; G. Schwarzenberger, International Law, 3rd edn (London: Stevens & Sons, 1957); P.
Guggenheim, 'What is positive international law?', in G. Lipsky (ed.), Law and Politics in
the World Community: Essays on Hans Kelsen's Pure Theory and Related Problems of
International Law (Berkley: University of California Press, 1953), pp. 15–30.

[23] A. Pellet, 'Cours général: le droit international entre souveraineté et communauté international' (2007) 2 Anuário Brasileiro de Direito Internacional 12 at 15, 19 and 31. See also
G. Buzzini, 'La théorie des sources face au droit international général' (2002) 106 Revue
générale de droit international public 581, esp. 584–90.

[24] In the same sense, see E. Jouannet, 'Regards sur un siècle de doctrine française du droit
international' (2000) 46 Annuaire français de droit international 1. See, generally, D.
Kennedy, 'International law and nineteenth century: history of an illusion' (1996) 65
Nordic Journal International Law 385 at 387; D. Kennedy, 'A new stream of international
legal scholarship' (1988–89) 7 Wisconsin International Law Journal 1 at 6; N. Purvis,
'Critical legal studies in public international law' (1991) 32 Harvard Journal of
International Law 81 at 84; M. Reisman, 'Lassa Oppenheim's nine lives' (1994) 19 Yale
Journal of International Law 255 at 271; See N. Onuf, 'Global law-making and legal
thought', in N. Onuf (ed.), Law-Making in the Global Community (Durham, NC: Carolina
Academic Press, 1982), p. 1 at p. 13; A. D'Amato, 'What "counts" as law?', in N. Onuf
(ed.), Law-Making in the Global Community (Durham, NC: Carolina Academic Press,

into a study of the 'ontology' of the doctrine of sources.[25] Although this growing dominant 'anti-theoretical'[26] posture can probably be explained by the growing self-assurance gained by international legal scholars after their branch of law was recognised as equal to other legal disciplines,[27] the perpetuation of this theoretical paucity in the twentieth century can be construed as a manifestation of the consolidation of the international belief system and, more specifically, the generalisation of self-referentiality. For these reasons, it can be argued that the sophistication of the doctrine of sources of international law and the consolidation of self-referentiality at the heart of the belief system are deeply – and unsurprisingly – intertwined. Be that as it may, with the rise of the modern doctrine of sources in the twentieth century and the idea that modes of legal reasoning associated with the sources constitute rules, a great deal of the self-referentiality of the international belief system at the level of the formation of the fundamental doctrines has thus been put in place, thereby allowing the formation of all fundamental doctrines of international law to be explained through the sources of international law.

2 Explaining the Functioning of the Fundamental Doctrines through Interpretation

While the doctrine of sources allows self-referentiality to operate at the level of the formation of the foundational doctrines, it is argued here that the doctrine of interpretation – as it is organised in Articles 31 and 32 of the Vienna Convention on the Law of Treaties – makes self-referentiality possible at the level of the functioning of the fundamental doctrines.

Before elaborating on the interpretation-based self-referentiality at work in international legal thought and practice, the way in which

---

1982), p. 83 at pp. 83–107; M. Koskenniemi, 'Repetition as reform' (1998) 9 *European Journal of International Law* 405; J. Klabbers, 'Constitutionalism and the making of international law' (2008) 5 *NoFo* 84 at 94.

[25] A classical example is R. Jennings and A. Watts, *Oppenheim's International Law*, 9th edn, vol. 1 (London: Longmans, 1992).

[26] The expression is from M. Koskenniemi, 'Repetition as reform' (1998) 9 *European Journal of International Law* 405 at 406.

[27] T. O. Elias, 'Problems concerning the validity of treaties' (1971-III) 133 *Collected Courses of the Hague Academy of International Law* 333 at 341. See K. Zemanek, 'The legal foundations of the international system' (1997) 266 *Collected Courses of the Hague Academy of International Law* 9 at 131 et seq.

interpretation is construed here needs to be elucidated.[28] For the sake of the discussion conducted here, interpretation is understood as a performative[29] and constitutive activity[30] that contributes to the making of what it purports to find.[31] So construed, interpretation is an ubiquitous phenomenon,[32] all practices and discourses about international law having an interpretive dimension.[33] In that sense, any engagement in legal argumentation necessarily has an interpretive dimension. The object of interpretation as it is understood thus can be very diverse. What is interpreted in international legal discourses includes the legal pedigree of rules, the content of rules, modes of legal reasoning, facts, etc. Interestingly, the various objects of interpretation are not necessarily subjected to the same regime or method of interpretation.[34] Each of these interpretive processes is

---

[28] I have expounded on my understanding of interpretation elsewhere. See Jean d'Aspremont, 'The multidimensional process of interpretation: content-determination and law-ascertainment distinguished', in A. Bianchi, D. Peat and M. Windsor (eds.), *Interpretation in International Law* (Oxford: Oxford University Press, 2015), pp. 111–29.

[29] On the idea that legal interpretation is a creative activity that contributes to the making of what it purports to find, see I. Venzke, 'The travails of legal positivism from post-modern perspectives: performativity, deconstructions and governmentality', in J. Kammerhofer and J. d'Aspremont (eds.), *International Legal Positivism in a Postmodern World* (Cambridge: Cambridge University Press, 2014). See in the same volume, G. Hernandez, 'Interpretation'.

[30] See N. Onuf: '[S]aying is doing; talking is undoubtedly the most important way that we go about making the world what it is'. See N. Onuf, 'Constructivism: a user's manual', in V. Kublakova, N. Onuf and P. Kowert (eds.), *International Relations in a Constructed World* (New York: Sharpe, 1998), p. 59.

[31] I. Venzke, 'The travails of legal positivism from post-modern perspectives: performativity, deconstructions and governmentality', in J. Kammerhofer and J. d'Aspremont (eds.), *International Legal Positivism in a Postmodern World* (Cambridge: Cambridge University Press, 2014).

[32] Robert Cover, 'The Supreme Court 1982 term – foreword: nomos and narrative' (1983) 97 *Harvard Law Review* 4 at 4–5.

[33] Interpretation, in that sense, is said to permeate all of legal life. See G. Hernandez, 'Interpretation', in J. Kammerhofer and J. d'Aspremont (eds.), *International Legal Positivism in a Postmodern World* (Cambridge: Cambridge University Press, 2014), pp. 317–48. See, however, the claims that legal reasoning and interpretation cannot be conflated and that no all legal reasoning involve interpretation. See Timothy Endicott, 'Legal Interpretation', in A. Marmor (ed.), *Routledge Companion to Philosophy of Law* (London: Routledge, 2012), p. 109.

[34] The most common approach (i.e. the textualist interpretation) relies heavily on the mechanics of induction and allows the interpreter to infer the command from the text itself. According to the intentionalist technique, the interpreter strives to resuscitate the actual intention of the law maker and extrapolates an answer to the question at stake on the basis of the reconstructed intention of the legislator. By virtue of a purposive interpretation, the interpreter entrusts to herself the task of continuing in the legislative task according to the purpose pursued by an idealised legislator and to give effect to the

also the site of a very distinct and uneven distribution of interpretive power where different actors compete for interpretive authority.[35]

Whilst acknowledging the multidimensional and ubiquitous character of interpretation, the argument made here in relation to interpretation-based self-referentiality zeroes in on a specific dimension of interpretation, namely, the interpretation of the fundamental doctrines and the modes of legal reasoning they put in place. More specifically, interpretation is discussed here in relation to the determination of the modes of legal reasoning prescribed by the fundamental doctrines as they are enunciated in the international instruments that serve as their formal repository. It is argued that such interpretation of the formal repository of fundamental doctrines generates self-referentiality because it is subjected to the modes of legal reasoning put in place by one of the fundamental doctrines themselves, namely, the doctrine of interpretation. Indeed, once the fundamental doctrines are construed as rules derived from international instruments, the determination of the content thereof comes to be guided by the fundamental doctrine of interpretation as is found in Articles 31 and 32 of the Vienna Convention on the Law of Treaties. Although the fundamental doctrine of interpretation as it is enunciated in Articles 31 and 32 of the Vienna Convention is not always deemed fully applicable to instruments that are not of a conventional nature – such as articles adopted by the International Law Commission – the regime of interpretation of all instruments providing a formal repository to fundamental doctrines continues to be informed by the same interpretive constraints of the fundamental doctrine of interpretation. As a result, most international lawyers deem that the interpretation of the instruments that serve as the formal repository of fundamental doctrines is subject to the rules of the fundamental doctrine of interpretation.[36]

---

policy goals pursued in the specific case concerned. On this account, see A. Marmor, 'Textualism in context', *USC Gould School of Law Legal Studies Research Paper Series* No. 12–13, 18 July 2012.

[35] See, generally, J. d'Aspremont, *Epistemic Forces in International Law* (London: Edward Elgar, 2015), pp. 1–30. See also J. d'Aspremont, 'Wording in international law' (2012) 25 *Leiden Journal of International Law* 575.

[36] For an example pertaining to the regime of interpretation of the Articles on State Responsibility, see G. Gaja, 'Interpreting articles adopted by the International Law Commission' (2016) 85 *British Yearbook of International Law* 10 at 18 (While claiming that Articles 31 and 32 of the Vienna Convention on the Law of Treaties are inapplicable, he claims that the general rule of interpretation stated in Article 31, paragraph 1, according to which 'a treaty shall be interpreted in good faith and in accordance with the ordinary meaning to be given to the terms of the treaty in their context and in the light of its object and purpose' is a rule applicable to all international instruments.) In the same

The contribution of the doctrine of interpretation to the self-referentiality of the international belief system warrants three observations. First, it must be highlighted that, like sources, the doctrine of interpretation presents all the common features of a fundamental doctrine. It prescribes modes of legal reasoning which are supposed to be systematically organised. Likewise, it is held to be derived from an international instrument, namely, Articles 31 and 32 of the Vienna Convention on the Law of Treaties to which they are genealogically bound. Alternatively, it is commonly derived from customary international law.[37]

Second, the modes of legal reasoning associated with the doctrine of interpretation are also meant to be rules.[38] Indeed, it does not seem controversial to claim that mainstream international legal scholarship has always promoted a predominantly rule-based approach to the doctrine of interpretation. According to such an approach, the

---

vein, see G. Abi-Saab, 'La Commission du Droit International, la codification et le processus de formation du droit international', in *Making Better International Law: The International Law Commission at 50* (New York: United Nations, 1998), pp. 181 at 196.

[37] R. Gardiner, *Treaty Interpretation* (Oxford: Oxford University Press, 2008), p. 13S. See, generally, J. M. Sorel, 'Article 31', in P. Klein and O. Corten (eds.), *Les Conventions de Vienne sur le Droit des Traités: Commentaire Article par Article* (Bruxelles: Bruylant, 2006), pp. 1289–334; M. E. Villiger, *Customary International Law and Treaties: A Study of their Interactions and Interrelations with Special Consideration of the 1969 Vienna Convention on the Law of Treaties* (Dordrecht: Martinus Nijhoff, 1985), pp. 334ff; see Torrez Bernardez, 'Interpretation of treaties by the International Court of Justice following the adoption of the 1963 Vienna Convention on the Law of Treaties', in G. Hafner et al. (eds.), *Liber Amicorum Seidl-Hohenveldern* (The Hague: Kluwer, 1998), p. 723.

[38] Whilst this seems self-evident today, this has not always been the case. In this respect, it is worth recalling the doubts expressed by some of the drafters of the Vienna Convention on the Law of Treaties. For instance, Alfred Verdross raised the question of the nature of the rules of interpretation which the International Law Commission intended to codify, arguing that 'the Commission ought first to decide whether it recognised the existence of such rules' (ILC, 726th Meeting, UN Doc A/CN.4/167, reproduced in *Yearbook of the International Law Commission*, vol. I (1964), pp. 20–21, para. 15). In his view, '[I]t was highly controversial whether the rules established by the case-law of arbitral tribunals and international courts were general rules of international law or merely technical rules' (*ibid.*, para. 15). In the same vein, Sir Humphrey Waldock conceded that he 'was decidedly lukewarm on rules on interpretation, including them more because he thought this was expected of him than out of genuine expectation that rules on interpretation would be of much use' (cited by J. Klabbers, 'Virtuous Interpretation', in Malgosia Fitzmaurice et al. (eds.), *Treaty Interpretation and the Vienna Convention on the Law of Treaties: 30 Years On*, vol. 1 (Leiden: Martinus Nijhoff, 2010), p. 18). On these earlier doubts in the codification of rules on interpretation, see the remarks of Fuad Zarbiyev, *Le Discours Interprétatif en Droit International Contemporain: Un Essai Critique* (Bruylant, 2015), pp. 23–28.

doctrine of interpretation, like all other fundamental doctrines,[39] is construed as being composed of formal rules, those enshrined in the Vienna Convention on the Law of Treaties.[40] In fact, most of the studies produced on the interpretation of treaties in recent years understand the doctrine of interpretation as a set of rules found in the 1969 and 1986 Vienna Conventions on the Law of Treaties.[41] International courts and tribunals have endorsed a similar position.[42] The same holds for the interpretation of other international legal acts.[43] Here, too, there are jurisprudential problems associated with the ruleness of the doctrine of interpretation[44] or its customary

---

[39] See Chapter 2.

[40] For a similar reading of the mainstream scholarship, see A. Bianchi, 'Textual interpretation and (international) law reading: the myth of (in) determinacy and the genealogy of meaning', in P. Bekker (ed.), *Making Transnational Law Work in the Global Economy: Essays in Honour of Detlev Vagts* (Cambridge: Cambridge University Press, 2010), p. 35 ('current reflection of mainstream international legal scholarship remains imbued with traditional rule-based approaches to legal interpretation'). See also Fuad Zarbiyev, *Le Discours Interprétatif en Droit International Contemporain: Un Essai Critique* (Bruylant, 2015), pp. 23–35.

[41] For a review of recent works on interpretation, see M. Waibel, 'Demystifying the art of interpretation' (2011) 22 *European Journal of International Law* 571. See also the works cited by A. Bianchi, D. Peat and M. R. Windsor (eds.), *Interpretation in International Law* (Oxford: Oxford University Press, 2015). For an approach that construes rules on interpretation as guiding principles or directives, see I. Van Damme, *Treaty Interpretation by the WTO Appellate Body* (Oxford: Oxford University Press, 2009), p. 35.

[42] *Territorial Dispute (Libyan Arab Jamahiriya v. Chad)* ICJ Rep 1994, 6; *Kasikili/Sedudu Island (Botswana v. Namibia)* ICJ Rep 1999, 1059; *LaGrand (Germany v. United States of America)* ICJ Rep 2001, 501, para. 99; *Legal Consequences of the Construction of a Wall in the Occupied Palestinian Territory* (Advisory Opinion), ICJ Rep 2004, 136, para. 94. See also *Iron Rhine ('Ijzeren Rijn') Railway (Belgium v. The Netherlands)*, 20 September 2005, p. 23, para. 45; WTO Appelate Body, *Japan-Alcoholic Beverages* (4 October 1996) II WT/DS8, 10–11/AB/R, part D, 10–12; WTO Appelate Body, *United States – Standards for Reformulated and Conventional Gasoline* (29 April 1996) WT/DS2/AB/R, 16–17; *Golder v. United Kingdom* App No 4451/70 (ECtHR, 21 February 1975), para. 32.

[43] *Accordance with International Law of the Unilateral Declaration of Independence in Respect of Kosovo* (Request for Advisory Opinion), ICJ Rep 2010, 404, para. 94. See E. Papstavridis, 'Interpretation of security council resolutions under chapter VII in the aftermath of the Iraqi crisis' (2007) *International and Comparative Law Quarterly* 83.

[44] If construed as rules by mainstream international legal scholarship, such constraints on content-determination interpretation correspond to what Fiss calls 'disciplining rules'. See O. Fiss 'Objectivity and interpretation' (1982) 34 *Stanford Law Review* 739. It is well known that the idea of disciplining rules has been the object of very extensive criticism. For Fish, such rules 'are in need of interpretation and cannot themselves serve as constraints on interpretation'. This objection led Fish to understand constraints on interpretation not as rules but as practices of an 'interpretive community'. See S. Fish, 'Fish v. Fiss' (1984) 36 *Stanford Law Review* 1325 at 1336. See also A. Bianchi, 'Textual interpretation and (international) law reading: the myth of (in) determinacy and the

nature.[45] Yet these problems have not prevented international lawyers from wholeheartedly embracing the ruleness of the doctrine of interpretation.[46]

Third, the doctrine of interpretation and its application to the formal repositories of fundamental doctrines are not only meant to explain interpretive moves in the application of all fundamental doctrines. They also justify the inevitable changes and adjustments

genealogy of meaning', in P. Bekker (ed.), *Making Transnational Law Work in the Global Economy: Essays in Honour of Detlev Vagts* (Cambridge: Cambridge University Press, 2010), p. 48. This is a criticism made by H. L. A. Hart, *The Concept of Law*, 2nd edn (Oxford: Oxford University Press, 1994), p. 126. For some mitigating factors, see G. Hernandez, 'Interpretation', in J. Kammerhofer and J. d'Aspremont (eds.), *International Legal Positivism in a Postmodern World* (Cambridge: Cambridge University Press, 2014). On the specific problem of infinite regress, see I. Venzke, 'Language games: topography and traction of a metaphor'; I. Venzke, 'The travails of legal positivism from post-modern perspectives: performativity, deconstructions and governmentality', in J. Kammerhofer and J. d'Aspremont (eds.), *International Legal Positivism in a Postmodern World* (Cambridge: Cambridge University Press, 2014). See also G. Letsas, 'Strasbourg's interpretive ethic: lessons for the international lawyer' (2010) 21 *European Journal of International Law* 509 at 534; Fuad Zarbiyev, *Le Discours Interprétatif en Droit International Contemporain: Un Essai Critique* (Bruylant, 2015), pp. 28–35.

[45] Aside from the belief system to which it belongs, the customary character of the doctrine of interpretation could be challenged from the very perspective of the doctrine of sources of international law. Indeed, if the doctrine of customary international law is applied in an orthodox manner, it is not at all certain that the constraints on interpretation of international law meet the traditional requirements for customary law. First, it seems that the practice is mostly that of authoritative judicial bodies in their own right. It is true that some of them constitute organs of international organisations. Yet it is not clear that such a practice qualifies as practice attributable to subjects of international law for the sake of the formation of customary law. Second, it is not obvious that the 'anthropomorphic' requirement of opinio juris can ever be extracted from the attitude of international courts and tribunals that have been applying – albeit religiously – the law on interpretation. Third, it is not certain that those rules on interpretation could ever pass the elementary 'Continental Shelf' test whereby any potential standard is required to be of a 'fundamentally norm-creating character such as could be regarded as forming the basis of a general rule of law' to ever generate customary law (see ICJ Rep 1969, 3, para 72; see also *Asylum (Colombia v. Peru)*, ICJ Rep 1950, 6, para. 277). In this respect, it does not seem controversial to say that the rules on interpretation do not dictate any specific behaviour to states and international organisations. Moreover, the specific interpretive constraints they put forward remain rather loose and vague. For all these reasons, it seems implausible that the unanimous claims about the customary status of the interpretive constraints found in the Vienna Conventions would ever survive a careful application of the orthodox doctrine of customary law.

[46] For some criticisms of the rule-based approach in interpretation, see A. Bianchi, 'The game of interpretation in international law: the players, the cards, and why the game is worth the candle', in Andrea Bianchi, Daniel Peat and Matthew Windsor (eds.), *Interpretation in International Law* (Oxford: Oxford University Press, 2015), pp. 35.

undergone by the fundamental doctrines. Indeed, as was recalled earlier,[47] fundamental doctrines are fluid and are also subject to adjustment when they are applied. Self-referentiality at the level of the functioning of fundamental doctrines allows the fundamental doctrine of interpretation to explain the dynamism of the content of all fundamental doctrines.[48] In this respect, interpretive modes such as the principle of systemic integration[49] or subsequent practice[50] generally play a crucial role.

With the doctrine on interpretation being construed as rules that are applicable to the interpretation of the rules composing other fundamental doctrines, the self-referentiality of the belief system is put into effect when it comes to the functioning of the fundamental doctrines. It is noteworthy that international lawyers have fallen short of claiming that the doctrine of interpretation itself ought to be interpreted along the lines of its own modes of legal reasoning. In that sense, the contribution to self-referentiality of the doctrine of interpretation is not as absolute as that of the doctrine of sources, which is supposed to explain its own formation.[51] Yet the doctrine of interpretation is made one of the linchpins of self-referentiality at

---

[47] See Chapter 2, Section 1.

[48] As a result of self-referentiality, international law 'erases its own doubts, negates its own inadequacies, denies its own internal instability'. See P. Schlag, *Laying Down the Law* (New York: New York University Press, 1996), p. 12.

[49] See, generally, C. McLachlan, 'The principle of systemic integration and article 31(3)(c) of the Vienna Convention' (2005) 54 *International and Comparative Law Quarterly* 279; I. Van Damme, 'Some observations about the ILC Study Report on the Fragmentation of International Law: WTO treaty interpretation against the background of other international law' (2006) 17 *Finnish Yearbook of International Law* 21; see also V. Tzevelekos, 'The use of Article 31(3)(c) of the VCLT in the case law of the ECtHR: an effective anti-fragmentation tool or a selective loophole for the reinforcement of human rights teleology? Between evolution and systemic integration' (2010) 31 *Michigan Journal of International Law* 621; A. Orakhelashvili, *The Interpretation of Acts and Rules in Public International Law* (Oxford: Oxford University Press, 2008), pp. 366–69.

[50] See, generally, the four reports of the Special Rapporteur of the International Law Commission on subsequent agreements and subsequent practice in relation to interpretation of treaties, First report of the Special Rapporteur, Mr Georg Nolte, 65th session of the ILC (2013), UN Doc A/CN.4/660, Second report of the Special Rapporteur, Mr Georg Nolte, 66th session of the ILC (2014), UN Doc A/CN.4/671, Third report of the Special Rapporteur, Mr Georg Nolte, 67th session of the ILC (2015), UN Doc A/CN.4/683, Fourth report of the Special Rapporteur, Mr Georg Nolte, 68th session of the ILC (2016), UN Doc A/CN.4/694.

[51] See Chapter 1.

the heart of the belief system. Together sources-based self-referentiality and interpretation-based self-referentiality ensure that the formation and functioning of all fundamental doctrines are explained by fundamental doctrines themselves and that fundamental doctrines operate as transcendental validators generating an experienced sense of constraint.

4

Manifestations of the International Belief System

The preceding chapters have exposed the structure of the international belief system and explained how, within that belief system, the fundamental doctrines are construed as rules derived from some key international instruments, thereby allowing them to invent their origin and dictate their functioning. In so doing, the preceding chapters have thus laid bare the role of self-referentiality by virtue of which the formation and functioning of the rules composing fundamental doctrines come to be explained by the doctrines of sources and interpretation. This chapter seeks to illustrate how this belief system works in contemporary international thought and practice. The fundamental doctrines of sources and interpretation having already been discussed in Chapter 3. This chapter does so in relation to four other specific fundamental doctrines, namely, responsibility, statehood, *jus cogens* and customary international law. This discussion is also accompanied by examples of some of the specific features of the international belief system as it was exposed in the previous chapters. The four fundamental doctrines examined here have been chosen for the extent to which they illustrate specific manifestations of the international belief system.[1] Such a choice does not prejudge the existence of other key fundamental doctrines. This book leaves it to the reader to generalise the observations provided here to other fundamental doctrines of international law.[2]

The chapter starts with a discussion of the fundamental doctrine of responsibility and shows that fundamental doctrines do not coalesce

---

[1] It can be added that the fundamental doctrines examined here are positive doctrines in that they differ from fundamental doctrines of contestation, such as self-determination, the right to development, sovereign equality or permanent sovereignty on natural resources. These fundamental doctrines of contestation are fundamental doctrines in their own right, similarly construed as rules and equally understood as putting in place formal modes of legal reasoning that are resorted to produce international legal discourse.

[2] This remark originated in an exchange with Mark Pollack and Pamela Bookman.

naturally or accidentally but are often the product of a carefully orchestrated design process meant to create a fundamental doctrine (1). The attention then turns to the doctrine of statehood and the 1933 Convention on Rights and Duties of States, which illustrate how some international instruments are elected with a view to offering a formal repository to fundamental doctrines and allow their universalisation (2). The invention of a genealogical link with an international instrument to offer a formal repository is also illustrated with the doctrine of customary international law and the derivation of the two-element approach from Article 38 of the Statute of the Permanent Court of International Justice (3). Finally, the doctrine of *jus cogens* is briefly discussed to show the justificatory space provided by the international belief system (4).

1   Orchestrated Design Process: The Doctrine of Responsibility

The doctrine of international responsibility is construed here as an organised cluster of modes of reasoning through which the battle for the determination and allocation of the burden of compensation for a prior harm is fought as well as for the exercise of constraints to restore and protect legality.[3] Common understandings of this cluster of modes of legal reasoning manifest the same type of ruleness as the one we witnessed in connection with all other fundamental doctrines in that the doctrine of responsibility is construed as a set of – mostly customary[4] – rules. Like the other fundamental doctrines in the international belief system, responsibility is presented and argued as derived from an instrument playing the role of formal repository,[5] which, in this case, is composed of two sets of articles[6] codified by a subsidiary organ of the

---

[3]   The restorative understanding of legality is usually traced back to Roberto Ago. See also R. Ago, 'Le délit international' (1939-II) 69 *Collected Courses of the Hague Academy of International Law* 426 at 426–7, 429. See 'Second report of the Special Rapporteur Mr. Roberto Ago', in *Yearbook of the International Law Commission*, 1970, vol. II, pp. 178–79.

[4]   On the making of rules of responsibility under the cover of customary international law, see Fernando Lusa Bordin, 'Reflections on customary international law: the authority of codification conventions and ILC Draft Articles in International Law' (2014) 63 *International and Comparative Law Quarterly* 535.

[5]   For a list of references made by the International Court of Justice to the Articles on State Responsibility, see J. Crawford, 'Chance, order, change: the course of international law. general course on public international law' (2013) 365 *Collected Courses of the Hague Academy on International Law* 108, n. 263.

[6]   See 'Report of the Commission to the General Assembly on the work of its 53rd session', in *Yearbook of the International Law Commission*, 2001, vol. II, part 2. See also *Yearbook of the International Law Commission*, 2011, vol. II, part 2.

General Assembly of the United Nations, namely, the International Law Commission (ILC).[7]

While illustrating all the main traits of the international belief system, the doctrine of responsibility further demonstrates that fundamental doctrines do not emerge accidentally or naturally but are often the product of a very carefully orchestrated design process. The making of the doctrine of responsibility has indeed followed a well-engineered process whereby some key professionals consciously weighed the various patterns of argumentative structures available and engaged in negotiations to promote the modes of legal reasoning that would perform what they understand to be the role of responsibility. There is no doubt that the architects of the doctrine of responsibility were very much aware of their doctrine-making responsibilities.[8] This is fabulously illustrated by the candidness of Roberto Ago in his famous course on the 'international delict' at the Hague Academy in 1938 – which paved the way for the subsequent codification of the subject after the Second World War – and where he bluntly recognised that doctrine-making is a matter of scholarly choices.[9] As is well known, reaching a compromise on the final

---

[7] The formalisation of the modes of legal reasoning on state responsibility by the ILC led some authors to speak of the ILC as an 'instrument of formalization of international law'. See O. Corten and P. Klein, 'La Commission du droit international comme agent de la formalisation du droit de la responsabilité', in D. Alland, V. Chetail, O. de Frouville and J. Vinuales (eds.), *Unity and Diversity of International Law: Essays in Honour of Professor Pierre-Marie Dupuy* (Leiden: Martinus Nijhoff, 2014), p. 415.

[8] See, however, Crawford and Grant, who speak of an 'unspoken bargain, a jural construction' between states: see J. Crawford and T. Grant, 'Responsibility of states for injuries to foreigners', in J. P. Grant and J. Craig Barker (eds.), *The Harvard Research in International Law: Contemporary Analysis and Appraisal* (Buffalo: Hein, 2007), p. 84.

[9] See e.g. R. Ago, 'Le délit international' (1939-II) 69 *Collected Courses of the Hague Academy of International Law* 426. At p. 423, he writes: 'la qualité de fait juridique, et de fait juridique illicite plus particulièrement, n'est pas une qualité naturelle, inhérente à une certaine conduit humaine, considérée exclusivement dans ses elements de fait et dans son essence matérielle, mais c'est une qualité octroyée par une consideration juridique: c'est une qualification juridique.' Later, however, he creates some ambiguity by playing down the creative character of system design by referring to the comparative observation of domestic legal orders that will provide the foundation of rules of international responsibility. See pp. 425, 433, 435–40. At p. 433, Ago writes: 'Encore une fois, naturellement, c'est l'observation directe des ordres juridiques et des règles qui y qualifient certains faits comme illicites qui va nous donner la notion requise.' In the same vein, see Alejandro Alvarez, *Le Continent Américain et la Codification du Droit International Law: Une Nouvelle 'Ecole' du Droit des Gens* (Paris: Pedone, 1938), pp. 52–53; Manfred Lachs, *Le Monde la Pensée en Droit International* (Paris: Economica, 1989), p. 9. On the idea that modes of legal reasoning of responsibility have been justified via reliance on a wide number arbitral awards that put forward modes of legal reasoning that were not accepted at the time, see O. Corten and P. Klein, 'La Commission du droit international comme

configuration of that doctrine of responsibility and the functions it ought to perform took longer than expected, for more than fifty years were necessary to draft 127 provisions – not to mention the handful of preceding private and public codification enterprises of the first half of the twentieth century. This is certainly more than the time and effort invested by the Committee of Jurists – which was equally aware of its doctrine-making responsibilities – which prepared the Statute of the Permanent Court of International Justice.[10] In that sense, although some of its modes of legal reasoning may well have been a bit hurried,[11] the making of the doctrine of responsibility has been the object of some unprecedented care and attention by all the international lawyers who contributed to its design, whether they were members of the ILC, judges, arbitrators or scholars.[12]

In this process, a handful of legal scholars imposed their views on others and managed to keep the upper hand in the making of the cognitive and definitional choices that shaped international responsibility and its formal modes of legal reasoning.[13] Indeed, the design of the modes of legal reasoning around which the establishment of responsibility and the determination of its contents must be articulated were never the result of 'neutral' empirical and comparative observations, as is often presented in the literature[14] or in the work of the codifying

---

agent de la formalisation du droit de la responsabilité', in D. Alland, V. Chetail, O. de Frouville and J. Vinuales (eds.), *Unity and Diversity of International Law: Essays in Honour of Professor Pierre-Marie Dupuy* (Leiden: Martinus Nijhoff, 2014), esp. pp. 402–415.

[10] O. Spiermann, '"Who attempts too much does nothing well": the 1920 Advisory Committee of Jurists and the Statute of the Permanent Court of International Justice' (2002) 73 *British Yearbook of International Law* 187.

[11] See J. d'Aspremont, 'The articles on the responsibility of international organizations: magnifying the fissures in the law of international responsibility' (2012) 9 *International Organizations Law Review* 15.

[12] On the making of the rules on responsibility and the question of their authority, see Fernando Lusa Bordin, 'Reflections on customary international law: the authority of codification conventions and ILC Draft Articles in International Law' (2014) 63 *International and Comparative Law Quarterly* 535.

[13] It has been argued that the current modes of legal reasoning associated with responsibility manifests an autonomous and abstract approach that is characteristic of the European understanding of responsibility, especially that inherited from German public law thinking. It is said that this model gained currency at the expense of the more ad hoc and pragmatic approach informed by American practice of investment protection. See, generally, A. Nissel, 'The duality of state responsibility' (2013) 44 *Columbia Human Rights Law Review* 793.

[14] R. Ago, 'Le délit international' (1939-II) 69 *Collected Courses of the Hague Academy on International Law* 420–21, 425, 433, 435–40 (At p. 433, Ago writes: 'Encore une fois, naturellement, c'est l'observation directe des orders juridiques et des règles qui y qualifient certains faits comme illicites qui va nous donner la notion requise').

bodies.[15] Instead, it was the perceptions of the social needs (or their own interests) of these architects that consciously and conspicuously informed the way in which some specific unfavourable consequences were associated with conduct that was seen as undesirable.[16] It was with a similar awareness and care that the modes of legal reasoning on determining and allocating the burden of compensation for a prior harm and the exercise of constraints to restore and protect legality were organised in an attempt to be simple, plain and easily operable.[17] That model – constructed by Anzilotti and his disciples but which also bears the marks of German public law thinking[18] – was officially confirmed in 1975.[19] Such an approach postulates that wrongfulness is an interface between the origin of responsibility – built on a distinction between non-conformity (violation) – and its

---

[15] 'First report of the Special Rapporteur Mr. Roberto Ago, 21st session of the ILC' in *Yearbook of the International Law Commission*, pp. 138–39.

[16] In the same vein, R. Ago, 'Le délit international', 420–21, where he speaks of behaviour that is socially useful ('conduite socialement utile') and behaviour that is socially harmful ('conduite socialement nuisible').

[17] For some critical remarks, see D. Alland, *Anzilotti et le droit international public* (Paris: Pedone, 2012), pp. 123–70.

[18] See August Wilhem Heffter, *Le droit international de l'Europe*, trans. Bergson, 4th edn (Cotillon, 1883), p. 225. See G. Jellinek, *Die rechtliche Natur der Staatenvertrage* (Holder, 1880), pp. 46–61. See the reference of Anzilotti to German public law in Dioniso Anzilotti, 'Teoria generale della responsibilita dello stato' (1902), cited by A. Nissel, 'The duality of state responsibility' (2013) 44 *Columbia Human Rights Law Review* 793 at 804. There is some debate as to the actual influence of German public law thinking on the Italian designers of the modes of legal reasoning associated with responsibility. For the claim that German public law thinking had a direct impact on Anzilotti and other Italian scholars, see A. Nissel, 'The duality of state responsibility' (2013) 44 *Columbia Human Rights Law Review* 793. For him, German public law thinking brought the idea of the autonomy of responsibility as a legal institution as well as an abstraction. See also O. Spiermann, *International Legal Argument in the Permanent Court of International Justice: The Rise of the International Judiciary* (Cambridge: Cambridge University Press, 2005), p. 41. For a more nuanced account of the influence of German legal thought on Anzilotti, see G. Nolte, 'From Dionisio Anzilotti to Roberto Ago: the classical international law of state responsibility and the traditional primacy of a bilateral conception of inter-state relations' (2002) 13 *European Journal of International Law* 1083 esp. 1084–86; J. Crawford and T. Grant, 'Responsibility of states for injuries to foreigners', in J. P. Grant and J. Craig Barker (eds.), *The Harvard Research in International Law: Contemporary Analysis and Appraisal* (Buffalo: Hein, 2007), pp. 80–86; see also Federica Paddeu, 'A genealogy of force majeure in international law' (2013) 82 *British Yearbook of International Law* 381 esp. 403–5. See also Clyde Eagleton, *The Responsibility of States in International Law* (New York: New York University Press, 1928), p. 19 (for whom August Wilhem Heffter's influence, in particular, should not be exaggerated).

[19] Report of the ILC on the work of its twenty-seventh session, 30 GAOR Supp. (No. 10), at 7, reproduced in the *Yearbook of the International Law Commission*, 1975, vol. 2, para. 56.

consequences.[20] Distinguishing between a violation *stricto sensu* and wrongfulness rather than creating equivalence between the two was meant to limit or exclude the consequences of responsibility when violations are less undesirable or socially harmful.[21] The gap between violation and wrongfulness was purposely filled with the notion of circumstances precluding wrongfulness.[22] Furthermore, all subjective elements, such as *dolus*, fault and (un)due diligence,[23] were – sometimes artificially and temporarily[24] – left out with a view to creating an allegedly uniform and objective standard of determination of responsibility based on wrongfulness that, in the end, is supposed to be easy to wield.[25] It is with the same awareness and care that numerous exceptions were made to the above-mentioned original binary system of establishment of responsibility. Indeed, the simplicity of the concept fell short of providing a sufficiently wide accountability net when applied to the complexity of contemporary relations. In other words, in many situations, the system did not prove adequate to apprehend

[20] P. Weil, 'Le droit international en quête de son identité: Cours général de droit international public' (1992) 237 *Collected Courses of the Hague Academy on International Law* 334.

[21] R. Ago, 'Le délit international', 434.

[22] On the development of that notion, see H. Aust, 'Circumstances precluding wrongfulness', in A. Nollkaemper and I. Plakokefalos (eds.), *Principles of Shared Responsibility in International Law* (Cambridge: Cambridge University Press, 2014), pp. 174–77. For a more specific study on the development of the notion of force majeure in the law of state responsibility, see Federica Paddeu, 'A genealogy of force majeure in international law' (2013) 82 *British Yearbook of International Law* 381.

[23] For a different understanding of international responsibility that retains the notion of fault, see the views defended by Gaetano Morelli. For a reproduction of some of Morelli's most important work, see R. Kolb, *Notions de Gaetano Morelli* (Paris: Pedone, 2013), pp. 255–60.

[24] The argument can be made that psychological elements have not been completely obliterated from the system and still pervade many aspects of the regime. It suffices to mention all the hypotheses of attribution of responsibility – already mentioned earlier – that presuppose that participation is accompanied by the knowledge of the circumstances of the wrongful act. See Articles 14–19 and 58–63, Draft Articles on the Responsibility of International Organisations, Report of the ILC, GAOR 66th session, suppl. 10, UN Doc. A/66/10, 54ff. On the oscillation between intention and knowledge of the facts in the concept of complicity, see O. Corten and P. Klein, 'The limits of complicity as a ground for responsibility', in K. Bannelier, T. Christakis and S. Heathcote (eds.), *The ICJ and the Evolution of International Law: The Enduring Impact of the Corfu Channel Case* (London: Routledge, 2012), pp. 315–34.

[25] R. Ago, 'Second report on state responsibility', in *Yearbook of the International Law Commission*, 1970, vol. II, UN Doc. A/CN.4/233, p. 185; J. Crawford and S. Olleson, 'The nature and forms of international responsibility', in M. Evans (eds.), *International Law* (Oxford: Oxford University Press, 2003), p. 451. On the conceptual 'revolution' that such an objectification may have constituted, see Alain Pellet, 'The ILC's articles on state responsibility', in James Crawford et al. (eds.), *The Law of International Responsibility* (Oxford: Oxford University Press, 2010), pp. 76–77.

all the dimensions of non-conforming behaviours – and exercises of power – that were supposed to be subjected to the law of international responsibility. It is with the awareness that this 'Anzilottian' concept of responsibility did not capture all the socially harmful situations that the creators wanted to subdue[26] that the architects of the law of international responsibility came to design a conceptual hotchpotch for all situations that did not fit with the binary concept of wrongfulness but were still deemed sufficiently problematic to be included into the law of international responsibility.[27] This residual subterfuge took the form of attribution of responsibility (also sometimes called, albeit unconvincingly, 'indirect responsibility' to differentiate it from attribution of conduct).[28] Other conceptual adjustments were also forged by Roberto Ago and his followers,[29] who resorted to private law concepts – such as injury[30] – to make the law of international responsibility perform public law functions[31] and give it a communitarian content.[32]

---

[26] See R. Ago, 'Second report on state responsibility', p. 186, para. 29.

[27] See, generally, James Fry, 'Attribution of responsibility', in A. Nollkaemper and I. Plakokefalos (eds.), *Principles of Shared Responsibility in International Law* (Cambridge: Cambridge University Press, 2014), pp. 98–133. For a use of that distinction in connection with specific issues of responsibility, see J. d'Aspremont, 'Abuse of the legal personality of international organizations and the responsibility of member states' (2007) 4 *International Organizations Law Review* 91; or J. d'Aspremont, 'Rebellion and state responsibility' (2009) 58 *International and Comparative Law Quarterly* 427.

[28] Rather surprisingly, the commentary on the Articles on State Responsibility provisions on attribution of responsibility indicates that 'the idea of the implication of one State in the conduct of another is analogous to problems of attribution, dealt with in chapter II.' See J. Crawford, *The International Law Commission's Articles on State Responsibility: Introduction, Text and Commentaries* (Cambridge: Cambridge University Press, 2002), p. 147.

[29] See G. Nolte, 'From Dionisio Anzilotti to Roberto Ago: the classical international law of state responsibility and the traditional primacy of a bilateral conception of inter-state relations' (2002) 13 *European Journal of International Law* 1083.

[30] On the declaratory function of injury, see J. Crawford, 'Overview of part three of the Articles on State Responsibility', in J. Crawford, A. Pellet and S. Olleson (eds.), *The Law of International Responsibility* (Oxford: Oxford University Press, 2010), p. 931.

[31] See, generally, B. Stern, 'The elements of an internationally wrongful act', in J. Crawford, A. Pellet and S. Olleson (eds.), *The Law of International Responsibility* (Oxford: Oxford University Press, 2010), p. 194. A good illustration is the introduction of sanction regulation in the regime of responsibility aimed at the restoration of legality but conditioned upon injury. See Articles 42 and 50 of the Articles on State Responsibility. On the idea that the inclusion of the faculty to take countermeasures led to a distortion of the notion of injury, see A. Nollkaemper, 'Constitutionalization and the unity of the law of international responsibility' (2009) 16 *Journal of Global Legal Studies* 535 at 555.

[32] G. Nolte, 'From Dionisio Anzilotti to Roberto Ago: the classical international law of state responsibility and the traditional primacy of a bilateral conception of inter-state relations'

The foregoing shows that the political ambitions[33] of the architects of international responsibility, as well as the conceptual and practical difficulties[34] of the various ways in which the modes of legal reasoning pertaining to the determination and allocation of the burden of compensation for a prior harm as well as to the exercise of constraints to restore and protect legality could be organised, were all carefully weighted during the design process of the fundamental doctrine of responsibility. Their translation into a cluster of modes of legal reasoning was thus well engineered and controlled, thereby showing that the organisation of the modes of legal reasoning and the emergence of fundamental doctrines are not the offspring of an unbridled and dishevelled process. As is well known, the final result of this carefully orchestrated process took the form of two sets of articles famously known as the Articles on Responsibility of States for Internationally Wrongful Acts (hereafter ASR)[35] and the Articles on the Responsibility of International Organisations (hereafter ARIO).[36] From the perspective of the belief system discussed herein, these two texts constitute the formal repository of the organised cluster of modes of legal reasoning on the determination and allocation of the burden of compensation for a

---

(2002) 13 *European Journal of International Law* 1083. See also A. Nollkaemper and D. Jacobs, 'Shared responsibility in international law: a conceptual framework' (2013) 34 *Michigan Journal of International Law* 359 at 401–2.

[33] See M. Koskenniemi, 'Doctrines of state responsibility', in James Crawford, Alain Pellet and Simon Olleson (eds.), *The Law of International Responsibility* (Oxford: Oxford University Press, 2010), pp. 47–50. P.-M. Dupuy, 'Dionisio Anzilotti and the law of international responsibility of states' (1992) 3 *European Journal of International Law* 139; G. Nolte, 'From Dionisio Anzilotti to Roberto Ago: the classical international law of state responsibility and the traditional primacy of a bilateral conception of inter-state relations' (2002) 13 *European Journal of International Law* 1083. Cf. the political ambitions that informed the creation of international criminal mechanisms. See D. Wippman, 'The International Criminal Court', in C. Reus-Smit (ed.), *The Politics of International Law* (Cambridge: Cambridge University Press, 2004), pp. 151.

[34] B. Stern, 'Et si on utilisait la notion de préjudice juridique? Retour sur une notion délaissée à l'occasion de la fin des travaux de la C.D.I sur la responsabilité des États' (2001) 47 *Annuaire français de droit international* 3; see A. Nollkaemper, 'Constitutionalization and the unity of the law of international responsibility' (2009) 16 *Indiana Journal of Global Legal Studies* 535.

[35] 'Report of the Commission to the General Assembly on the work of its 53rd session', in *Yearbook of the International Law Commission*, 2001, vol. II, part 2. The text reproduced as it appears in the annex to General Assembly Resolution 56/83 of 12 December 2001 and corrected by UN Doc. A/56/49(vol. I)/corr. 4.

[36] *Yearbook of the International Law Commission*, 2011, vol. II, part 2.

prior harm and the exercise of constraints to restore and protect legality are nested.

2 The Finding of a Formal Repository: The Doctrine of Statehood

Attention now turns to the fundamental doctrine of statehood, which illustrates how fundamental doctrines are derived from an international instrument by virtue of imaginary genealogy. This section more specifically shows how the modes of legal reasoning associated with statehood and recognition came to be presented as a derivative of the 1933 Convention on Rights and Duties of States in the second half of the twentieth century.[37]

A preliminary remark is warranted concerning the fundamental character of the doctrine of statehood. It must be acknowledged that this doctrine, as it was designed and systematised in the twentieth century, has at present become very contested. Many international lawyers today question the very modes of legal reasoning put in place by the doctrine of statehood and regularly call for its amendment or even replacement. I submit that the contested nature of the doctrine of statehood is not sufficient to strip it of its character as a fundamental doctrine.[38] Being fundamental has never meant that a doctrine is uncontested.[39] What is contested is usually not a doctrine's fundamental character but its content and the modes of legal reasoning it puts in place. It could even be argued that the doctrine of statehood is severely contested precisely because it is held as fundamental and still plays a defining role in relation to the modes of legal reasoning about statehood in contemporary legal thought and practice. In this sense, the fact that the doctrine of statehood is contested is a confirmation – rather than a refutation – of its role as fundamental doctrine.

To introduce the point made in this section, it is useful to recall the common posture of international lawyers, which views the doctrine of statehood – which, for the sake of discussion, is broadly construed as comprising modes of legal reasoning on both the definition of states and

---

[37] For a discussion of the various regulatory agendas at work in the fundamental doctrine of statehood, see J. d'Aspremont, *Epistemic Forces in International Law* (London: Elgar, 2015), pp. 33–60. See also J. d'Aspremont, 'The international law of statehood: craftsmanship for the elucidation and regulation of births and deaths in the international society' (2014) 29 *Connecticut Journal of International Law* 201.

[38] This is a remark that I owe to an exchange with Mari Takeuchi.

[39] See Chapter 2, Section 2.

the role of recognition – as based on the 1933 Montevideo Convention on Rights and Duties of States.[40] Indeed, this international instrument is commonly held by international lawyers as the repository of the modes of legal reasoning associated with the so-called statehood criteria, namely, population, territory and *effectivité*, as well as, to some extent, the declarative nature of recognition.[41] It is no surprise that it has been contended that invoking the Montevideo Convention boils down to a 'reflex' for anyone articulating a legal claim about statehood or recognition.[42] States generally abide by the same narrative, indicating that the Montevideo Convention is the starting point of any legal argument relationing to statehood.[43] From the perspective of the belief system, the Montevideo Convention can be considered, in contemporary international legal scholarship and practice, to be the

---

[40] K. Knop, 'Statehood', in J. Crawford and M. Koskenniemi (eds.), *The Cambridge Companion to International Law* (Cambridge: Cambridge University Press, 2012), p. 95; V. Degan, 'Création et disparition de l'etat (a la lumière du démembrement des trois fédérations multiethniques en europe)' (1999) 279 *Collected Courses of the Hague Academy on International Law* 199 at 227; C. Tomuschat, 'International law: ensuring the survival of mankind on the eve of a new century – general course on public international law' (1999) 281 *Collected Courses of the Hague Academy on International Law* 96; J. Vidmar, 'Explaining the legal effects of recognition' (2012) 61 *International and Comparative Law Quarterly* 361 at 382; M. Shaw, *International Law*, 7th edn (Cambridge: Cambridge University Press, 2014), p. 144; D. Harris, *Cases and Materials on International Law*, 7th edn (London: Sweet & Maxwell/Thomson Reuters (Legal), 2010), p. 95; T. Grant, 'Defining statehood: the Montevideo Convention and its discontents' (1998–99) 37 *Columbia Journal of Transnational Law* 403; Jure Vidmar, 'Territorial integrity and the law of statehood' (2013) 44 *George Washington International Law Review* 101; B. Broms, 'States', in M. Bedjaoui (ed.), *International Law: Achievements and Prospects* (New York: UNESCO, 1991), p. 43; K. Doehring, 'States', in R. Bernhardt (ed.), *Encyclopedia of Public International Law*, vol. IV (New York: Elsevier, 2000), p. 601. Cf. J. Crawford, *Brownlie's Principles of Public International Law*, 8th edn (Oxford: Oxford University Press, 2012), p. 128.
[41] For the idea that Montevideo put an end to the constitutive theory and the 'standard of civilization', see Arnulf Becker Lorca, *Mestizo International Law: A Global Intellectual History 1842-1933* (Cambridge: Cambridge University Press, 2014), pp. 305–52; see also J. L. Brierly, *The Law of Nations: An Introduction to the International Law of Peace*, 5th edn (Oxford: Clarendon Press, 1955), p. 129; A. Cassese, *International Law*, 2nd edn (Oxford: Oxford University Press, 2005), pp. 71–80.
[42] T. Grant, 'Defining statehood: the Montevideo Convention and its discontents' (1998–1999) 37 *Columbia Journal of Transnational Law* 403 at 414.
[43] See the numerous written statements submitted by states in April 2009 in the framework of the request for advisory opinion on the accordance with international law of the unilateral declaration of independence in respect of Kosovo. See e.g. 'Written Statement of Argentina', para. 48; 'Written Statement of Austria', para. 26; 'Written Statement of Cyprus', paras. 166–69; 'Written Statement of Egypt', para. 26; 'Written Statement by the United States of America', p. 34.

repository of the doctrine of statehood,[44] itself construed as a set of customary rules.[45]

It is noteworthy that the Montevideo Convention, as the repository of the fundamental doctrine of statehood, is sometimes supplemented with other authoritative instruments. In fact, the invocation of the 1933 Montevideo Convention on Rights and Duties of States is, at least as far as recognition is concerned, often accompanied by references to the opinions delivered between 1991 and 1993 by the Arbitration Commission of the Conference on Yugoslavia (commonly known as the Badinter Commission).[46] As explained in Chapter 2, that the repository of a fundamental doctrine is complemented by auxiliary repositories is not unheard of. In the case of the doctrine of statehood, it remains that, although supplemented by auxiliary repositories such as the Opinions of the Badinder Commission, the 1933 Montevideo Convention on Rights and Duties of States continues to be the central repository when it comes to the universalisation of the doctrine of statehood.

The specific aspect of the belief system at work behind the doctrine of statehood discussed in this section is the imaginary genealogy that allows the derivation of fundamental doctrines from an international instrument. In particular, I submit that the derivation of the doctrine of statehood from the Montevideo Convention and the construction of an imaginary genealogical link between them constitutes a rather recent endeavour. For a long time, international lawyers did not seek any common understanding of the modes of legal reasoning behind statehood

---

[44] See also the literature cited by T. Grant, 'Defining statehood: the Montevideo Convention and its discontents' (1998–1999) 37 *Columbia Journal of Transnational Law* 403 at 414

[45] See e.g. Cedric Ryngaert and Sven Sobrie, 'Recognition of states: international law or realpolitik? The practice of recognition in the wake of Kosovo, South Ossetia, and Abkhazia' (2011) 24 *Leiden Journal of International Law* 467; see also David Bederman, *The Spirit of International Law* (Atlanta: University of Georgia Press, 2002), p. 49. See, however, Jure Vidmar, 'The concept of the state and its right of existence' (2015) 4 *Cambridge Journal of International and Comparative Law* 547 (for Vidmar, it is the status of state that is customary under international law and not the statehood criteria).

[46] See e.g. Cedric Ryngaert and Sven Sobrie, 'Recognition of states: international law or realpolitik? The practice of recognition in the wake of Kosovo, South Ossetia, and Abkhazia' (2011) 24 *Leiden Journal of International Law* 467. See also the written statement of Slovenia submitted in April 2009 in the framework of the request for advisory opinion on the accordance with international law of the unilateral declaration of independence in respect of Kosovo, pp. 1–2. The opinions are reprinted in Alain Pellet, 'The opinions of the Badinter Arbitration Committee. A second breath for the self-determination of peoples' (1992) 3 *European Journal of International Law* 178 at 182; and in Danilo Turk, 'Recognition of states: a comment' (1993) 4 *European Journal of International Law* 66 at 90.

and recognition, let alone a universal repository where such modes of legal reasoning could be found. Indeed, in the literature of the nineteenth century and the beginning of the twentieth century, authors would either abstain from defining the state and the role of recognition[47] or simply fail to seek to design common modes of legal reasoning, limiting themselves to their own personal definitions without any ambition to universalise them.[48] At the time, the only matter of interest was the systematisation of the modes of exclusion of non-European and non-Christian nations from the remit of international law, not how states were defined.[49] It is interesting to note in this regard that the adoption of the 1933 Montevideo Convention on Rights and Duties of States had very little effect on such passivity, neither at the time of its adoption nor at the time of its entry into force. In fact, in the 1930s and 1940s, the authors who came with their own definitions still did not feel any need to universalise the doctrine of statehood by anchoring it in an authoritative instrument and, hence, never referred to the 1933 Montevideo Convention.[50] It is true that the 1940s evidenced some early expressions of a need to find a repository for the doctrine of statehood as a result of the growing inclination of international lawyers at the time to ground the definition

---

[47] See e.g. J. Lorimer, *Principes de Droit International*, trans. E. Nys (Brussels: Merzbach and Falk, 1884).

[48] See e.g. T. D. Woolsey, *International Law* (New York: Scribner, Armstrong, 1877), p. 49; H. Wheaton. *Elements of International Law*, vol. 1 (London: B Fellowes, 1836), p. 62; F. F. Martens, *Traité de Droit International*, vol. 1, trans. A. Léo (Paris: Librairie Maresco Aîné, 1883), p. 273; T. J. Lawrence, *The Principles of International Law*, 7th edn (London: Macmillan, 1923), p. 48; W. E. Hall, *A Treatise on International Law*, 3rd edn (Oxford: Clarendon Press, 1890), p. 18.

[49] See Antony Anghie, *Imperialism, Sovereignty and the Making of International Law* (Cambridge: Cambridge University Press, 2004), pp. 32–114 (for whom it is exclusion that shaped the modes of legal reasoning of the time). See also M. Koskenniemi, *The Gentle Civilizer of Nations: The Rise and Fall of International Law 1870–1960* (Cambridge: Cambridge University Press, 2001), pp. 98–178.

[50] See e.g. L. Le Fur, *Précis de Droit International Public*, 3rd edn (Paris: Dalloz, 1937), p. 64; J. L. Brierly, *The Law of Nations*, 4th edn (Oxford: Clarendon Press, 1949), p. 111; H. Lauterpacht, *Recognition in International Law* (Cambridge: Cambridge University Press, 1947), p. 26. For a different reading, see T. Grant, who claims that the references to Montevideo to articulate claims on statehood and recognition started in the 1940s. See T. Grant, 'Defining statehood: the Montevideo Convention and its discontents' (1998–99) 37 *Columbia Journal of Transnational Law* 403 at 414. See also the declaration of the United Kingdom of 24 August 1948, reproduced in ILC, 'Preparatory study concerning a Draft Declaration on the Rights and Duties of States – memorandum submitted by the Secretary General on Fundamental Rights and Duties of States', UN Doc. A/CN.4/2, 15 December 1948, pp. 185–86 (according to which there is no accepted definition).

of states in 'international practice'.[51] Yet such endeavours remained limited. It was only in the 1950s and 1960s that one began to witness more regular contentions that the doctrine of statehood and the declaratory approach to recognition were derived from the 1933 Montevideo Convention on Rights and Duties of States.[52] The intensification of this quest for the elaboration of a formal doctrine of statehood in the 1960s is certainly not fortuitous. While it is not the aim of this section to explain the driving forces and agendas behind the design of a doctrine of statehood by international lawyers, it is possible to surmise that decolonisation and the unprecedented surge of new states at the time prodded international lawyers into feeling the need to invent a sophisticated tool to regulate the birth of states and formalise the modes of legal reasoning about statehood.[53]

Interestingly, in parallel with the consolidation of the status of the 1933 Montevideo Convention as a formal repository of the fundamental doctrine of statehood in the second half of the twentieth century, the origin of the definition of a state prescribed by the 1933 Montevideo Convention happened to be ascribed to the German publicist Georg Jellinek and, in particular, to his work, *Das Recht Des Modernen Staates*.[54] This paternity

---

[51] See e.g. H. Lauterpacht, *Recognition in International Law* (Cambridge: Cambridge University Press, 1947). See also ILC, 'Draft Declaration on Rights and Duties of States with commentaries', in *Yearbook of the International Law Commission*, 1949, para. 49 at para. 289. The Commission concluded that no useful purpose would be served by an effort to define the term 'State', though this course had been suggested by the governments of the United Kingdom and India. In the Commission's draft, the term 'State' is used in the sense commonly accepted in international practice. For an earlier expression of that position, see C. C. Hyde, *International Law Chiefly as Interpreted and Applied by the United States* (Boston: Little Brown, 1922), p. 17. It is interesting to note that the three-element doctrine received some judicial support in 1929 in the award of the Germano-Polish Mixed Arbitral Tribunal. See '*Deutsche Continental Gas-Gesellschaft v. Polish State*' (1929) 5 *Annual Digest* 11. For a more recent expression of that empirical approach, see R. Higgins, *The Development of International Law through the Political Organs of the United Nations* (Oxford: Oxford University Press, 1963), p. 14; or P. Malanczuk, *Akehurst's Modern Introduction to International Law*, 7th rev. edn (London: Routledge, 1997), p. 75.

[52] Philip Jessup, *A Modern Law of Nations: An Introduction* (New York: Macmillan, 1956) at 43; N. Mugerwa 'Subjects of international law', in M. Sørensen (ed.), *Manual of Public International Law* (New York: Macmillan/St. Martin's Press, 1968), p. 250; D. P. O'Connell, *International Law*, 2nd edn (London: Stevens & Sons, 1970), p. 284; D. P. O'Connell, *International Law for Students* (London: Stevens & Sons, 1971) at p. 120.

[53] I have discussed the agendas behind the so-called law of statehood elsewhere. See J. d'Aspremont, 'The International Law of Statehood: craftsmanship for the elucidation and regulation of births and deaths in the international society' (2014) 29 *Connecticut Journal of International Law* 201.

[54] Georg Jellinek, *Allgemeine Staatslehre*, vol. I: *Das Recht des Modernen Staates* (O. Häring, 1905), pp. 381–420.

warrants an observation. This account of the origin of the Montevideo definition[55] is inevitably bewildering because very few authors at the beginning of the twentieth century actually drew on Jellinek to define the state.[56] This German parentage of the Montevideo definition is also unsettling because it does not seem that the work of Jellinek actually influenced the jurists who did the groundwork for 1933 Montevideo Convention.[57] Be that as it may, for the sake of the argument made herein, it suffices to highlight that the finding of a formal repository for the doctrine of statehood and the choice of the Montevideo Convention came with a specific historical narrative whereby the systematisation of statehood found in that instrument was traced back to German public law thinking.[58]

It must be acknowledged that despite its role as a formal repository of the fundamental doctrine of statehood, the 1933 Montevideo Convention is regularly the object of criticism by scholars. Indeed, in the late twentieth century and early twenty-first century, it has become rather common to deride the Montevideo definition either from an empirical or a normative vantage point.[59] Irrespective of the merits of such claims, it is

---

[55] See e.g. A. Verdross and B. Simma, *Universelles Völkerrecht: Theorie und Praxis (dritte Auflage)*, 3rd edn (Berlin: Duncker & Humblot, 1984), pp. 379–80; P. Malanczuk, *Akehurst's Modern Introduction to International Law*, 7th rev. edn (New York: Routledge, 1997), p. 75; K. Doehring, 'State', in R. Bernhardt (ed.), *Encyclopedia of Public International Law*, vol. IV (New York: Elsevier, 2000), p. 601; Jure Vidmar, 'Territorial integrity and the law of statehood' (2013) 44 *George Washington International Law Review* 101 at 104–5; T. Grant, 'Defining statehood: the Montevideo Convention and its discontents' (1998–99) 37 *Columbia Journal of Transnational Law* 403 at 418; Jure Vidmar, 'The concept of the state and its right of existence' (2015) 4 *Cambridge Journal of International and Comparative Law* 547.

[56] See the writers discussed by T. Grant, 'Defining statehood: the Montevideo Convention and its discontents' (1998–99) 37 *Columbia Journal of Transnational Law* 403 at 416–18.

[57] See the account made of the process leading to the adoption of the Montevideo Convention provided by Arnulf Becker Lorca, *Mestizo International Law: A Global Intellectual History 1842–1933* (Cambridge: Cambridge University Press, 2014), chap. 9.

[58] On how the idea of system trickled into international legal thought from German public law thought, see the remarks in Chapter 1, Section 4.

[59] J. Crawford, *The Creation of States* (Oxford: Oxford University Press, 2007), at 62–89; 'Kosovo and the Criteria for Statehood in International Law', in M. Milanovic and M. Wood (eds.), *The Law and Politics of the Kosovo Advisory Opinion* (Oxford: Oxford University Press 2015) at 281; J. Crawford, *Brownlie's Principles of Public International Law*, 8th edn (2012), at 128; A. Peters, 'Does Kosovo lie in the lotus-land of freedom?' (2011) 24 *Leiden Journal of International Law* 95–108; Jure Vidmar, 'Territorial integrity and the law of statehood' 44 *George Washington International Law Review* (2013) 101; Jure Vidmar, *Democratic Statehood in International Law: The Emergence of New States in Post-Cold War Practice* (London: Hart, 2013); D. Raic, *Statehood and the Law of Self-Determination* (Alphen aan den Rijn, Netherlands: Kluwer Law, 2002), pp. 151–58; D. Harris, *Cases and Materials on International Law*, 7th edn (London: Sweet & Maxwell/Thomson Reuters (Legal), 2010), at 95. See also the written

noteworthy, for the sake of the argument made herein, that such criticism continues to be premised on the very idea that the 1933 Montevideo Convention is the repository of the fundamental doctrine of statehood and recognition. It could even be said that the contemporary discontent with the Montevideo Convention reaffirms – rather than contradicts – the status of formal repository for that instrument.

A salient aspect of the imaginary genealogical link built in the second half of the twentieth century between the fundamental doctrine of statehood and the 1933 Montevideo Convention lies with its counter-intuitiveness. In this regard, it should be recalled that the Montevideo codification process, in line with Alvarez's approach,[60] was meant to be the public international law code of the Americas and not a restatement of a universal international law.[61] It is well known in this respect that the codification of international law in the Americas had always been construed as a tool to claim autonomy and emancipate the continent from a form of universality perceived as 'too European'.[62] With respect to statehood

---

statement of Slovenia submitted in April 2009 in the framework of the request for advisory opinion on the accordance with international law of the unilateral declaration of independence in respect of Kosovo, pp. 1–2. For an overview of some of these criticisms, see T. Grant, 'Defining statehood: the Montevideo Convention and its discontents' (1998–99) 37 *Columbia Journal of Transnational Law* 403 at 434–47.

[60] A. Alvarez, *Considérations Générales sur la Codification du Droit International Américain* (Rio de Janeiro: Imprensa Nacional, 1927).

[61] See Alejandro Alvarez, *Le Continent Américain et la Codification du Droit International Law: Une Nouvelle 'Ecole' du Droit des Gens* (Paris: Pedone, 1938), pp. 20–21 ('Ces Etats ont estimés ... que le Droit International en vigueur en Europe leur était ... applicable mais qu'ils pouvaient réglementer les rapports internationaux en toute liberté, conformément aux conditions et besoins du Nouveau Monde, notamment pour assurer leur independance et leur libre développement, et que dans ce but ils pouvaient aller jusqu'à proclamer des principes contraires aux principes juridiques et au système politique en vigueur en Europe à cette époque. C'est la conscience juridique américaine.' See also p. 21: 'Il est hors de doute que les Etats d'un continent, voire même d'une région, peuvent élaborer un Droit International continental ou régional, c'est-à-dire des principes et des règles destinées à régir leurs rapports réciproques. Il est hors de doute aussi, que ces Etats peuvent procéder non seulement à la codification de ces Droits particuliers mais aussi à celle du Droit International en général, – mais seulement pour ce qui concerne aussi leur rapports réciproques.'

[62] See, generally, J. L. Esquirol, 'Latin America', in B. Fassbender and A. Peters (eds.), *Oxford Handbook on the History of International Law* (Oxford: Oxford University Press, 2012), pp. 562–66; H. Caminos, 'The Latin American contribution to international law' (1986) 80 *American Society of International Law Proceedings* 157 at 157–60; Alejandro Alvarez, 'La method du droit international à la veille de sa codification' (1913) 20 *Revue générale de droit international public* 725. See the remarks of Arnulf Becker Lorca, *Mestizo International Law: A Global Intellectual History 1842–1933* (Cambridge: Cambridge University Press, 2014), pp. 327–34. See the criticisms of Brierly of the pan-American

in particular, the Montevideo Convention sought an explicit departure from some of the common criteria of statehood – such as civilisation[63] or recognition.[64] The ambition never was to draft a universal code. What is more, as the earlier rejection of the project to codify American international law at Habana shows, the main thrust of the Montevideo codification process was not statehood but non-intervention.[65] It is no coincidence that it took a change in the American position on non-intervention to make the adoption of what became the Montevideo Convention possible,[66] the definition of a state drawing almost no attention during the negotiations.[67] This is why it is rather remarkable that the product of a codification of American public international law on non-intervention was turned, in the second half of the twentieth century, into the repository for the fundamental doctrine of statehood.[68]

codification project for the flattening of history and international relations: J. L. Brierly 'The draft code of American international law', reproduced in H. Lauterpacht and C. H. M. Waldock (eds.), *The Basis of Obligation in International Law and Other Papers by J. L. Brierly* (Oxford: Clarendon Press, 1958), pp. 117–26.

[63] The move away from civilisation had already been witnessed in the practice of the League of Nations. See, generally, Arnulf Becker Lorca, *Mestizo International Law: A Global Intellectual History 1842–1933* (Cambridge: Cambridge University Press, 2014), pp. 263–304. See also A. Verdross and B. Simma, *Universelles Völkerrecht: Theorie und Praxis*, 3rd edn (Berlin: Duncker & Humblot, 1984), para. 379. Cf. Gerrit W. Gong, *The Standard of 'Civilisation' in International Society* (Oxford: Clarendon Press, 1984), p. 26 (who argues that Montevideo puts in place a new standard of civilisation). The real value of that practice is, however, difficult to gauge as criteria for statehood and criteria for membership to the League of Nations were not always clearly distinguished. On the idea that we have witnessed today a return to the standard of civilisation, see D. Fidler, 'The return of the standard of civilization' (2001) 2 *Chicago Journal of International Law* 137.

[64] See the remarks of Arnulf Becker Lorca, *Mestizo International Law: A Global Intellectual History 1842–1933* (Cambridge: Cambridge University Press, 2014), p. 339.

[65] J. L. Esquirol, 'Latin America', in B. Fassbender and A. Peters (eds.), *Oxford Handbook on the History of International Law* (Oxford: Oxford University Press, 2012), pp. 566–70; see also Arnulf Becker Lorca, *Mestizo International Law: A Global Intellectual History 1842–1933* (Cambridge: Cambridge University Press, 2014), p. 341.

[66] Arnulf Becker Lorca, *Mestizo International Law: A Global Intellectual History 1842–1933* (Cambridge: Cambridge University Press, 2014), p. 349

[67] The elaboration of the Montevideo Convention partly drew on the so-called Pessôa Code, which contained a definition of state (a state is a permanent grouping of individuals that inhabit a defined territory and obey the same government that is in charge of the administration of justice and the preservation of order). See E. Pessôa, *Projecto de Codigo de Direito Internacional Publico* (Rio de Janeiro: Imprensa Nacional, 1911).

[68] In the same vein, Arnulf Becker Lorca, *Mestizo International Law: A Global Intellectual History 1842–1933* (Cambridge: Cambridge University Press, 2014), p. 351; or J. L. Esquirol, 'Latin America', in B. Fassbender and A. Peters (eds.),

3 The Invention of an Imaginary Genealogy: The Doctrine of Customary Law

This section addresses the manner in which customary international law was given a formal repository thanks to the imaginary genealogical link created with Article 38 of the Statute of the Permanent Court of International Justice. Although the doctrine of custom is part of the more general doctrine of sources and plays the same explanatory function for all fundamental doctrines as sources,[69] customary international law, for the sake of this section, is discussed as a distinct and self-standing doctrine.

'Custom' is known to most legal systems, where it refers to an unwritten process in which normativity is behaviourally generated short of any written instrument. The potential to generate legal normativity through behaviours rather than formal instruments has proved very popular in international legal argumentation.[70] The reasons for the popularity of this fundamental doctrine in international legal argumentation need no discussion here.[71] It is more germane to draw attention to the extent to which the fundamental doctrine of custom is given a formal repository thanks to the invention of a genealogical link with Article 38 of the Statute of the Permanent Court of International Justice.

Oxford Handbook on the History of International Law (Oxford: Oxford University Press, 2012), p. 576.

[69] See e.g. D. J. Bederman, *Custom as a Source of Law* (Cambridge: Cambridge University Press, 2010), pp. 136–37: 'Finally, and (perhaps) most influentially, customary international law norms dictate the construction and application of "meta-norms" of public international law. These include what H. L. A. Hart would call secondary rules of recognition for other international law sources, as with principles of treaty formation, interpretation, and termination. Likewise, the substance of international law of state responsibility and the procedures under which states make claim for redress of international wrongs are dictated by custom.'

[70] This is in contrast with domestic legal orders. See François Ost, *Le Temps du Droit* (Paris: Les Éditions Odile Jacob, 1999), p. 86 ('la coutume paraît toujours en suris').

[71] A few of these reasons can be mentioned here. First, customary international law performs a safeguarding function for international law as a whole. Indeed, thanks to its generation of normativity through the behaviour of states, custom always guarantees *a minimal content to international law*. Second, custom seems to allow the continuous updating of international law and its congruence with the rapidly changing dynamics of the international society. Third, customary international law provides all international lawyers with a formidable argumentative tool by virtue of which they universalise almost any legal claim. For a further examination of the pull of custom, see J. d'Aspremont, 'The decay of modern customary international law in spite of scholarly heroism', in G. Capaldo (ed.), *Global Community: Yearbook of International Law and Jurisprudence* (Oxford: Oxford University Press, 2015).

To introduce this argument, it must be recalled that in contemporary international legal discourse, the dominant modes of legal reasoning to determine the existence and content of a rule of customary international law are articulated around the establishment of two distinct facts, that is, practice and *opinio juris* (acceptance as law). This is the so-called two-element doctrine of customary international law[72] that, despite some continuous emancipatory and fragmentary forces,[73] came to dominate contemporary legal argumentation about customary international law in the twentieth century.[74] The recent work of the International Law Commission (ILC) has confirmed that the two-element approach continues to be the dominant articulation of the modes of legal reasoning related to determining the existence and content of customary rules in the twenty-first century.[75]

This two-element approach is riddled with conceptual and practical problems that have been discussed extensively in the literature.[76] This is

---

[72] The first authoritative manifestation of such doctrine in international case law dates back to the famous judgment in *The Case of the S.S. Lotus (France v Turkey)* PCIJ, series A, no.10, p. 28. For some early contestations of this two-element doctrine, see H. Kelsen, 'Théorie du droit international coutumier' (1939) 1 *Revue Internationale de Théorie du Droit* 253 at 263.

[73] J d'Aspremont, 'An autonomous regime of identification of customary international humanitarian law: do not say what you do or do not do what you say?', in R. van Steenberghe (ed.), *Droit International Humanitaire: Un Régime Spécial de Droit International?* (Bruylant, 2013), pp. 72–101, available at SSRN: http://ssrn.com/abstract=2230345; S. H. Choi, and M. Gulati, 'Customary international law: how do courts do it?', 9 February 2015, available at SSRN: https://papers.ssrn.com/sol3/papers.cfm?abstract_id=2561900; R. Kolb, 'Selected problems in the theory of customary international law' (2003) 50 *Netherlands International Law Review* 119, at 128.

[74] On the rise of the two-element doctrine, see also P. Haggenmacher, 'La doctrine des deux éléments en droit coutumier dans la pratique de la Cour internationale' (1986) 90 *Revue Générale de Droit International Public* 5.

[75] See the text of the draft conclusions on identification of customary international law adopted by the Commission on first reading; ILC, 'Draft report: Chapter V – Identification of customary international law', 68th session (2016), UN Doc. A/CN.4/L.883/Add.1. See also ILC, 'Third report on the identification of customary international law', UN Doc. A/CN.4/682, 27 March 2015, para. 15. The claim of a fragmentation of the doctrine of customary law has been rejected by the ILC, which has continued to see unity in the practice: ILC, 'First report of the Special Rapporteur, Sir Michael Wood', 65th session, A/CN.4/663, 17 May 2013, para. 19: unity – no fragmentation. See also ILC, 'Second report on identification of customary international law by the Special Rapporteur Michael Wood', UN Doc. A/CN.4/672, 22 May 2014, para. 28: only a difference in interpretation and application (second report, para. 28).

[76] J. Kammerhofer, 'Uncertainty in the formal sources of international law: customary international law and some of its problems' (2004) 15 *European Journal of International Law* 523; Vassilis Tzevelekos, 'Juris dicere: custom as matrix, custom as a

not a discussion that ought to be rehashed here. What matters here is that the two-element approach is, in mainstream international legal discourses, held as being derived from Article 38 of the Statute of the Permanent Court of International Justice. Indeed, this provision is continuously invoked as the repository of the two-element variant of the fundamental doctrine of custom.[77] Yet it is argued here that although the two elements were not absent from international legal thought in the nineteenth century and early twentieth century,[78] this genealogical

norm, and the role of judges of (their) ideology in custom making', in N. Rajkovic, T. Aalberts and T. Gammeltoft-Hansen (eds.), *Power of Legality: Practices of International Law and Their Politics* (Cambridge: Cambridge University Press, 2016), pp. 188–208; Sienho Yee, 'Article 38 of the ICJ statute and applicable law: selected issues in recent cases' (2016) 7 *Journal of International Dispute Settlement* 472 esp. 479-87; J. P. Kelly, 'The twilight of customary international law' (2000) 40 *Virginia Journal of International Law* 449; C. Bradley, 'A state preferences account of customary international law adjudication', 10 October 2014, available at SSRN: http://ssrn.com/abstract=2508298; Lazlo Blutman, 'Conceptual and methodological deficiencies: some ways that theories on customary international law fail' (2014) 25 *European Journal of International Law* 529. See the famous contradiction highlighted by M. Sørensen, 'Principes de droit international public' (1960-III) 101 *Collected Courses of the Hague Academy on International Law* 1 at 50. In the same sense, see A. d'Amato, *The Concept of Custom in International Law* (Ithaca, NY, Cornell University Press, 1971), p. 7. On this paradox, see the comments of R. Kolb, 'Selected problems in the theory of customary international law' (2003) 50 *Netherlands International Law Review* 119 at 137ff; M. Byers, *Custom, Power and the Power of Rules: International Relations and Customary International Law* (Cambridge: Cambridge University Press, 1999), pp. 129–46 ; M. Koskenniemi, *From Apology to Utopia*, pp. 388–473; J. Klabbers, 'The curious condition of custom' (2002) 8 *International Legal Theory* 29; James Crawford, *Chance, Order, Change: The Course of International Law: General Course on Public International Law* (The Hague: Pocketbooks of the Hague Academy of International Law, 2013), pp. 82–84. For a criticism from general legal theory perspective, see e.g. A. Somek, 'Defective law', in *University of Iowa Legal Studies Research Papers*, no. 10–33, December 2010.

[77] See e.g. D. J. Bederman, *Custom as a Source of Law* (Cambridge: Cambridge University Press, 2010), pp. 135, 137, 166. (at p. 137, he write that custom 'involves a searching analysis of what has been taken as a canonical set of elements for the proof of any customary international law norm: ICJ Statute Article 38's requirements of a "general practice" of states, which is "accepted as law"'). In the same vein, A. Pellet, 'Article 38', in A. Zimmermann, C. Tomuschat and K. Oellers-Frahm (eds.), *The Statute of the International Court of Justice* (Oxford: Oxford University Press, 2002), p. 813. For some examples, M. H. Mendelson, 'The formation of customary international law' (1998) 272 *Collected Courses of the Hague Academy on International Law* 159 at 187; I. Brownlie, *Principles of Public International Law* (Oxford: Oxford University Press, 2003), p. 6; A. Cassese, *International Law* (Oxford: Oxford University Press, 2005), p. 156.

[78] Alphonse Rivier is credited with the first use of the modern concept of opinio juris as an essential element of custom. See A Rivier, *Principles du droit des Gens* (1896), p. 35. For a recognition of such paternity, A. Carty, *Philosophy of International Law* (Edinburgh: Edinburgh University Press, 2007), p. 50.

narrative by which international lawyers root their two-element doctrine is imaginary.[79] Indeed, a scant review of the *travaux préparatoires* of the drafting of this provision indicates that in 1920 there was little discussion on the very notion of customary international law in the debates of the Advisory Committee of Jurists and, subsequently, of the Council or Assembly of the League.[80] Most discussions relating to the sources of international law revolved around the need for a provision on the sources,[81] the need to address *non liquet* and general principles.[82] The drafting history of Article 38 even shows that the drafters did not seriously discuss what was meant by customary international law and certainly not the need to distinguish between practice and *opinio juris*.[83] They simply 'had no very clear idea as to what constituted international custom'.[84] In other words, they 'did not have in mind a splitting-up of the definition of custom into two distinct elements'.[85] Thus the *travaux préparatoires* of Article 38 are, as far as the two-element variant of the doctrine of customary international law is concerned, rather inconsequential.[86] This is certainly not surprising, as the purpose of including a provision on the applicable law by the Permanent Court of International Justice was not to define each source mentioned therein but rather to

---

[79] In the same vein, C. Tams, 'Meta-custom and the court: a study in judicial law-making' (2015) 14 *Law and Practice of International Courts and Tribunals* 51 at 54–57.

[80] Ole Spiermann, '"Who attempts too much does nothing well": the 1920 Advisory Committee of Jurists and the Statute of the Permanent Court of International Justice' (2002) 73 *British Yearbook of International Law* 187 esp. 212–218. In the same vein, see D. J. Bederman, *Custom as a Source of Law* (Cambridge: Cambridge University Press, 2010), p. 141. See also ILC, 'First report on formation and evidence of customary international law by Sir Michael Wood', UN Doc. A/CN.4/663, 17 May 2013, para. 30.

[81] Procès-verbaux, pp. 286ff, 293ff.   [82] *Ibid.*, pp. 311–12, 331–38.

[83] In the same vein, See P. Haggenmacher, 'La doctrine des deux éléments en droit coutumier dans la pratique de la Cour international' (1986) 90 *Revue Générale du Droit International Public* 5 at 30–31; C. Tams, 'Meta-custom and the court: a study in judicial law-making' (2015) 14 *Law and Practice of International Courts and Tribunals* 51 at 59; A. Pellet, 'Article 38', in A. Zimmermann, C. Tomuschat, K. Oellers-Frahm (eds.), *The Statute of the International Court of Justice* (Oxford: Oxford University Press, 2002), p. 813.

[84] *Yearbook of the International Law Commission* 1950, vol. I, p. 6, para. 45.

[85] A. Pellet, 'Article 38', in A. Zimmermann, C. Tomuschat, K. Oellers-Frahm (eds.), *The Statute of the International Court of Justice* (Oxford: Oxford University Press, 2002), p. 813.

[86] This was confirmed by the report of Hammarskjöld (report of 2 July 1920), Hammarskjöldska Arkivet, p. 480, cited by Ole Spielmann, '"Who attempts too much does nothing well": the 1920 Advisory Committee of Jurists and the Statute of the Permanent Court of International Justice' (2002) 73 *British Yearbook of International Law* 187 at 216–17.

provide the new court with some guidance.[87] This being said, it remains that grounding the two-element doctrine of custom in a provision that was not meant to carry any specific understanding of customary law reinforces the imaginariness of the genealogical link established with Article 38.

The idea that the two-element variant of the doctrine of custom can be derived from Article 38 by virtue of such imaginary genealogy can even turn more idiosyncratic when approached from a purely textual perspective. It is hardly contested that the very text of Article 38[88] – provided that it can be construed in an intelligible way[89] – does not lend any support to the dominant two-element doctrine of custom embraced by international lawyers.[90] Interestingly, international lawyers usually explain the discrepancy between their genealogical claim and the text of Article 38 by virtue of an argument of poor drafting.[91] Like the incongruence of the *travaux préparatoires*, the discrepancy with the text does not prevent them from continuing to assert that Article 38 provides the foundations for the two-element doctrine of

---

[87] L. Ferrari, Méthodes de recherche de la coutume internationale dans la pratique des etats (1965) 192 *Collected Courses of the Hague Academy on International Law* 243. Ole Spielmann, '"Who attempts too much does nothing well": the 1920 Advisory Committee of Jurists and the Statute of the Permanent Court of International Justice' (2002) 73 *British Yearbook of International Law* 187 at 212–18; A. Pellet, 'Article 38', in A. Zimmermann, C. Tomuschat, K. Oellers-Frahm (eds.), *The Statute of the International Court of Justice* (Oxford: Oxford University Press, 2002), p. 813.

[88] The original Root-Philimoore formulation read 'international custom, as evidence of a common practice in use between nations and accepted by them as law' before being slightly amended to read 'international custom, as evidence of a general practice accepted as law'. See Procès-Verbaux of the Proceedings of the Advisory Committee of Jurists (1920), p. 306, annex no. 3.

[89] For a recent criticism, see James Crawford, *Chance, Order, Change: The Course of International Law: General Course on Public International Law* (The Hague: Pocketbooks of the Hague Academy of International Law, 2013), p. 84. See also C. Tams, 'Meta-custom and the court: a study in judicial law-making' (2015) 14 *Law and Practice of International Courts and Tribunals* 51 at 52.

[90] A. Pellet, 'Article 38', in A. Zimmermann, C. Tomuschat, K. Oellers-Frahm (eds.), *The Statute of the International Court of Justice* (Oxford: Oxford University Press, 2002), p. 813. C. Bradley, 'A state preferences account of customary international law adjudication', 10 October 2014, available at SSRN: http://ssrn.com/abstract=2508298; J. L. Kunz, 'The nature of customary international law' (1953) 47 *American Journal of International Law* 662 at 664.

[91] See e.g. D. J. Bederman, *Custom as a Source of Law* (Cambridge: Cambridge University Press, 2010), pp. 142–43.

customary international law.[92] With Article 38, customary international law is provided with a formal repository and is able to prescribe the modes of legal reasoning pertaining to the determination of the existence and content of international customary rules.

4   The Supply of a Justificatory Space: The Doctrine of jus cogens

As with responsibility, statehood and customary law, the fundamental doctrine of *jus cogens* presents most of the common features of a fundamental doctrine reduced to rules derived from an international instrument thanks to imaginary genealogy.[93] With an emphasis on the fundamental doctrine of *jus cogens*, this section grapples with the extent to which the international belief system allows international lawyers to debate the content of their fundamental doctrines without having to inquire about their foundations, thereby fully benefitting from the international belief system and especially its sources-based self-referentiality.[94]

The fundamental doctrine of *jus cogens*, after having been battered for few decades, has now secured almost unanimous acceptance, and the doubts vented at its inception have ebbed away. Such consensus has been significantly shored up by the increasing number of judicial authorities referring to – and, more importantly, relying on – *jus cogens* not only in

---

[92] A. Pellet, 'Article 38', in A. Zimmermann, C. Tomuschat, K. Oellers-Frahm (eds.), *The Statute of the International Court of Justice* (Oxford: Oxford University Press, 2002), p. 813.

[93] While the belief system behind the notion of *jus cogens* has never been examined, scholars have often expressed the idea that there is something mystical at work in international legal argumentation in relation to *jus cogens*. Gerry Simpson reported that the idea was used by J. Shand Watson in a presentation at the American Society of International Law. See G. Simpson, 'Book review of *Peremptory Norms (Jus Cogens) in International Law: Historical Developments, Criteria, Present Development* by Lauri Hannikainen' (1991) 13 *Australia Yearbook of International Law* 180, n. 2), but the expression did not make its way to the written transcript of the contribution. See J. Watson, 'State consent and the sources of international obligation jurisprudence of international law: classic and modern views' (1992) 86 *American Society of International Law Proceedings* 108. Authors also often speak about the 'mystery' of *jus cogens*. A. Bianchi, 'Human rights and the magic of jus cogens' (2008) 19 *European Journal of International Law* 491 at 493; Asif Hameed, 'Unravelling the mystery of jus cogens in international law' (2014) 84 *British Yearbook of International Law* 52; Enzo Cannizzaro, 'Peremptory law-making', in Rain Liivoja and Jarna Petman (eds.), *International Law-making: Essays in Honour of Jan Klabbers* (London: Routledge, 2014), p. 270; T. Weatherall, *Jus Cogens: International Law and Social Contract* (Cambridge: Cambridge University Press, 2015), pp. 112–113.

[94] On sources-based self-referentiality, see Chapter 3, Section 1.

cosmetic *obiter dicta* but also as kingpins of their legal reasoning.[95] This success of the fundamental doctrine of *jus cogens* probably originates in the projection of a more systemic and organised image of an otherwise rather rambling legal order, the representation of a more morally cohesive international legal order and the creativity that it unlocks among international lawyers.[96] I submit that *jus cogens*, like other fundamental doctrines, constitutes a cluster of modes of legal reasoning about non-derogation[97] and normative hierarchy[98] that is commonly considered to be a set of rules derived from two provisions of an international instrument, namely, Articles 53 and 64 of the Vienna Convention on the Law of Treaties. That *jus cogens* is construed as a set of rules derived from an international instrument thanks to imaginary genealogy does not mean that it is devoid of controversy. As indicated earlier,[99] the international belief system does not provide any determinacy as to the content of the fundamental doctrines. It thus should not be surprising that the content of this fundamental doctrine, whether the determination of norms to which a *jus cogens* character is recognised[100] or the effects attached to the *jus cogens*

[95] See e.g. ILC, Study Group on the Fragmentation of International Law, UN Doc A/CN.4/ L.682, 13 April 2006, p. 183, para. 363 and p. 190, para. 377; Theodor Meron, 'International law in the age of human rights: general course on public international law' (2003) 301 *Collected Courses of the Hague Academy of International Law* 202; M. E. O'Connell, 'Jus cogens, international law's higher ethical norms', in Donald Earl Childress III (ed.), *The Role of Ethics in International Law* (Cambridge: Cambridge University Press, 2012), p. 79; G. Danilenko, 'International jus cogens: issues of law-making' (1990) 2 *European Journal of International Law* 42 at 43. For a recent overview of the judicial decisions affirming the existence of *jus cogens*, see T. Weatherall, *Jus Cogens: International Law and Social Contract* (Cambridge: Cambridge University Press, 2015), pp. 162–74.

[96] See J. d'Aspremont, 'Jus cogens: a social construct without pedigree' (2015) 46 *Netherlands Yearbook of International Law* 85. See also A. Bianchi, 'Human rights and the magic of jus cogens' (2008) 19 *European Journal of International Law* 491.

[97] See, generally, Robert Kolb, *Théorie du jus cogens international* (Paris: Publication de IUHEI, 2001). For a criticism, see P.-M. Dupuy, 'L'unité de l'ordre juridique international: cours général de droit international public' (2002) 297 *Collected Courses of the Hague Academy on International Law* 9 at 281. For a rebuttal of the argument of Pierre-Marie Dupuy, see R. Kolb, *Peremptory International Law (Jus Cogens): A General Inventory* (Oxford: Hart Publishing, 2015), esp. Introduction.

[98] P.-M. Dupuy, 'L'unité de l'ordre juridique international: cours général de droit international public' (2002) 297 *Collected Courses of the Hague Academy on International Law* 9.

[99] See Chapter 2, Section 1.

[100] For a discussion of this question, see e.g. ILC, 'Report of the International Law Commission', 66th session, UN Doc. A/69/10, Annex: Report by M. Dire D. Tladi; A. Gomez Robledo, 'Le ius cogens international: sa genèse, sa nature, ses fonctions' (1981) 172 *Collected Courses of the Hague Academy of International Law* 9 at 167; L. A. Alexidze, 'Legal nature of jus cogens in contemporary international law' (1981) 172

character,[101] remains the object of very passionate debate. What the international belief system provides, however, is a comfort zone where international lawyers can afford to debate the content of the fundamental doctrine without having to inquire about its foundations. Indeed, most of the time, they take advantage of the self-referentiality that allows the formation of the doctrine of *jus cogens* to be explained by virtue of the

     Collected Courses of the Hague Academy on International Law 219 at 259; M. Saul, 'Identifying jus cogens norms: the interaction of scholars and international judges' (2015) 5 *Asian Journal of International Law* 26; M. E. O'Connell, 'Jus cogens, international law's higher ethical norms', in Donald Earl Childress III (ed.), *The Role of Ethics in International Law* (Cambridge: Cambridge University Press, 2012), p. 79; Cezary Mik, 'Jus cogens in contemporary law' (2013) 33 *Polish Yearbook of International Law* 27. Enzo Cannizzaro, 'Peremptory law-making', in Rain Liivoja and Jarna Petman (eds.), *International Law-Making: Essays in Honour of Jan Klabbers* (London: Routledge, 2014), p. 270. For an extensive discussion, see T. Weatherall, *Jus Cogens: International Law and Social Contract* (Cambridge: Cambridge University Press, 2015), pp. 200–265.

[101] International lawyers have quickly envisaged a wide variety of new legal effects beyond the traditional non-derogability in the law of treaties or the consequences in the law of state responsibility in case of serious breaches of *jus cogens*. Such a promotion of *jus cogens* beyond the law of treaties or the law of responsibility not only pertains to the non-existence (or voidness) of customary rules or unilateral acts contradictory to *jus cogens* – an extension that had been anticipated. It is well known that *jus cogens* is nowadays frequently invoked to deny state immunity in cases of violation of *jus cogens* obligations. Yet many new possibilities and impossibilities have been advocated. The range of legal effects associated with *jus cogens* includes the bindingness of *jus cogens* norms on all parties to succession, its impact on the recognition of states, the duty of judicial notice of a contradiction to *jus cogens* in the absence of invocation by the parties, its consequences on the legality of domestic policies and actions related to a breach of *jus cogens*, the obligations to nullify domestic law manifestly contrary to *jus cogens*, a duty to investigate and prosecute crimes of *jus cogens*, an assumption of universal jurisdiction (for *jus cogens* crimes), an obligation *aut dedere aut iudicare*, the interdiction or invalidity of amnesties, the invalidation of popular initiatives in favour of legislation in contradiction to *jus cogens*, a duty to exercise diplomatic protection, universal bindingness on non-state actors, the invalidity of UN Security Council resolutions contrary to *jus cogens*, the disqualification of a sovereign act, the increased competence of executive bodies of international organisations or possible new constraints (or argumentative empowerment) in the doctrine of interpretation. Other specific legal effects have been discussed in the law of the sea or international investment law. Even in its 'breeding areas' such as the law of treaties and the law of responsibility, new legal effects have been envisaged, like the provisional non-application of treaty norms that are in contradiction to *jus cogens*, the inadmissibility of treaty reservations contrary to *jus cogens*, a new sort of exception of non-execution or new aggravated responsibility for violations of human rights of *jus cogens* character beyond the consequences already provided by the Articles on State Responsibility. Regarding the world of possibilities created by *jus cogens*, see the idea of '*notion à tout faire*' mentioned by A. Pellet, 'Conclusions', in C. Tomuschat and J.-M. Thouvenin (eds.), *The Fundamental Rules of the International Legal Order: Jus Cogens and Obligations Erga Omnes* (Leiden: Martinus Nijhoff, 2006), p. 422; see also A. Bianchi, 'Human rights and the magic of jus cogens' (2008) 19 *European Journal of International Law* 491.

doctrine of sources. As a result, beyond the idea that the formation of *jus cogens* is explained by the sources of international law, the foundations of the notion has been left floating and in want of any further reflection.[102]

To appreciate the justificatory space provided by the international belief system on the basis of which international lawyers can concentrate their debates on the content of the notion rather than its foundations, a distinction must be made between the foundations of the rules by which a *jus cogens* character is recognised and the foundations of the mechanism by which the legal effects attached to a *jus cogens* character are produced.[103] It goes without saying that this distinction between *jus cogens* norms and the mechanism of *jus cogens* itself is not new.[104] In the

---

[102] The idea that the notion of *jus cogens* is in want of clear foundations is regularly heard in the literature. See e.g. G. Danilenko, 'International jus cogens: issues of law-making' (1991) 2 *European Journal of International Law* 4 at 43. B. Simma, 'The contribution of Alfred Verdross to the theory of international law' (1995) 6 *European Journal of International Law* 33 at 53; M. Saul, 'Identifying jus cogens norms: the interaction of scholars and international judges' (2014) 5 *Asian Journal of International Law* 1 (first view); see also the account of Carlo Focarelli, 'Promotional jus cogens: a critical appraisal of jus cogens' legal effects' (2008) 77 *Nordic Journal of International Law* 429. See also Karl Zemanek, 'The metamorphosis of jus cogens: from an institution of treaty law to the bedrock of the international legal order?', in E. Cannizzaro, (ed.), *The Law of Treaties Beyond the Vienna Convention* (Oxford: Oxford University Press, 2011), p. 409.

[103] It must be acknowledged that the notion of *jus cogens* mechanism – as opposed to *jus cogens* norms – is not self-evident. Indeed, all the legal effects of *jus cogens* are usually scattered across various regimes. Even the non-controversial and traditional legal effects of *jus cogens* are found in two distinct regimes, that is, the law of treaties and the law of responsibility. In this sense, it may seem idiosyncratic to speak of a *jus cogens* mechanism as a self-standing and unitary notion. I submit, however, that the fact that the legal effects are found in several specific 'areas' does not automatically pluralise and fragment the question of the foundations of the *jus cogens* mechanism. It is not because such legal effects are produced under different umbrellas that the whole mechanism of *jus cogens* needs, for the sake of its foundations, to be similarly disaggregated. In this sense, this chapter adopts a holistic concept of the *jus cogens* mechanism by which it is seen as one single construct in need of the same foundations. For a similar point, see Enzo Cannizzaro, 'A higher law for treaties?', in E. Cannizzaro (ed.), *The Law of Treaties beyond the Vienna Convention* (Oxford: Oxford University Press, 2011), p. 440.

[104] In the literature, a wide variety of dichotomies have been put forward to capture the difference between the mechanism of *jus cogens* itself and the rules at the advantage of which such a mechanism produces its legal effects. For instance, distinctions are made between first-order rules of *jus cogens* and second-order rules of *jus cogens* (U. Linderfalk, 'The creation of jus cogens: making sense of Article 53 of the Vienna Convention' (2011) 71 *Zeitschrift für ausländisches öffentliches Recht und Völkerrecht* 359; U. Linderfalk, 'The source of jus cogens obligations: how legal positivism copes with peremptory international law' (2013) 82 *Nordic Journal of International Law* 369, or between the rules belonging to the public order and the mechanism of public order; see J.

literature, this distinction is usually made to show that the mechanism of *jus cogens* itself is not necessarily of a *jus cogens* character.[105] For the sake of this section, the distinction is made with a view to showing that the international belief system has provided international lawyers, albeit in different ways, with justificatory space with respect to both dimensions of this fundamental doctrine.

International lawyers have fully taken advantage of the sources-based self-referentiality of the international belief system when it comes to the foundations of norms benefitting from *jus cogens* status in the international legal order. Indeed, they commonly establish their legal foundations by virtue of the doctrine of sources. This does not mean that no variations are observed in the way the doctrine of sources is deployed to explain *jus cogens* norms. Actually, diverging sources-based constructions have been designed in this respect and must be outlined here.[106] There is a first group of international lawyers who claim that *jus cogens*–making operates as a distinct source of law.[107] In the same vein, some scholars contend

Verhoeven, 'Considérations sur ce qui est commun: cours général de droit international public' (2008) 334 *Collected Courses of the Hague Academy on International Law* 9 at 231.

[105] On the idea that second-order rules are not *jus cogens* but customary rules (as a result, customary law can explain the effect of *jus cogens* without a self-explanatory and self-referential detour to *jus cogens* to explain the effect of *jus cogens*); see U. Linderfalk, 'The Creation of jus cogens: making sense of Article 53 of the Vienna Convention' (2011) 71 *Zeitschrift für ausländisches öffentliches Recht und Völkerrecht* 359 at 375–76; U. Linderfalk, 'The source of jus cogens obligations: how legal positivism copes with peremptory international law' (2013) 82 *Nordic Journal of International Law* 369. For the exact opposite position, see A. Cassese, *International Law*, 2nd edn (Oxford: Oxford University Press, 2005), p. 205; see, generally, Lauri Hannikainen, *Peremptory Norms (Jus Cogens) in International Law: Historical Development, Criteria, Present Status* (Helsinki: Finnish Lawyers' Publishing Company, 1988); D. Shelton, 'Normativity hierarchy in international law' (2006) 100 *American Journal of International Law* 291; Carlo Focarelli, 'Promotional jus cogens: a critical appraisal of jus cogens' legal effects' (2008) 77 *Nordic Journal of International Law* 429.

[106] See also the recent overview provided by T. Weatherall, *Jus Cogens: International Law and Social Contract* (Cambridge: Cambridge University Press, 2015), pp. 124–74.

[107] G. Onuf and R. K. Birney, 'Peremptory norms of international law: their source, function and future' (1974) 4 *Denver Journal of International Law and Policy* 187 at 195; G. A. Christenson, 'Jus cogens: guarding interests foundational to international society', (1988) 28 *Virginia Journal of International Law* 585 at 592; R. Monaco, 'Observations sur la hiérarchie des normes du droit international', in *Liber Amicorum Hermann Mosler* (Berlin: Springer, 1983), p. 606; J. Vidmar, 'Norm conflicts and hierarchy in international law: towards a vertical international legal system', in E. De Wet and J. Vidmar, (eds.), *Hierarchy in International Law: The Place of Human Rights* (Oxford: Oxford University Press, 2012) p. 13; A. Orakhelashvili, *Peremptory Norms in*

that *jus cogens* norms are made by virtue of a special process where a double consent is expressed[108], that they depend on *jus cogens*-specific manifestations of consensus[109] or that they constitute a special type of customary law where *opinio juris* is understood differently[110] or where state practice is downplayed.[111] Such views are sometimes echoed in judicial practice.[112] It is well known that despite the fact that such understanding of *jus cogens*-making did not seem to enjoy much support during the Vienna Conference,[113] it is the possibility of introducing a new form of law-making that would be less dependent on state consent that led some countries such as France to reject the Vienna Convention on the Law of Treaties.[114]

The idea that *jus cogens* norms are made through new and specific sources is, however, not the dominant sources-based approach to the foundations of *jus cogens* norms. The great majority of scholars

International Law (Oxford: Oxford University Press, 2006), pp. 104–5; G. Hernandez, *The International Court of Justice and the Judicial Function*, (Oxford: Oxford University Press, 2014), pp. 218–19.

[108] A. Gomez Robledo, 'Le ius cogens international: sa genèse, sa nature, ses fonctions' (1981) 172 *Collected Courses of the Hague Academy on International Law* 9 at 105; Erika de Wet, 'Jus cogens and obligations erga omnes', in Dinah Shelton (ed.), *Oxford Handbook on Human Rights* (Oxford: Oxford University Press, Oxford, 2013), pp. 541–61; A. de Hoog, *Obligations Erga Omnes and International Crimes* (The Hague: Kluwer Law, 1996), pp. 45–46.

[109] A. Verdross and B. Simma, *Universelles Völkerrecht* (Berlin: Duncker & Humblot, 1984), p. 324; R. Kolb, 'The formal source of ius cogens in public international law' (1998) 53 *Zeitschrift for öffenliches Recht* 69 at 93.

[110] Ulf Linderfalk, 'The effects of jus cogens norms: whoever opened Pandora's box, did you ever think about the consequences?' (2008) 5 *European Journal of International Law* 853 at 862; Paul Reuter, *Introduction to the Law of Treaties*, 2nd edn (London: Routledge, 1995), p. 143.

[111] L. Henkin, 'International law: politics, values and functions: general course on public international law' (1989) 216 *Collected Courses of the Hague Academy of International Law* 9 at 60, 216; O. Schachter, 'Entangled treaty and custom', in Y. Dinstein (ed.), *International Law at a Time of Perplexity: Essays in Honour of Shabtai Rosenne* (Dordrecht: Martinus Nijhoff, 1988), p. 734; S. Sur, 'Discussion', in A. Casesse and J. Weiler (eds.), *Change and Stability in International Law-Making* (Berlin: de Gruyter, 1988), p. 128; A. Orakhelashvili, *Peremptory Norms in International Law* (Oxford: Oxford University Press, 2006), pp. 301–2; C. Tomuschat, 'Obligations arising from states without or against their will' (2013) 241 *Collected Courses of the Hague Academy on International Law* 195 at 307.

[112] Inter-American Commission, *Michael Domingues v United States*, rep. no. 62/02, Merits, Case 12.285, 22 October 2002, para. 5.

[113] G. Danilenko, 'International jus cogens: issues of law-making' (1991) 2 *European Journal of International Law* 42 at 49.

[114] United Nations Conference on the Law of Treaties, 1st session, 26 March–24 May 1968, p. 94.

establish the foundations of *jus cogens* norms through the traditional sources of international law without resorting to the idea of a specific or distinct source. Most of these scholars resort to the doctrine of customary international law,[115] sometimes claiming that *jus cogens* existed by virtue of customary law even before the adoption of the Vienna Convention.[116] It is even occasionally said that the insertion of the reference to the acceptance and recognition by the international community of states as a whole was a means to anchor Article 53 in Article 38 of the Statute of the International Court of Justice and especially in the doctrine of customary international law.[117] Those scholars usually find support for their customary law–based approach in a few decisions of international courts, most notably the International Court of Justice's decision in the case on questions related to the *Obligation to*

---

[115] Restatement of the Foreign Relations Law of the United States, Revised (1985); M. Ragazzi, *The Concept of International Obligations Erga Omnes* (Oxford: Clarendon Press, 1997), p. 53. Jordan Paust, 'The reality of jus cogens' (1981) 7 *Connecticut Journal of International Law* 81 at 82; D'Amato, *The Concept of Custom in International Law* (Ithaca, NY: Cornell University Press, 1971), pp. 111, 132; T. Meron, 'The Geneva Conventions as customary law' (1987) 81 *American Journal of International Law* 348 at 350; U. Linderfalk, 'The creation of jus cogens: making sense of Article 53 of the Vienna Convention' (2011) 71 *Zeitschrift für ausländisches öffentliches Recht und Völkerrecht* 359; U. Linderfalk, 'The source of jus cogens obligations: how legal positivism copes with peremptory international law' (2013) 82 *Nordic Journal of International Law* 369; M. Byers, 'Conceptualising the relationship between jus cogens and erga omnes' (1997) 66 *Nordic Journal of International Law* 220; P.-M. Dupuy, 'L'unité de l'ordre juridique international: cours général de droit international public' (2002) 297 *Collected Courses of the Hague Academy on International Law* 9 at 275–76; J. Verhoeven, 'Considérations sur ce qui est commun: cours général de droit international public' (2008) 334 *Collected Courses of the Hague Academy on International Law* 9 at 231; J. Sztucki, *Jus Cogens and the Vienna Convention on the Law of Treaties: A Critical Appraisal* (Wein: Springer-Verlag, 1974), p. 75; B. Conforti, 'Cours général de droit international public' (1988) 212 *Collected Courses of the Hague Academy on International Law* 9 at 129. For a criticism of this *jus cogens*–based approach, see M. Janis, 'The nature of jus cogens' (1988) 3 *Connecticut Journal of International Law* 359 at 360; D. Dubois, 'The authority of peremptory norms in international law: state consent or natural law' (2009) 78 *Nordic Journal of International Law* 133. Thomas Weatherall, 'Against fragmentation: international common law and the development of jus cogens' (2014), available at SSRN: http://ssrn.com/abstract=2565165; J. Verhoeven, 'Invalidity of treaties: anything new in/under the Vienna Conventions?', in E. Cannizzaro (ed.) *The Law of Treaties Beyond the Vienna Convention* (Oxford: Oxford University Press, 2011), p. 305.

[116] L. A. Alexidze, 'Legal nature of jus cogens in contemporary international law' (1981) 172 *Collected Courses of the Hague Academy on International Law* 219 at 230–32; R. St. J. Macdonald, 'Fundamental norms in contemporary international law' (1987) 25 *Canadian Yearbook of International Law* 115 at 132.

[117] This reading of the *travaux* is put forward by M. Ragazzi, *The Concept of International Obligations Erga Omnes* (Oxford: Clarendon Press, 1997), p. 53.

prosecute or extradite (Belgium v. Senegal).[118] Others have found that general principles constitute a better breeding ground for *jus cogens* norms.[119] In addition, there are scholars who claim that *jus cogens* can be grounded on a variety of sources at the same time.[120] Whatever its variants, grounding *jus cogens* in the existing formal sources seems to have been the dominant view during the Vienna Conference[121] and what the ILC seems to have supported in its subsequent work.[122]

Among all the scholars resorting to the doctrine of sources to anchor *jus cogens* rules in the international legal order, a third group of scholars can be identified that adopts a series of blended approaches. According to them, *jus cogens* norms are the result of deductive and inductive processes in that they are deduced from positive values and allegedly validated by formal sources,[123] courts and tribunals usually having a very

---

[118] See *Questions Relating to the Obligation to Prosecute or Extradite (Belgium v Senegal)*, ICJ Rep. 2012, 422, para. 99. For Saul, this judgment seems to indicate that *jus cogens* comes from customary law. See M. Saul, 'Identifying jus cogens norms: the interaction of scholars and international judges' (2014) 5 *Asian Journal of International Law* 1 (first view) at 7; see also *Arbitral Award of 31 July 1989 (Guinea-Bissau v Senegal)*, XX RSA 119, para. 44. For a detailed discussion of the case law of the ICJ in relation to *jus cogens*, see G. Hernandez, *The International Court of Justice and the Judicial Function* (Oxford: Oxford University Press, 2014), pp. 229–36.

[119] 'Report on the law of treaties by Mr. H. Lauterpacht, Special Rapporteur', in *Yearbook of the International Law Commission 1953*, vol. II, p. 155; Paul Reuter, *Introduction to the Law of Treaties*, 2nd edn (London: Routledge, 1995), p. 145; P. Alston and B. Simma, 'The sources of human rights law: custom, jus cogens, general principles' (1988) 12 *Australian Yearbook of International Law* 102. See also the award in *Guinea-Bissau v Senegal*, para. 44, cited in note 118.

[120] L. A. Alexidze, 'Legal nature of jus cogens in contemporary international law' (1981) 172 *Collected Courses of the Hague Academy on International Law* 219 at 256; R. Kolb, 'The formal source of ius cogens in public international law' (1998) 53 *Zeitschrift for öffenliches Recht* 69.

[121] This is the opinion of G. Danilenko, 'International jus cogens: issues of law-making' (1991) 2 *European Journal of International Law* 42 at 49, citing the statement of Greece, Cuba, Poland, Italy, Ivory Coast, Cyprus, USA, and Bulgaria (United Nations Conference on the Law of Treaties, Official Records, I, at 295, 297, 302, 311, 321, 387 and United Nations Conference on the Law of Treaties, Official Records, II, 102).

[122] Report of the Commission to the General Assembly on the work of its 28th session, *Yearbook of the International Law Commission*, 1976 vol. II, p. 86.

[123] A. Verdross, 'Forbidden treaties in international law' (1937) 31 *American Journal of International Law* 571 at 573; Asif Hameed, 'Unravelling the mystery of jus cogens in international law' (2014) 84 *British Yearbook of International Law* 52 at 78; B. Simma, 'The contribution of Alfred Verdross to the theory of international law' (1995) 6 *European Journal of International Law* 33 at 34 and 53; D. Dubois, 'The authority of peremptory norms in international law: state consent or natural law' (2009) 78 *Nordic Journal of International Law* 133; Report on the Law of Treaties by Mr. H. Lauterpacht, Special Rapporteur, *Yearbook of the International Law Commission 1953*, vol. II, p. 154;

prominent role in the verification of such blended criteria.[124] A variant of this reconciliatory approach is also found in recent constructions articulated around social contract theory.[125]

The foregoing shows that as far as *jus cogens* norms are concerned, the doctrine of sources has sufficed to explain, albeit in a variety of ways, the foundations of *jus cogens* norms, allowing self-referentiality to provide international lawyers with justificatory space and sparing them any further foundational debates about *jus cogens* norms. I submit that self-referentiality has provided some similar transcendental comfort in relation to the foundation of the *jus cogens* mechanism. Indeed, the doctrine of sources has provided an explanation for the foundation of the *jus cogens* mechanism in the eyes of a large number of international lawyers. First, there are those who do not distinguish between the question of the foundations of *jus cogens* norms and that of the foundations of the *jus cogens* mechanism and for whom the explanation of the former covers the latter. Second, there are scholars for whom the mechanism of

---

see M. Ragazzi, *The Concept of International Obligations Erga Omnes* (Oxford: Clarendon, 1997), p. 57; Lauri Hannikainen, *Peremptory Norms (Jus Cogens) in International Law: Historical Development, Criteria, Present Status* (Helsinki: Finnish Lawyers' Publishing Company, 1988), part II.

[124] A Cassese, 'For an enhanced role of jus cogens', in A. Cassese, *Realising Utopia: The Future of International Law* (Oxford: Oxford University Press, 2012), pp. 158, 164. See the critical remarks of Hélène Ruiz Fabri, 'Enhancing the rhetoric of jus cogens' (2012) 23 *European Journal of International Law* 1049.

[125] T. Weatherall, *Jus Cogens: International Law and Social Contract* (Cambridge: Cambridge University Press, 2015), pp. 175–82, esp. p. 183 ('In the context of jus cogens, a hybridised source of international law renders intelligible the way customary law and general principles, together, account for the emergence of norms necessary for the social existence of the international community apart from the direct consent of individual states. In practice, this process is based principally upon *opinio juris sive necessitatis*, expressive of the higher interest of the international community, as a proxy for mankind that gives rise to the positive rules of *jus cogens*. As such, the emergence of peremptory norms is as much social contract as it is international law'). Interestingly, it is this specific blended understanding of the foundations of *jus cogens* norms that, albeit not being necessarily dominant, had caught the attention of those critical works that have sought to highlight the contradiction at the heart of legal argumentation on *jus cogens*. Gerry Simpson writes: 'The scoffing of the voluntarist is never far away when the phrase "common good" is invoked.' See G. Simpson, 'Book review of *Peremptory Norms (Jus Cogens) in International Law: Historical Developments, Criteria, Present Development* by Lauri Hannikainen' (1991) 13 *Australia Yearbook of International Law* 182. See also Martti Koskenniemi, *From Apology to Utopia* (Cambridge: Cambridge University Press, Cambridge, 2005), pp. 322–25 (Martti Koskenniemi understands *jus cogens* as being built on ascending (consensualist) and descending (non-consensualist) modes of argumentation and inevitably condemned to collapse in either naturalism or voluntarism).

jus cogens was 'positivised' by the 1969 Vienna Convention on the Law of Treaties without any further indication as to the specific means by which the *jus cogens* mechanism is anchored in the international legal order.[126] For them, Articles 53 and 64 suffice to provide foundations to the fundamental doctrine and justify the proper embodiment of the mechanism of *jus cogens* in international law. Others invoke customary international law.[127]

It must be acknowledged, however, that resort to the doctrine of sources to explain the foundations of the *jus cogens* mechanism has not been as omnipresent as is witnessed in relation to *jus cogens* norms. Indeed, there are a number of international lawyers who have developed a great indifference towards the question of the foundations of the *jus cogens* mechanism.[128] This has been possible by virtue of a series of foundation-avoidance moves.[129] This section is not the place to systematically review the great variety of foundation-avoidance moves observed in the literature.[130] For the

---

[126] G. Danilenko, 'International jus cogens: issues of law-making' (1991) 2 *European Journal of International Law* 42 at 46; A. Gomez Robledo, 'Le ius cogens international: sa genèse, sa nature, ses fonctions' (1981) 172 *Collected Courses of the Hague Academy on International Law* 9 at 105, 109; J. Verhoeven, 'Considérations sur ce qui est commun: cours général de droit international public' (2008) 334 *Collected Courses of the Hague Academy on International Law* 9 at 230; ILC, Study Group on the Fragmentation of International Law, UN Doc. A/CN.4/L.682, p. 183, para. 362.

[127] For an exception, see U. Linderfalk, who anchors the *jus cogens* mechanism in the international legal order by virtue of the mechanism of customary international law; see U. Linderfalk, 'The creation of jus cogens: making sense of Article 53 of the Vienna Convention' (2011) 71 *Zeitschrift for öffentliches Recht* 359 at 375–76; U. Linderfalk, 'The source of jus cogens obligations: how legal positivism copes with peremptory international law' (2013) 82 *Nordic Journal of International Law* 369.

[128] This indifference has sometimes been bemoaned. See U. Linderfalk, 'The creation of jus cogens: making sense of Article 53 of the Vienna Convention' (2011) 71 *Zeitschrift for öffenliches Recht* 359 at 363. See also A. D'Amato, 'It's a bird, it's a plane, it's jus cogens' (1990) 6 *Connecticut Journal of International Law* 1 (for whom the impossibility of providing such a definition invalidates the notion). See also the rationale for the proposal to include the question of the nature to the agenda of the ILC, 'Report of the International Law Commission', 66th session, UN Doc. A/69/10, Annex: Report by M. Dire D. Tladi.

[129] These foundation-avoidance arguments include the claim that the question of the foundation of *jus cogens* has been clinched once and for all by the extensive use of *jus cogens* by courts and tribunals, the claim that *jus cogens* is derived from natural law or universal values, the claim that *jus cogens* is an inherent element of the legal system, the claim that *jus cogens* is the expression of international public order or the expression of international public policy or the claim that *jus cogens* is a social product of the system.

[130] This has been done elsewhere. See J. d'Aspremont, 'Jus cogens as a social construct without pedigree' (2015) 46 *Netherlands Yearbook of International Law* 85. For a comprehensive overview of the various approaches found in the literature, see R. Kolb, 'The formal source of ius cogens in public international law' (1998) 53 *Zeitschrift for*

sake of the argument made here, it suffices to say that for many international lawyers, it has not seemed necessary to make use of the self-referentiality provided by the international belief system and explain the *jus cogens* mechanism through sources.[131] It is argued here that such disinterest and lack of an explicit use of the sources-based self-referentiality do not fault the belief system discussed in this book but, on the contrary, uphold it. Indeed, it can be argued that it is because international lawyers feel that the international belief system provides sufficient justificatory space that they can afford not to bother about explaining the formation of the *jus cogens* mechanism though sources and focus on debates about the content of the doctrine only. In this sense, utter foundational indifference and the absence of an explicit use of sources-based self-referentiality may simply be construed as the expression of the justificatory space of the belief system at its height. Thus, whether they engage with *jus cogens* norms or with the *jus cogens* mechanism, international lawyers are fully reaping the benefits of the international belief system and the justificatory space it supplies.

öffenliches Recht 69; or Robert Kolb, *Théorie du jus cogens international* (Paris: Publications de IUHEI, 2001); R. Kolb, *Peremptory International Law (Jus Cogens): A General Inventory* (Oxford: Hart, 2015), esp. chap. 3; Enzo Cannizzaro, 'Peremptory law-making', in Rain Liivoja and Jarna Petman (eds.), *International Law-Making: Essays in Honour of Jan Klabbers* (London: Routledge, 2014), pp. 261–70; K. Zemanek, 'The metamorphosis of jus cogens': from an institution of treaty law to the bedrock of the international legal order?', in Enzo Cannizzaro (ed.), *The Law of Treaties Beyond the Vienna Convention* (Oxford: Oxford University Press, 2011), pp. 381–410; Asif Hameed, 'Unravelling the mystery of jus cogens in international law' (2014) 84 *British Yearbook of International Law* 52; Evan J. Criddle and Evan Fox-Decent, 'A fiduciary theory of jus cogens' (2009) 34 *Yale Journal of International Law* 331.

[131] It should be stressed that claiming that the *jus cogens* mechanism has been left floating without an agreed foundation does not mean that it is a construct without history. The way in which the concept emerged is thus well known, and its historical origins are easily traceable by most international lawyers. For some historical account of the notion, see A. Gomez Robledo, 'Le ius cogens international: sa genèse, sa nature, ses fonctions' (1981) 172 *Collected Courses of the Hague Academy on International Law* 9 at 17–68; Lauri Hannikainen, *Peremptory Norms (Jus Cogens) in International Law: Historical Development, Criteria, Present Status* (Helsink: Finnish Lawyers' Publishing Company, 1981), part I; E. Suy, 'The concept of jus cogens in public international law', in *Lagonissi Conference: Papers and Proceedings*, vol. II (Geneva: Carnegie Endowment for International Peace, 1967), p. 17; Evan J. Criddle and Evan Fox-Decent, 'A fiduciary theory of jus cogens' (2009) 34 *Yale Journal of International Law* 331. For some historical considerations from a soviet perspective, see L. A. Alexidze, 'Legal nature of jus cogens in contemporary international law' (1981) 172 *Collected Courses of the Hague Academy on International Law* 219 at 228–232; T. Weatherall, *Jus Cogens. International Law and Social Contract* (Cambridge: Cambridge University Press, 2015), pp. 111–23.

5

Suspension of the International Belief System

The previous four chapters have produced an image of international law as a belief system. This international belief system is built on self-referentiality on the basis of a reduction of fundamental doctrines to rules derived from some key international instruments and whose formation and functioning are explained through the fundamental doctrines themselves. It was shown simultaneously that it is such self-referentiality that guarantees a justificatory space in which international lawyers can experience a sense of constraint towards the fundamental doctrines without interference from any evidentiary demands from the outside world. While the doctrines of sources and interpretation were more systematically examined in relation to their contribution to self-referentiality, the way in which the fundamental doctrines of responsibility, statehood, customary law and *jus cogens* are reduced to rules derived from an international instrument by virtue of imaginary genealogy also was discussed with a view to illustrating some of the contemporary manifestations of the international belief system.

Exposing the international belief system at work behind the fundamental doctrines of international law has constituted a central ambition of this book. This is what the four preceding chapters have tried to achieve. Yet, as mentioned earlier,[1] the image of international law that was produced in the preceding chapters is also envisaged as an invitation to international lawyers to temporarily suspend the belief system at work in their common understanding of the formation and functioning of the fundamental doctrines. Suspending the belief system means engaging in an exercise of unlearning one's understanding of the formation and functioning of the fundamental doctrines of international law that these lawyers have been trained to continuously reproduce and respond to. This concretely calls for a rupture of the self-referentiality on which the international belief system is built and thus a flight from an

---

[1] See Chapter 1.

explanation of the formation and functioning of fundamental doctrines in their own terms.

In carrying out such an unlearning exercise of the explanation provided by sources and interpretation, this chapter aims at discontinuing the 'miscognising'[2] effect of the belief system and re-imagining international law and its fundamental doctrines outside the box of sources- and interpretation-based self-referentiality. As will be shown, such a rupture in particular helps us to re-imagine fundamental doctrines as designed and shaped by a series of interventions by a great number of actors and based on processes that are not captured by the fundamental doctrines themselves.

This chapter starts with a discussion of the interventions that are laid bare by a rupture with sources-based self-referentiality, that is, an explanation of the formation of the fundamental doctrines provided by the doctrine of sources of international law (1). It continues with an examination of the interventions which are revealed by the suspension of interpretation-based self-referentiality, that is, an explanation of the functioning of the fundamental doctrines by the doctrine of interpretation (2).

1   Unlearning Sources-Based Self-Referentiality

In the international belief system, as discussed in Chapter 3, the formation of fundamental doctrines is explained via the doctrine of sources. This means that fundamental doctrines, including the fundamental doctrine of sources itself, are held to be the product of the rule-making processes recognised by the doctrine of sources. In the international belief system, the formation of fundamental doctrines is 'de-personified' and reduced to the adoption of the international instruments from which those doctrines are supposedly derived. In the belief system, sources-based self-referentiality obfuscates the multitude of individual and collective interventions in the design of the fundamental doctrines that disappear behind these instruments from which they are allegedly derived.

If one suspends the belief system and does away with such a self-referential explanation of the formation of the fundamental

---

[2] On the notion of 'miscognition' (*méconnaissance*), see Chapter 1, Section 3. See, generally, Pierre Bourdieu, 'A lecture on the lecture', in Pierre Bourdieu, *In Other Words: Essays towards a Reflexive Sociology* (1990), pp. 176, 183.

doctrines, their making can no longer be construed as rule-making[3] whereby the international instruments from which they are derived are assembled and promulgated in a manner recognised by the doctrine of sources. Instead, suspending the belief system and separating from sources-based self-referentiality turn the emphasis to the interventions[4] that shape the fundamental doctrines and the modes of legal reasoning they prescribe. More precisely, such suspension allows one to capture a wide variety of distinct interventions in the formation of fundamental doctrines.[5] One witnesses, among others, interventions to design modes of legal reasoning, interventions to axiomise modes of legal reasoning and package them in a fundamental doctrine, interventions to elevate a given instrument in a repository of a fundamental doctrine, interventions to create imaginary genealogy and derive fundamental doctrines

---

[3] For a critical review of the literature on international law-making, see J. d'Aspremont, 'Cognitive conflicts and the making of international law: from empirical concord to conceptual discord in legal scholarship' (2009) 46 *Vanderbilt Journal of Transnational Law* 1119.

[4] It is well known that for Carl Schmitt the making of concepts such as sovereignty and community originated in a genesis that witnessed an arbitrary intervention *ex nihilo*. See Carl Schmitt, *Political Theology: Four Chapters on the Concept of Sovereignty*, trans. George Schwab (Chicago: University of Chicago Press, 1985), p. 38.

[5] This is what differentiates the account here from the occasional, sparse, rare and unsystematic recognitions of the role of a multitude of actors in the formation of international lawyers' modes of legal reasoning that are witnessed in the international legal literature. See e.g. Olivier Corten, *Le Discours du Droit International: Pour un Positivisme Critique* (Paris: Pedone, 2009), pp. 153–76, esp. 176 ('L'image d'un ordre juridique unifié et pacificateur est en effet mieux assure si l'on évoque une codification des règles existantes que si l'on admet qu'un texte prétendumment codificateur n'est en réalité que le fruit d'une volonté de son ou de ses auteurs.' '[L]a codification offer un moyens à certains acteurs politiques de faire prévaloir leurs positions en le parant des vertus du droit et de l'universalité.'). On the idea that sources are complicit in obfuscating the work of international courts, see Ingo Venzke, 'The role of international courts as interpreters and developers of the law: working out the jurisgenerative practice of interpretation' (2011) 34 *Loyola of Los Angeles International and Comparative Law Review* 99; see also Lianne Boer, 'The greater part of "jurisconsults": on consensus claims and their footnotes in legal scholarship' (2016) 29 *Leiden Journal of International Law* 1021. See also R. Ago, 'Le délit international' (1938) 68 *Collected Courses of the Hague Academy on International Law* 420; Alejandro Alvarez, *Le Continent Américain et la Codification du Droit International Law: Une Nouvelle 'Ecole' du Droit des Gens* (Paris: Pedone, 1938), pp. 52–53. It is sometimes acknowledged that the first organised packages of modes of legal reasoning were the product of philosophical reflections and not the product of rules. See Manfred Lachs, *Le Monde la Pensée en Droit International* (Paris: Economica, 1989) (French translation, Manfred Lachs, *The Teacher in International Law: Teachings and Teaching*), p. 7. On the variety of actors engaged in axiomisation in systematisation of modes of legal reasoning, see also Michel van de Kerchove and François Ost, *Legal System between Order and Disorder*, trans. Iian Stewart (Oxord: Clarendon Press, 1995), pp. 84, 89–90.

from international instruments and interventions to adjust or improve existing modes of legal reasoning.

Although the exercise could prove extremely valuable, it would be of no use here to seek to trace the causal relationships between each of the specific modes of legal reasoning that are organised by the fundamental doctrines examined in previous chapters and the interventions that have shaped them.[6] It is more important to stress that the account of the formation of fundamental doctrines produced by a suspension of the belief system envisaged here also brings about a radical *sequential* rupture from sources-based self-referentiality. Indeed, the whole process of fundamental doctrine formation is actually reversed, and the design of modes of legal reasoning can no longer be construed as a top-down process by which some modes of legal reasoning are derived from an international instrument. Nor can it be understood as a state-centric law-making process. Instead, the formation of fundamental doctrines must be construed as a bottom-up process by which modes of legal reasoning are organised into axiomatic packages that are genealogically linked with an international instrument that is meant to be their repository and from which they are supposedly derived.[7] Said differently, the making of fundamental doctrines thus can no longer be seen as a question of law-making but rather as a process of inventing tradition.[8] The suspension of sources-based self-referentiality simultaneously results in a discontinuation of the – often overblown – idea of state-centricism in the making of fundamental doctrines.

It is important to highlight that the result of this sequential rupture provoked by the unlearning of sources is not only descriptive. It also bears on international lawyers' evaluative enterprises. In fact, this reversal of the sequence makes it more obvious that

---

[6] For an illustration of such an exercise, see David Kennedy, 'Primitive legal scholarship' (1986) 27 *Harvard International Law Journal* 1. See also some of the observations made by Manfred Lachs, *Le Monde la Pensée en Droit International* (Paris: Economica, 1989) (French translation, Manfred Lachs, *The Teacher in International Law: Teachings and Teaching*).

[7] There are some interesting parallels with biblical gospels. See Regis Debray, *Transmitting Culture*, trans. Eric Rauth (New York: Columbia University Press, 1997), p. 20 ('The holy speech of Jesus did not come first, only to be gathered and set down by apostle-mediators subsequently and then finally broadcast on all fronts (omnes gentes) by members of the priestly body serving as mere relays').

[8] On the notion of invention of tradition, see Eric Hobsbawn, 'Introduction: inventing traditions', in E. Hobsbawn and T. Ranger (eds.), *The Invention of Tradition* (Cambridge: Cambridge University Press, 1983), pp. 1–14.

the decisive site of struggle where actors fight to determine the modes of legal reasoning of international legal discourse[9] cannot be reduced to the arena where the repositories of fundamental doctrines are promulgated and adopted. Instead, the decisive sites of struggle become those where the modes of legal reasoning and the axiomisation thereof are actually debated and produced, as well as the sites where repositories for fundamental doctrines are chosen and the imaginary genealogy created. The sites of struggle warranting the attention of international lawyers thus change once the belief system has been suspended.

It must be acknowledged that this account of the interventions punctuating the formation of the fundamental doctrines draws on a wide and pluralistic conception of actors who can potentially intervene in international legal discourse[10] and shape fundamental

---

[9] On the pursuit of collective interest as one of the drivers in such struggles even in situations of private codification, see Nils Jansen, *The Making of Legal Authority: Non-legislative Codifications in Historical and Comparative Perspective* (Oxford: Oxford University Press, 2010), p. 7. On the various agendas pursued by some of the key fundamental doctrines of international law, see Jean d'Aspremont, *Epistemic Forces in International Law: Foundational Doctrines and Techniques of International Legal Argumentation* (London: Elgar, 2015).

[10] For the sake of the interventions discussed here, the notion of international legal discourse remains widely defined. For instance, international legal discourse is not restricted to judicial processes (see e.g. Fredrich V. Kratochwil, *Rules, Norms, and Decisions: On the Conditions of Practical and Legal Reasoning in International Relations and Domestic Affairs* (Cambridge: Cambridge University Press, 1989), p. 209) ('judicial decision-making is only one part of rule-handing and of "lawyering"'). See also James Crawford and Martti Koskenniemi, 'Introduction', in J. Crawford and M. Koskenniemi (eds.), *Cambridge Companion to International Law* (Cambridge: Cambridge University Press, 2012), p. 1. See also Yasuaki Onuma, *Le Droit International et le Japon: Une Vision Trans-Civilisationnelle du Monde* (Paris: Pedone, 2016), pp. 120–23. Likewise, international legal discourse is construed as being dependent on at least one of the stakeholders being a legal official of some sort (See Pierre Bourdieu, 'The force of law: toward a sociology of the juridical field' (1987) 38 *Hastings Law Journal* 805 at 843 ('The power of law is special. It extends beyond the circle of those who are already believers')). Instead, a huge variety of actors acting a wide range of capacities can potentially produce and participate in international legal discourse. This should suffice to make clear that for the understanding of international legal discourse adopted here, the category of legal officials – developed in British analytical jurisprudence – is unhelpful to apprehend what is at work in the making of international legal arguments. In the same vein, see Mario Prost, *The Concept of Unity in Public International Law* (Oxford: Hart, 2012), p. 128. See also J. d'Aspremont, *Formalism and the Sources of International Law* (Oxford: Oxford University Press, 2011), chap. 8. Even in analytical jurisprudence, the notion has been very much criticised. See e.g. K. Culver and M. Giudice, *Legality's Borders: An Essay in General Jurisprudence* (Oxford: Oxford University Press, 2010), esp. pp. 8–14. See also

doctrines.[11] Indeed, interventions are construed here as being conducted by any actor who is sufficiently socialised[12] as an international lawyer and who is sufficiently well versed in the modes of legal reasoning recognised and practised by international legal professionals.[13] In this sense, the mastery of some of the currently accepted fundamental doctrines conditions the possibility of intervening in the formation of new fundamental doctrines or in the refinement and adjustment of current fundamental doctrines. This also means that the potential to intervene in the formation of fundamental doctrines or their adjustment is restricted and depends on a certain degree of socialisation of actors as international lawyers. Yet, being socialised as an international lawyer does not suffice to actually affect the design of the modes of legal reasoning of fundamental doctrines or their axiomisation. Certain other institutional and social parameters – which

---

B. Tamanaha, *A General Jurisprudence of Law and Society* (Oxford: Oxford University Press, 2001), p. 142.

[11] It is not denied that such an understanding of international legal discourse comes with constructivist overtones. See, generally, N. Onuf, *World of Our Making: Rules and Rules in Social Theory and International Relations* (Columbia: University of South Carolina Press, 1989); N. Onuf, 'The constitution of international society' (1994) 5 *European Journal of International Law* 1 at 6; N. Onuf, 'Do rules say what they do? From ordinary language to international law' (1985) 26 *Harvard Journal of International Law* 385; J. Brunnée and S. J. Toope, 'International law and constructivism: elements of an international theory of international law' (2000–1) 39 *Columbia Journal of Transnational Law* 19. On the great variety of strands in constructivism and their possible contribution to international legal theory, see F. Dos Reis and Oliver Kessler, 'Constructivism and the politics of international law', in A. Orford and F. Hoffmann (eds.), *The Oxford Handbook of the Theory of International Law* (Oxford: Oxford University Press, 2016), pp. 345–64.

[12] On this notion, see J. d'Aspremont, *Epistemic Forces in International Law: Foundational Doctrines and Techniques of International Legal Argumentation* (London: Elgar, 2015), pp. 9–22.

[13] Fredrich V. Kratochwil, *Rules, Norms, and Decisions: On the Conditions of Practical and LegalRreasoning in International Relations and Domestic Affairs* (Cambridge: Cambridge University Press, 1989), p. 11 ('not only must an actor refer to rules and norms when he/she wants to make a choice, but the observer, as well, must understand the normative structure underlying the action in order to interpret and appraise choices. Norms are therefore not only "guidance devices" but also the means which allow people to pursue goals, share meanings, communicate with each other, criticize assertions, and justify actions'). On the constitutive role of international legal arguments, see Christian Reus-Smit, 'Introduction', in Christian Reus-Smit (ed.), *The Politics of International Law* (Cambridge: Cambridge University Press, 2004), p. 5. In this respect, it is a truism to say that descriptive frameworks are performative because they allow the construction of certain realities. See Alasdair McIntyre, *Whose Justice? Which Rationality?* (Notre Dame, IN: Notre Dame University Press, 1988), p. 333.

have been called 'capital'[14] – bear upon the capacity to intervene in the formation of fundamental doctrines.[15] The same holds for the changes of fundamental doctrines.

It is equally relevant to highlight here that even if the design of fundamental doctrines is carefully orchestrated and engineered, as was discussed in relation to the doctrine of responsibility,[16] the numerous interventions that are revealed by a suspension of the belief system do not follow any systemic or linear pattern and often unfold in a rather chaotic fashion. For instance, the interventions to choose an international instrument and make it the repository of a fundamental doctrine – as was illustrated in relation to the doctrine of statehood and the doctrine of customary international law[17] – may not be simultaneous to interventions aimed at designing the modes of legal reasoning of the fundamental doctrine concerned.[18]

This non-systematic nature of the articulation of the various interventions in the formation of fundamental doctrines is not exclusive to interventions in the formation of fundamental doctrines that are informed by certain strong power structures, overarching agendas and hierarchies. In this respect, it should be made clear that interventions in the formation of fundamental doctrines constitute huge exercises of power that are not devoid of hegemony because they seek to universalise

---

[14] On the notion of capital, see P. Bourdieu, 'The forms of capital', in J. Richardson (ed.) *Handbook of Theory and Research for the Sociology of Education* (New York, Greenwood, 2001), pp. 241–58. On this notion, see, generally, Rob Moore, 'Capital', in Michael Grenfell (ed.), *Pierre Bourdieu: Key Concepts*, 2nd edn (London: Routledge, 2012), pp. 98–113.

[15] This does not mean, however, that interventions are reserved to state officials or legal officials. The departure from the idea that only state or legal officials can contribute to the design of fundamental doctrines constitutes one of the main claims of my earlier work, *Formalism and the Sources of International Law* (Oxford: Oxford University Press, 2011), esp. chap. 8. See also J. d'Aspremont, 'Non-state actors and the social practice of international law', in Math Noortmann, August Reinisch and Cedric Ryngaert (eds.), *Non-State Actors in International Law* (Oxford: Hart, 2015), pp. 11–31.

[16] See Chapter 4, Section 3.

[17] See Chapter 4, Sections 2 and 3. It happens that the intervention to design the modes of legal reasoning is more or less simultaneous with the intervention to elect the formal repository and universalise the doctrine concerned, as exemplified by the doctrine of responsibility examined earlier. On the doctrine of responsibility, see Chapter 4, Section 1.

[18] For a further illustration in relation to the doctrine of interpretation, see Fuad Zarbiyev, *Le Discours Interprétatif en Droit International Contemporain: Un Essai Critique* (Brussels: Bruylant, 2015), pp. 129–59.

specific modes of legal reasoning.[19] Some of these exercises of power are surely problematic.[20] Some of them could even be seen as acts of 'violence'[21] that are forgotten by virtue of sources-based self-referentiality.[22] In the same vein, such interventions may take place against a backdrop of some extensive form of 'complicity'[23] among all those who partake in international legal discourse. These dimensions of interventions in the formation of fundamental doctrines have been the object of occasional sociological studies.[24] Although much remains to be said about the

---

[19]   See, generally, E. Laclau, Emancipation(s) (London: Verso, 2007).

[20]   They could even be construed as pursing and serving the imperialism of international law. See, generally, China Miéville, *Between Equal Rights: A Marxist Theory of International Law* (London: Pluto Press, 2005). See also Antony Anghie, *Imperialism, Sovereignty and the Making of International Law* (Cambridge: Cambridge University Press, 2004).

[21]   Derrida famously understands law as being mystical by reference to 'a silence walled up in the violent structure of the founding acts'. He adds: 'the founding or grounding, the positing of the law cannot by definition rest on anything but themselves, they are themselves a violence without ground.' See J. Derrida, 'Force of law: the "mystical foundation of authority"', in Gil Anidjar (ed.), *Acts of Religion: Jacques Derrida* (London: Routledge, 2002), p. 242; Pierre Bourdieu sees a form of violence in the formalism of law. For him, to submit to the power of form is to submit to 'the symbolic violence'. China Miéville, *Between Equal Rights: A Marxist Theory of International Law* (London : Pluto Press, 2005), p. 286; Antony Anghie, *Imperialism, Sovereignty and the Making of International Law* (Cambridge: Cambridge University Press, 2004), p. 6. See also P. Schlag, *Laying Down the Law* (New York: New York University Press, 1996), p. 147. Cf. the notion of symbolic violence developed by Bourdieu. See P. Bourdieu and L. Wacquant, *An Invitation to Reflexive Sociology* (Chicago : University of Chicago Press, 1992), p. 15. See Pierre Bourdieu, 'The force of law: toward a sociology of the juridical field' (1987) 38 *Hastings Law Journal* 805 at 850. See the remarks of J. D. Schubert, 'Suffering/symbolic violence', in Michael Grenfell (ed.), *Pierre Bourdieu: Key Concepts*, 2nd edn (London : Routledge, 2012), pp. 179–94.

[22]   Pierre Schlag writes: 'For all those who are legally trained, the violence of law is extremely difficult to recall. It is difficult to recall because even where it emerges it does so in a legitimated form. The violence of law emerges everywhere under the guise of the already authorized or under the guise of the necessarily justified' (P. Schlag, *Laying Down the Law* (New York: New York University Press, 1996), p. 146).

[23]   See Pierre Bourdieu, 'The force of law: toward a sociology of the juridical field' (1987) 38 *Hastings Law Journal* 805 at 844. See also Michel Foucault, *Surveiller et Punir* (Gallimard, 1975) p. 35.

[24]   See e.g. Yves Dezalay, *Lawyers and the Rule of Law in an Era of Globalization* (London: Routledge, 2011). See also Y. Dezalay, *Marchands de droit: La restructuration de l'ordre juridique international par les multinationales du droit* (Paris: Fayard, 1992); or Yves Dezalay and Bryant Garth 'Merchants of law as moral entrepreneurs: constructing international justice from the competition for transnational business disputes' (1995) 29 *Law and Society Review* 27. For an introduction to sociological approaches to international law, see Moshe Hirsch, *Invitation to the Sociology of International Law* (Oxford: Oxford University Press, 2015).

sociological aspects of the structures of the interventions that shape the fundamental doctrines of international law, this chapter is not the place to inquire into this aspect of the formation of fundamental doctrines any further.[25]

Two additional observations are necessary to theorise the notion of intervention in the formation of fundamental doctrines as it is revealed by the unlearning exercise envisaged here. First, it must be acknowledged that the distinction between the notion of intervention and sources will appear rather thin for those who embrace a rather loose understanding of the notion of sources of law. For instance, from a traditional common-law perspective, sources could be understood in a much broader sense as to include judicial interventions or other behaviours that influence norm setting.[26] The same holds if one takes the informal approach of norm-setting centred on participation like the one advocated by the New Haven School of International Law.[27] The discussion conducted here, however, embraces neither a broad or a loose understanding of sources that would include such intervention nor the deformalisation promoted by the New Haven School.[28] As far as the latter is concerned, it should be added that although the suspension of belief envisaged here sets aside the explanatory value of the sources of international law for the formation of fundamental doctrines, it neither does away with the sources as an organised cluster of modes of legal reasoning nor shares the agenda of the deformalisation vindicated by the New Haven School.[29]

Second, it should be stressed that the suspension of the belief system advocated here and the focus on interventions cannot be reduced to a new theory of judicial law-making, of *stare decisis* or of path-dependency.[30] It is

---

[25] As indicated earlier, such a posture should not be construed as any form of complacency. See also Chapter 1, Section 3.

[26] This is a remark I owe to an exchange with Gareth Davies.

[27] See, generally, Harold D. Lasswell and Myres S. McDougal, *Jurisprudence for a Free Society* (The Hague: Martinus Nijhoff, 1992). See also M. W. Reisman, S. Wiessner and A. R. Willard, 'The New Haven School: a brief introduction' (2007) 32 *Yale Journal of International Law* 575.

[28] On the various types of deformalisation of the identification of legal rules, see Jean d'Aspremont, 'The politics of deformalization in international law' (2011) 3 *Goettingen Journal of International Law* 503.

[29] In particular, this discussion falls short of any reformist agenda and does not seek to determine the consequences of the unlearning advocated here, which constitutes a fundamental difference with the approach articulated by the New Haven School. See Chapter 6. This is a remark I owe to exchanges with John Haskell.

[30] See e.g. O. A. Hathaway, 'Path dependence in the law: the course and pattern of legal change in a common law system' (2001) 86 *Iowa Law Review* 101. This is a remark I owe

true that many of the interventions that punctuate the design of fundamental doctrines of international law could be understood as 'precedents'
that, after some chaotic encounters, eventually coalesce into a set of modes
of legal reasoning organised within a fundamental doctrine. Yet this does
not mean that the unlearning and the focus on interventions promoted
here bear any resemblance to theories of judicial law-making, *stare decisis*
or path-dependency commonly developed in relation to common-law
legal systems. In fact, as was indicated earlier, the interventions discussed
here are not necessarily of a judicial nature. Judicial interventions only
constitute a fraction of the interventions at work in the formation and
functioning of the fundamental doctrines of international law. Moreover,
the actual causal relationships and continuity between the various interventions that punctuate the design of the fundamental doctrines of international law and the specific modes of legal reasoning that are
encapsulated and organised in each of them fall outside the inquiry carried
out here.[31]

The foregoing has provided an overview of what the formation of
fundamental doctrines may come to look like after a rupture with
sources-based self-referentiality. Section 2 turns to the consequences of
such a separation from interpretation-based self-referentiality, that is, an
explanation of the functioning of fundamental doctrines by the fundamental doctrine of interpretation.

2   Unlearning Interpretation-Based Self-Referentiality

In the international belief system, as discussed in Chapters 2 and 3,
the functioning of fundamental doctrines, and thus the way in
which they are interpreted and applied by international lawyers,
is explained through one specific fundamental doctrine, namely,
the fundamental doctrine of interpretation. The doctrine of interpretation also governs the inevitable dynamism of fundamental
doctrines that are constantly adjusted and re-invented when they
are applied by international lawyers. In this way, the functioning of
fundamental doctrines is made the object of the fundamental doctrine of interpretation. I submit that a suspension of the belief

to an exchange with Jean Galbraith; R. A. Posner, 'Path-dependency, pragmatism, and a
critique of history in adjudication and legal scholarship' (2000) 67 *University of Chicago
Law Review* 573; S. J. Liebowitz and Stephen E. Margolis, 'Path-dependence, lock-in, and
history' (1995) 11 *Journal of Law, Economics, and Organization* 205.

[31] For some additional observations on this caveat, see Chapter 1, Section 4.

system at the level of the functioning of fundamental doctrines and thus a separation from interpretation-based self-referentiality produce an account of the functioning of fundamental doctrines that similarly puts the emphasis on a series of interventions by a multiplicity of actors that are similarly obfuscated by the belief system. Interventions at the level of the functioning of fundamental doctrines generally can be theorised in the same way as interventions that contribute to the formation of those doctrines.[32] For this reason, it is not necessary to iterate here how such interventions ought to be conceptualised and theorised. It is more relevant to outline some of the characteristics of those interventions that take place at the level of the functioning of fundamental doctrines and that distinguish them from the interventions witnessed at the level of the formation of the fundamental doctrines.

One aspect of these interventions in the functioning of fundamental doctrines is the fact that they generally *continue* the interventions witnessed in the formation of the fundamental doctrines. There often is an element of continuity between interventions in the formation of fundamental doctrines and interventions in the functioning of fundamental doctrines. Indeed, based on the unlearning of self-referentiality promoted here, the interventions that have been witnessed in the formation of modes of legal reasoning continue even after the fundamental doctrine has been nested in an international instrument and universalised.[33] This means, for instance, that the modes of legal reasoning of fundamental doctrines, after they have been axiomised and packaged in a fundamental doctrine (as well as derived from an international instrument), remain the object of new interventions to be maintained, preserved, streamlined and improved by a great variety of the actors involved in international legal discourse.[34] It may also happen that a fundamental doctrine fails to produce the efficient modes

---

[32] See Section 1.

[33] Here, too, there are some interesting parallels with biblical gospels. See Regis Debray, *Transmitting Culture*, trans. Eric Rauth (New York: Columbia University Press, 1997), p. 20 ('Holy writ is produced by particular communities making use of its as needed in order to communify. Hence, in the case of both Christianity and Islam, the belated character of their sacred scripture: following their faith, interpreters still found licence, for several centuries, to reinvent after their own fashion the revealed religious texts they claimed only to be quoting verbatim').

[34] See also the parallels with Ronald Dworkin's idea of the chain novel. See R. Dworkin, *Law's Empire* (London: Belknap Press, 1986), pp. 228–32.

of legal reasoning originally hoped for,[35] as illustrated by the current scholarship on customary international law.[36] In this case, the interventions in the formation of the doctrine are commonly followed by interventions aimed at salvaging or improving the malfunctioning axioms of legal reasoning of the fundamental doctrine concerned. It is important to note that because all such subsequent interventions usually follow the very axioms put in place by the fundamental doctrines, they reinforce those doctrines.[37] Even interventions meant to contest or reform fundamental doctrines, provided they use the same axiomisation of the modes of legal reasoning prescribed by the doctrine, help to buttress the doctrine concerned.[38]

Irrespective of this continuity between interventions in the formation and interventions in the functioning of fundamental doctrines, it is of great relevance to highlight that the interventions observed at the level of the functioning of fundamental doctrines are generally conducted by a multiplicity of actors who are not necessarily the same as those who intervened in the formation of fundamental doctrines.[39] This is so not only because such interventions may take place with intervals of several decades but also because the impact of the actors varies depending on what aspect of the functioning of fundamental doctrines they aimed to change.[40] A good example of this is provided by interventions in the

---

[35] On moments of self-reflectivity and the realisation by lawyers that their modes of legal reasoning do not lead anywhere, see Pierre Schlag, 'Normativity and the politics of form' (1991) 139 *University of Pennsylvania law Review* 801 at 930–31.

[36] This is a point that I have expounded on in J. d'Aspremont, 'The decay of modern customary international law in spite of scholarly heroism', in G. Capaldo (ed.), *Global Community: Yearbook of International Law and Jurisprudence* (Oxford: Oxford University Press, 2015).

[37] These interventions continue to fall within what A. McIntyre has called the 'tradition' and do not bring about any revolutionary change in the 'tradition'. See A. McIntyre, *Whose Justice? Which Rationality?* (London: Duckworthy, 1988), pp. 355–64.

[38] *Ibid.*, p. 364. See also M. Koskenniemi, 'International legal theory and doctrines', in *Max Planck Encyclopedia of Public International Law*, para. 33.

[39] As noted by Bianchi in relation to myths, once these actors' interventions materialise and generate authoritative doctrines, they may come to constrain the power of those from which they emanate. See Andrea Bianchi, 'Human rights and the magic of jus cogens' (2008) 19 *European Journal of International Law* 491 at 507.

[40] These variations are obviously contingent on social, institutional and personal parameters. For some remarks on these variations between interventions in the functioning of fundamental doctrines, see J. d'Aspremont, 'Wording in international law' (2012) 25 *Leiden Journal of International Law* 575; see also J. d'Aspremont, 'Non-state actors and the social practice of international law', in A. Reinisch, M. Noortmann and C. Ryngaert (eds.), *Non-State Actors in International Law* (Oxford: Hart, 2015), pp. 11–31. See also J. d'Aspremont, *Epistemic Forces in International Law* (London: Elgar, 2015), pp. 15–27.

functioning of the fundamental doctrines of statehood and customary law discussed previously.[41]

This discussion of the consequences of a rupture with interpretation-based self-referentiality and the emphasis on interventions rather than interpretation *stricto sensu* does not mean, however, that interpretation is totally absent from the account produced here of the functioning of fundamental doctrines. Actually, the interventions revealed by the unlearning exercise attempted here are all of an interpretive and performative nature.[42] In this sense, unlearning interpretation-based self-referentiality is not a denial of the phenomenon of interpretation.[43] The separation from interpretation-based self-referentiality entails a departure from interpretation in two specific regards only. First, it is a rejection of the idea that interpretive interventions at work in the functioning of the fundamental doctrine amounts to an interpretative process, as envisaged and governed by the fundamental doctrine of interpretation. Second, and more fundamentally, it is a repudiation of the idea that what is being interpreted when fundamental doctrines are applied and adjusted are the instruments where those fundamental doctrines are nested. The point is that international lawyers, when applying and adjusting fundamental doctrines, are not interpreting the international instruments from which they commonly derive the fundamental doctrines by virtue of imaginary genealogy. They exercise their interpretive craft in relation to the fundamental doctrine itself – and thus in relation to the content of the modes of legal reasoning they put in place – independently of the formal repository where the fundamental doctrine is located by virtue of imaginative genealogy.[44]

---

[41] See Chapter 4, Sections 2 and 3.

[42] This is a point I owe to a remark made by Emilyn Winkelmeyer. In that sense, unlearning interpretation-based self-referentiality is meant to acknowledge the creative, constitutive and performative character of interpretation. The image of an international belief system, albeit through a different route, thus produces similar findings as those made by Ingo Venzke in *How Interpretation Makes International Law: On Semantic Change and Normative Twists* (Oxford: Oxford University Press, 2012).

[43] As Pierre Schlag has argued, lawyers are constantly called upon to choose between interpretations, even at the level of their modes of legal reasoning. This is why, he explains, lawyers are not free. See Pierre Schlag, 'Normativity and the politics of form' (1991) 139 *University of Pennsylvania Law Review* 801 at 807.

[44] On the idea that the tradition is constantly interpreted and changed, see A. McIntyre, *Whose Justice? Which Rationality?* (London: Duckworth, 1988), pp. 359–65.

6

Epilogue

The chapters in this book have projected an image of international law that bears the characteristics of a belief system and by virtue of which international lawyers come to experience a sense of constraint towards fundamental doctrines such as sources, interpretation, responsibility, *jus cogens* and statehood. It was specifically argued that the experience of a sense of constraint towards fundamental doctrines is possible by virtue of ruleness (i.e. representation of a fundamental doctrine as rules) and imaginary genealogy (i.e. a fictive history allowing the derivation of fundamental doctrines from certain formal repositories), which, in turn, enable self-referentiality, that is, the explanation of the formation and functioning of fundamental doctrines in their own terms. So construed, this belief system constitutes a liberal pattern of legal thought inherited from the Enlightenment. After projecting such an image of international law and of its fundamental doctrines, Chapter 5 invited international lawyers to temporarily suspend the belief system at work in the common understanding of the formation and functioning of fundamental doctrines. It was argued that this suspension of the belief system requires the unlearning of the explanation of fundamental doctrines in their own terms and thus a rupture with the self-referentiality on which the international belief system is built. Such a separation from self-referentiality means that one must stop thinking about the formation and functioning of the fundamental doctrines in terms of sources or interpretation. This also includes a move away from the ideas of 'rules' or 'secondary rules' and 'state-centricism' in international lawyers' representations of the fundamental doctrines of international law. Only such a rupture with self-referentiality will allow one to falsify the transcendental character of the fundamental doctrines to which international lawyers turn to generate truth, meaning or sense in international legal discourse and secure a better capture of the multiple interventions, political choices and sites of struggles that shape modes of legal reasoning around which international legal discourse is articulated. This rupture also helps to do away with the common account of the history of the fundamental doctrines whose making can no longer be construed as following a linear and directional path punctuated by the adoption of certain key defining international instruments such as the Statute of the International Court of Justice, the Vienna Convention on the Law of Treaties or the Articles on State Responsibility.

It has been made clear that the discussion carried out in this book never aspired to provide an accurate depiction of the inner operation of international legal discourse. The modest ambition rather has been to make international lawyers sensitive to an image of what they are potentially thinking when they deploy the modes of legal reasoning prescribed by the fundamental doctrines of international law they are trained to apply. In this sense, this book has aimed primarily at providing new reflexive tools to professionals of international law with a view to allowing them to liberate themselves, albeit temporarily, from inherited patterns of legal thought they have been trained to reproduce and respond to.[1]

It must be acknowledged that engaging with the image of international law as a belief system is not a naive and purely formative, reflective exercise.[2] The consequences of such an undertaking can be potentially devastating.[3] These consequences range from rehabilitating the intolerable to encouraging heresy. Yet, because this book does not want its main claims to be held hostage to their consequences,[4] these final observations do not seek to prejudge or control what international lawyers make of the discussion contained in the preceding chapters. Thus the exercise conducted here is consciously stripped of any attempt to reconstruct international law in a certain way after the belief system

---

[1] Cf. the ambitions of Andrea Bianchi, *International Law Theories: An Inquiry into Different Ways of Thinking* (Oxford: Oxford University Press, 2016), pp. 16–20.

[2] As Martti Koskenniemi puts it, naiveté is anything but innocent. See M. Koskenniemi, 'The politics of international law: 20 years later' (2009) 20 *European Journal of International Law* 7.

[3] On the impact of theory, see the remarks of Andrea Bianchi, *International Law Theories: An Inquiry into Different Ways of Thinking* (Oxford: Oxford University Press, 2016), pp. 8–9.

[4] For a similar position, see Paul W. Kahn, *The Cultural Study of Law: Reconstructing Legal Scholarship* (Chicago, University of Chicago Press, 1999), p. 3 ('the intellectual project of understanding a culture of law should not be held hostage to the question of its practical consequence').

has been suspended.[5] While such a reflection probably will be continued elsewhere, it has been decided here to leave it to international
lawyers engaging with the image of international law as a belief system
and the suspension thereof to determine what they make of it, at least
for now.

Inevitably, the above-mentioned consequentialist agnosticism – that
is, the choice to abstain from controlling the consequences of the suspension of the international belief system – comes with a 'risk' – the risk that
the suspension of the international belief system and the drawing of
attention to the interventions obfuscated by self-referentiality result in
a consolidation of current power structures and forms of violence,[6]
thereby rehabilitating the inequalities consolidated and brought about
by contemporary international legal discourse.[7] Although this is unde-
niably among the possible consequences of the image of international law
projected here, this complacency is thwarted by the reformist potential
that simultaneously accompanies the suspension of the belief system, as
suggested here.[8] I submit that projecting an image of international law as
a belief system and immediately calling for its suspension come with an
unprecedented empowerment of reformers.[9] In fact, capturing and suspending the international belief system at work in the common understanding of the formation and functioning of fundamental doctrines of
international law provide not only a toolbox for reflection but also an

[5] This will probably be held against this book. The absence of account for change (an
account for change or failure to account for change?) is a criticism made by Ingo
Venzke towards David Kennedy's *A World of Struggle: How Power, Law, and Expertise
Shape Global Political Economy* (Princeton, NJ: Princeton University Press, 2016). See
Ingo Venzke, 'Cracking the frame? On the prospects of change in a world of struggle'
(2016) 27 *European Journal of International Law* 831.
[6] On the notion of symbolic violence, see P. Bourdieu and L. Wacquant, *An Invitation to
Reflexive Sociology* (Chicago: University of Chicago Press, 1992), p. 15. See the remarks of
J. D. Schubert, 'Suffering/symbolic violence', in Michael Grenfell (ed.), *Pierre Bourdieu:
Key Concepts*, 2nd edn (London: Routledge, 2012), pp. 179–94.
[7] This is a remark I owe to an exchange with Mikhail Xifaras. See also China Miéville,
Between Equal Rights: A Marxist Theory of International Law (London: Pluto Press, 2005),
esp. p. 318 ('To fundamentally change the dynamics of the system, it would be necessary
not to reform the institutions but to eradicate the forms of law – which means the
fundamental reformulation of the political-economic system of which they are the expressions. The project to achieve this is the best hope for global emancipation, and it would
mean the end of the law').
[8] Cf. Roberto Unger, *What Should Legal Analysis Become* (New York: Verso, 1996).
[9] Cf. Chantal Mouffe, *The Return of the Political* (New York: Verso, 1993), p. 140 ('To negate
the political does not make it disappear, it only leads to bewilderment in the face of its
manifestations and to impotence in dealing with them').

improved capacity of all professionals to situate themselves and their discourse, thereby reinforcing their capacity for political action.[10] In particular, it is only once they step outside sources- and interpretation-based self-referentiality that they maximise their capacity to reform through sources and interpretation as well as their chances of success. Likewise, the unlearning exercise proposed here also provides incentives for reform, for what has been unlearnt needs to be reinvented.[11] Indeed, outside self-referentiality, international lawyers find themselves in the unknown, and international law must be re-imagined. Unlearning vindicates reform and re-imagination.

Facilitating reform and empowering reformers are no trifling consequences of the exercise conducted here.[12] Nonetheless, this book, in line with it self-declared consequentalist agnosticism, does not go as far as offering a programme for reform, whether it is in terms of argumentative operativeness, legitimacy or distributive justice.[13] In this sense, this book

[10] See, generally, E. Laclau, *Emancipation(s)* (London: Verso, 2007), p. 27 ('It is a very well-known historical fact that an oppositionist force whose identity is constructed within a certain system of power is ambiguous vis-à-vis that system, because the latter is what prevents the construction of the identity and it is, at the same time, its condition of existence. And any victory against the system also destabilizes the identity of the victorious force'). See also Ingo Venzke, 'Cracking the frame? On the prospects of change in a world of struggle' (2016) 27 *European Journal of International Law* 831, at 846–47 (citing Menke, he writes: 'Entirely unsituated, the subject is not capable of political action'). In the same vein, Susan Marks, 'International judicial activism and the commodity-form theory of international law' (2007) 18 *European Journal of International Law* 199, at 202.

[11] As far as religious studies are concerned, the 1835 work of David Friedrich Strauss provides a good an illustration of the facilitation of re-invention through self-imposed unlearning process. Indeed, by exposing the baselessness of the supposed knowledge of the gospel history, he contributed to the rise of a new scholarly discipline alien to religious activities themselves. See David Friedrich Strauss, *The Life of Jesus Critically Examined*, trans. George Eliot, 4th edn (London [1835]).

[12] Cf. Bourdieusian sociology that does not change the world but encourages becoming aware of symbolic violence, domination and inequalities and therefore makes reconstructions possible. See P. Bourdieu, *In Other Words: Essays Towards a Reflexive Sociology* (Redwood City, CA: Stanford University Press, 1992). See the remarks of J. D. Schubert, 'Suffering/symbolic violence', in Michael Grenfell (ed.), *Pierre Bourdieu: Key Concepts*, 2nd edn (London: Routledge, 2012), p. 192.

[13] Cf. Paul Kahn, *The Cultural Study of Law: Reconstructing Legal Scholarship* (Chicago: University of Chicago Press, 1999), p. 30. See also J. von Bernstorff, 'International legal scholarship as a cooling medium in international law and politics' (2014) 25 *European Journal of International Law* 977; P. Schlag, 'Normative and nowhere to go' (1990) 43 *Stanford Law Review* 167 at 176, n. 23 ('The Thumper school of jurisprudence, like virtually all other jurisprudential schools, has taken a rather decisive instrumentalist turn lately. Accordingly, in the legal academy, Thumper's transcendental value in niceness has been transformed into the more instrumentalist value in being "constructive."

comes with no transformative urge.[14] This is an ambition that is left for later and for others. Such a choice shows, once again, that the discussion conducted here radically departs from existing scholarly enterprises that have similarly sought to shed light on the interventions at work in international legal discourse.[15] This does not mean, however, that future reformist ventures that would be informed by an unlearning exercise similar to the one advocated here can afford to remain silent on their rationale and agenda in terms of operativeness, legitimacy and distributive justice. Even after suspending the belief system informing the fundamental doctrines of international law, any would-be reformer is bound to provide the guarantee that a limping self-referential belief system is not simply replaced by a disaster.[16] In that sense, reform should never be idealised.

While abstaining from dictating what international lawyers should make of the claims articulated in this book, especially in terms of reform, these concluding remarks nonetheless warn against one potential use of

Thus, it is widely held among legal thinkers that one should not merely criticise or destroy, but try to be constructive as well. I find this sort of position perplexing – even on modernist terms. Consider a graphic example: If you take someone's neurosis away, are you being destructive (of that person's way of doing things) or are you being constructive (of a new organically healthy person)? If you were being destructive when you took away the person's neurosis, are you then obliged to do something more afterwards – something constructive? What would this additional constructive moment look like, and how would it help? Indeed, how often does a "cured" patient terminate therapy with the statement, "Yes, I understand I'm fine now. There's just one more question, doctor: What should I do?" But consider this instead: Just what is it that the academic routine is telling us when it advises legal thinkers to prescribe solutions? What is this – law and pharmacy? Are latent Langdellian science metaphors still channelling our thoughts? Should the AALS investigate? Should normative legal thought be registered under the Controlled Substances Act, 21 U.S.C. § § 801–904 (1982 & Supp. 1987)?'). This reference was suggested to me by Akbar Rasulov.

[14] The expression is from M. Koskenniemi, 'The politics of international law: 20 years later' (2009) 20 *European Journal of International Law* 7, at 15.

[15] In this respect, this book fundamentally differentiates itself from approaches to international law associated with the so-called New Haven School. In the same vein, see J. von Bernstorff, 'International legal scholarship as a cooling medium in international law and politics' (2014) 25 *European Journal of International Law* 977.

[16] Cf. Pierre Bourdieu, 'A Lecture on the lecture', in Pierre Bourdieu, *In Other Words: Essays Towards a Reflexive Sociology* (Redwood City, CA: Stanford University Press, 1990), p. 189: '[T]he magical ambition of transforming the social world without knowing the mechanisms that drive it exposes itself to the risk of replacing the "inert violence" of the mechanisms that its pretentious ignorance has destroyed with another and sometimes even more inhuman violence.' This is a reference to which Akbar Rasulov drew my attention.

the suspension of the belief system proposed herein. None of the preceding should ever be read as an invitation for apostasy, that is, a
renunciation by international lawyers of all their current beliefs in
terms of modes of legal reasoning.[17] In the light of the discussion conducted herein, apostasy seems neither possible nor desirable for international lawyers. First, belief systems inevitably replace one another, leaving
no possibility of a belief vacuum.[18] Second, and more important, belief
systems, including the belief system at work in international lawyers'
understanding of the formation and functioning of the fundamental
doctrines of international law, have undeniable merits. One of the merits
of the belief system examined in this book lies with the possibility of
communication.[19] After all, the international belief system, despite being
the manifestation of a liberal pattern of legal thought that obfuscates
interventions by a multitude of powerful actors and notwithstanding its
possible operative defectiveness, illegitimacy and injustice, is what makes
international legal discourse possible. This belief system is simultaneously the tool through which the international reformer or manager
can act. An apostate international lawyer would not be able to reform or
manage the world. This is why the suspension of the international belief
system suggested in this book is always meant to be temporary, apostasy
constituting no credible option.

It is of no avail to further discuss the general choice made here for not
seeking to control – to the exception of apostasy – the consequences of
the suspension of the international belief system. Indeed, it remains to be
seen whether the exercise proposed herein and, especially the suspension
of the belief system informing international lawyers' common understanding of fundamental doctrines, will find any consumer. If anything,

[17] See contra, Jerome Frank, *Law and the Modern Mind* (New Brunswick, NJ: Transaction
Publishers, 2009), p. 127: 'We have been inquiring into the reason for the persistence of
the basic illusion. It might be asked whether our question is worth answering. If an
illusion helps men live, if by acting on an erroneous dogma, men arrive at valuable results,
for the most part unmixed with evil, then to insist upon exposing the falsity of the illusion
or dogma is a best pedantry or bad manners and at worst malicious mischief or sadistic
morbidity ... But its harmful consequences are not few.'
[18] See Chapter 1, Section 3. See also Laclau, *Emancipation(s)*, p. 103 ('[T]he movement of
modernity to postmodernity ... will not necessarily involve the collapse of all the objects
and values contained within the horizon of modernity but, instead, will involve their
reformulation from a different perspective').
[19] On the possibility of communication in relation to the fundamental doctrine of sources,
see J. d'Aspremont, *Formalism and the Sources of International Law* (Oxford: Oxford
University Press, 2011). See also T. Meyer, 'Towards a communicative theory of international law' (2012) 13 *Melbourne Journal of International Law* 1.

this book is demanding for its readership because it requires a simultaneous familiarity with theoretical debates and literacy in the doctrinal intricacies of the modes of legal reasoning associated with the fundamental doctrines of international law. It may be that readers well versed in doctrinal debates end up being put off by the required literacy in theoretical discourse and vice versa. In that sense, and like many international law books before, it may happen that the consumers of the unlearning exercise promoted here may not simply be there at this time, either because they are no longer there or because they are not there yet.[20]

The absence of a readership amenable to the exercise proposed herein is plausible. In the age of pragmatism, concomitant literacy in both theory and doctrinal debates is a scarce resource. Traditionally construed as an inclination to concentrate exclusively on doctrinal debates away from theoretical controversies,[21] pragmatism can also manifest itself in the escape to the safe haven of theoretical debates away from tedious doctrinal developments. In that sense, and although it is rarely recognised as such, an exclusive focus on theory can also constitute a form of pragmatism. Be that as it may, pragmatism, in all its variants, has long frustrated the simultaneous yearning for theoretical and doctrinal intricacies,[22] thereby shrinking the possible interest in the image of international law as a belief system and a suspension thereof.

---

[20] This is a remark I owe to exchanges with Akbar Rasulov.

[21] This anti-theoretical pragmatism of contemporary legal scholarship has long been derided and criticised. For instance, Martti Koskenniemi has written that this is a pragmatism that sometimes 'involves an illegitimate naturalization of practitioner frameworks'. M. Koskenniemi, 'Doctrines of state responsibility', in James Crawford, Alain Pellet and Simon Olleson (eds.), *The Law of International Responsibility* (Oxford: Oxford University Press, 2010), p. 45 (citing S. Marks, *The Riddle of All Constitutions* (Oxford: Oxford University Press, 2000), pp. 66–67). This form of pragmatism has also been depicted as a 'surrender'. See G Simpson, 'On the magic mountain: teaching public international law' (1999) 10 *European Journal of International Law* 70 at 76. For some additional reflections on the reasons behind the anti-theoretical stance of mainstream legal scholarship, see J. Klabbers, 'Constitutionalism and the making of international law' (2008) 5 *No Foundations* 84 at 95. The famous British aversion of theory is sometimes traced back to Lauterpacht. See Carty, '"Why theory?" The implications for international law teaching', in P. Allott et al. (eds.), *Theory and International Law: An Introduction* (London: British Institute of International and Comparative Law, 1991), p. 77. For a contestation of this contention, see I. Scobbie, 'The theorist as judge: Hersch Lauterpacht's concept of the international judicial function' (1997) 2 *European Journal of International Law* 264.

[22] It is noteworthy that pragmatism can simultaneously be read as a sign of 'maturity' of a discipline. See T. Kuhn, *The Structure of Scientific Revolutions*, 50th anniv. edn (Chicago:

Whether this book eventually finds the consumers who can make sense of an image of international law as a belief system and who prove ready to suspend it for the sake of unlearning should be no matter of concern here. In fact, the high demands that this book has put on its readership in terms of critical attitude and doctrinal knowledge may themselves be constitutive of that readership. Of all possible consequences that the image of international law as a belief system and its suspension may engender, contributing to the consolidation of a readership that is both theoretically aware and doctrinally apt is maybe where the epistemological ambition of the intellectual exercise conducted here lies.

University of Chicago Press, 2012), p. 20: 'When the individual scientist can take a paradigm for granted, he need no longer, in its major works, attempt to build his field anew, starting from first principles and justifying the use of each concept introduced.'

BIBLIOGRAPHY

Abi-Saab, G., 'Les sources du droit international: essai de deconstruction', in M. Rama-Montaldo (ed.), *International Law in an Evolving World: Liber Amicorum in Tribute to Professor Eduardo Jiménez de Aréchaga*, vol. 1 (Montevideo: Fundacici de Cultura Universitaria, 1994)

'La Commission du Droit International, la codification et le processus de formation du droit international', in *Making Better International Law: The International Law Commission at 50* (New York: United Nations, 1998)

Adorno, T., and Horkheimer, M. (eds.), *Dialectic of Enlightenment* (London: Verso, 1997)

Ago, R., 'Le délit international' (1939-II) 69 *Collected Courses of the Hague Academy on International Law* 426

'Science juridique et droit international' (1956) 90 *Collected Courses of the Hague Academy on International Law* 851

Alexidze, L. A., 'Legal nature of jus cogens in contemporary international law' (1981) 172 *Collected Courses of the Hague Academy on International Law* 219

Alland, D., *Anzilotti et le droit international public* (Paris: Pedone, 2012)

Allott, P., 'Language, method and the nature of international law' (1971) 45 *British Yearbook of International Law* 79

'The true function of law in the international community' (1998) 5 *Indiana Journal of Global Studies* 391

'The idealist's dilemma' (International Law Association British Branch Conference, 23–24 May 2014)

Alston, P., and Simma, B., 'The sources of human rights law: custom, jus cogens, general principles' (1988) 12 *Australian Yearbook of International Law* 102

Alvarez, A., 'La method du droit international à la veille de sa codification' (1913) 20 *Revue générale de droit international public* 725

Considérations Générales sur la Codification du Droit International Américain (Rio de Janeiro: Imprensa Nacional, 1927)

Le Continent Américain et la Codification du Droit International Law: Une Nouvelle 'Ecole' du Droit des Gens (Paris: Pedone, 1938)

Alvarez, J., 'International organizations and the rule of law' (2016) Institute for International Law and Justice Working Paper 2016/4, available at www .iilj.org/wp-content/uploads/2016/07/alvarez-international-organizations -and-the-rule-of-law-iilj-wp-2016_4-gal.pdf (accessed 5 March 2017)

Anghie, A., *Imperialism, Sovereignty and the Making of International Law* (Cambridge University Press, 2004)

Anzilotti, D., 'Teoria generale della responsibilita dello stato' (1902) cited by A. Nissel, 'The duality of state responsibility' (2013) 44 *Columbia Human Rights Law Review* 793

   'La responsabilité internationale des États à raison des dommages soufferts par les étrangers' (1906) *Revue générale de droit international public* 5

   'Il diritto internazionale nei giudizi interni', reprinted in D. Anzilotti, *Scritti di Diritto Internazionale Pubblico* (Padua: CEDAM, 1956–7)

Aust, H., 'Circumstances precluding wrongfulness', in A. Nollkaemper and I. Plakokefalos (eds.), *Principles of Shared Responsibility in International Law* (Cambridge: Cambridge University Press, 2014)

Beckett, J., 'Countering uncertainty and ending up/down arguments: prolegomena to a response to NAIL' (2005) 16 *European Journal of International Law* 213

   'The politics of international law – twenty years later: a reply', *EJIL:TALK!*, 19 May 2009, available at www.ejiltalk.org/the-politics-of-international-law -twenty-years-later-a-reply/.

Bederman, D., 'The souls of international organizations: legal personality and the lighthouse at cape spartel' (1995–96) 36 *Virginia Journal of International Law* 275

   The Spirit of International Law (Atlanta: University of Georgia Press, 2002)

   Custom as a Source of Law (Cambridge: Cambridge University Press, 2010)

Bekker, P. (ed.), *Making Transnational Law Work in the Global Economy: Essays in Honour of Detlev Vagts* (Cambridge: Cambridge University Press, 2010)

Benjamin, W., 'Critique of violence', in *Selected Writings: Vol. 1: 1913–1926* (Cambridge, MA: Belknap Press of Harvard University Press, 1996)

Bentham, J., *An Introduction to the Principles of Morals and Legislation* (London: Kessinger, Whitefish, 2005, first published 1781)

Benvenisti, E., 'The conception of international law as a legal system' (2008) *Tel Aviv University Law Faculty Papers* 2008/83, 2

   'Comments on the systemic vision of national courts as part of an international rule of law' (2012) 4 *Jerusalem Review of Legal Studies* 42

   The Law of Global Governance (The Hague: Brill, 2014)

Benvenisti, E. and Downs, G. W., 'The empire's new clothes: political economy and the fragmentation of international law' (2007) 60 *Stanford Law Review* 595

Berman, N., 'In the wake of empire' (1999) 14 *American University International Law Review* 1521

   Passions et Ambivalences (Paris: Pedone, 2008)

Bernardez, T., 'Interpretation of treaties by the International Court of Justice following the adoption of the 1963 Vienna Convention on the Law of Treaties', in G. Hafner et al. (eds.), *Liber Amicorum Seidl-Hohenveldern* (The Hague: Kluwer, 1998)

Bianchi, A., 'Human rights and the magic of jus cogens' (2008) 19 *European Journal of International Law* 491

'Textual interpretation and (international) law reading: the myth of (in) determinacy and the genealogy of meaning', in P. Bekker (ed.), *Making Transnational Law Work in the Global Economy: Essays in Honour of Detlev Vagts* (Cambridge: Cambridge University Press, 2010)

'The game of interpretation in international law: the players, the cards, and why the game is worth the candle', in Andrea Bianchi, Daniel Peat and Matthew Windsor (eds.), *Interpretation in International Law* (Oxford: Oxford University Press, 2015)

International Law Theories: An Inquiry into Different Ways of Thinking (Oxford: Oxford University Press, 2016)

Bianchi, A., Peat, D., and Windsor, M. (eds.), *Interpretation in International Law* (Oxford: Oxford University Press, 2015)

Blumenberg, H., *The Legitimacy of the Modern Age* (Cambridge, MA: MIT Press, 1983)

Blutman, L., 'Conceptual and methodological deficiencies: some ways that theories on customary international law fail' (2014) 25 *European Journal of International Law* 529

Boer, L., 'The greater part of "jurisconsults": on consensus claims and their footnotes in legal scholarship' (2016) 29 *Leiden Journal of International Law* 1021

Bourdieu, P., 'The force of law: toward a sociology of the juridical field' (1987) 38 *Hastings Law Journal* 805

'A lecture on the lecture', in Pierre Bourdieu, *In Other Words: Essays Towards a Reflexive Sociology*, trans. Matthew Adamson (Redwood City, CA: Stanford University Press, 1990)

'The forms of capital', in J. Richardson (ed.) *Handbook of Theory and Research for the Sociology of Education* (New York, Greenwood, 2001)

Practical Reason, trans. R. Johnson (Cambridge, Polity, 1998)

Bourdieu, P. and Wacquant, L., *An Invitation to Reflexive Sociology* (Chicago: University of Chicago Press, 1992)

Bouriau, C., *Les fictions du droit: Kelsen, lecteur de Vaihinger* (Paris: Ens Éditions, 2013)

Bradley, C., 'A state preferences account of customary international law adjudication', 10 October 2014, available at SSRN: http://ssrn.com /abstract=2508298

Brierly, J. L., *The Law of Nations*, 4th edn (Oxford: Clarendon Press, 1949)

The Law of Nations: An Introduction to the International Law of Peace, 5th edn (Oxford: Clarendon Press, 1955)

'The draft code of American international law', in H. Lauterpacht and C. H. M. Waldock (eds.), *The Basis of Obligation in International Law and Other Papers by J. L. Brierly* (Oxford: Clarendon Press, 1958)

'The basis of obligations in international law', in H. Lauterpacht and C. H. M. Waldock (eds.), *The Basis of Obligation in International Law and Other Papers by the Late James Leslie Brierly* (Oxford: Clarendon Press, 1959)

Broms, B., 'States', in M. Bedjaoui (ed.), *International Law: Achievements and Prospects* (New York: UNESCO, 1991)

Brownlie, I., 'International law at the fiftieth anniversary of the United Nations: general course on public international law' (1995) 255 *Collected Courses of the Hague Academy on International Law* 9

Brunnee, J. and Toope, S. J., 'International law and constructivism: elements of an interactional theory of international law' (2000) 39 *Columbia Journal of Transnational Law* 19

Brunnée, J. and Toope, S. J., *Legitimacy and Legality in International Law* (Cambridge: Cambridge University Press, 2010)

Buzzini, G., 'La théorie des sources face au droit international general' (2002) 106 *Revue générale de droit international public* 581

Byers, M., 'Conceptualising the relationship between jus cogens and erga omnes' (1997) 66 *Nordic Journal of International Law* 220

Custom, Power and the Power of Rules: International Relations and Customary International Law (Cambridge: Cambridge University Press, 1999)

Çali, B., *The Authority of International Law: Obedience, Respect, and Rebuttal* (Oxford: Oxford University Press, 2015)

Caminos, H., 'The Latin American contribution to international law' (1986) 80 *American Society of International Law Proceedings* 157

Cannizzaro, E. (ed.), *The Law of Treaties Beyond the Vienna Convention* (Oxford: Oxford University Press, 2011)

'A higher law for treaties?', in E. Cannizzaro (ed.), *The Law of Treaties Beyond the Vienna Convention* (Oxford: Oxford University Press, 2014)

'Peremptory law-making', in Rain Liivoja and Jarna Petman (eds.), *International Law-making: Essays in Honour of Jan Klabbers* (London: Routledge, 2014), p. 270

Carty, A., *Post-Modern Law: Enlightenment, Revolution and the Death of Man* (Edinburgh: Edinburgh University Press, 1990)

'Why theory: the implications for international law teaching', in P. Allott et al. (eds.), *Theory and International Law: An Introduction* (London: Institute of International and Comparative Law, 1991)

Carty, T., *The Decay of International Law? A Reappraisal of the Limits of Imagination in International Affairs* (Manchester: Manchester University Press, 1986)

Cassese, A., *International Law*, 2nd edn (Oxford: Oxford University Press, 2005)
'For an enhanced role of jus cogens', in A. Cassese, *Realizing Utopia: The Future of International Law* (Oxford: Oxford University Press, 2012)

Castberg, F., 'La Méthodologie du droit international public' (1934) 43 *Collected Courses of the Hague Academy of International Law*

Chayes, A. and Handler Chayes, A., *The New Sovereignty: Compliance with International. Regulatory Agreements* (Cambridge, MA: Harvard University Press, 1995)

Choi, S. H. and M. Gulati, 'Customary international law: how do courts do it?', 9 February 2015, available at SSRN: https://papers.ssrn.com/sol3/papers.cfm?abstract_id=2561900

Christenson, G. A., 'Jus cogens: guarding interests foundational to international society', (1988) 28 *Virginia Journal of International Law* 585

Cohen, F., 'Transcendental nonsense and the functional approach' (1935) 35 *Columbia Law Review* 809

Collins, R., *The Institutional Problem in Modern International Law* (Oxford: Hart, 2016)

Conforti, B., 'Cours général de droit international public' (1988) 212 *Collected Courses of the Hague Academy on International Law* 9

Corten, O., *Le Discours du Droit International: Pour un Positivisme Critique* (Paris: Pedone, 2009)

Corten, O. and Klein, P., 'The limits of complicity as a ground for responsibility', in K. Bannelier, T. Christakis and S. Heathcote (eds.), *The ICJ and the Evolution of International Law: The Enduring Impact of the Corfu Channel Case* (London: Routledge, 2012)

Corten, O. and Klein, P., 'La Commission du droit international comme agent de la formalisation du droit de la responsabilité', in D. Alland, V. Chetail, O. de Frouville and J. Vinuales (eds.), *Unity and Diversity of International Law: Essays in Honour of Professor Pierre-Marie Dupuy* (Leiden: Martinus Nijhoff, 2014)

Cover, R., 'The Supreme Court 1982 term – foreword: nomos and narrative' (1983) 97 *Harvard Law Review* 4

Craven, M., 'Theorizing the turn to history in international law', in A. Orford and F. Hoffmann (eds.), *The Oxford Handbook of the Theory of International Law* (Oxford: Oxford University Press, 2016)

Crawford, J., 'Introductory remarks' (1994) 88 *Proceedings of the American Society of International Law* 22
The International Law Commission's Articles on State Responsibility: Introduction, Text and Commentaries (Cambridge: Cambridge University Press, 2002)

The Creation of States (Oxford: Oxford University Press, 2007)

'Overview of part three of the Articles on State Responsibility', in J. Crawford, A. Pellet and S. Olleson (eds.), *The Law of International Responsibility* (Oxford: Oxford University Press, 2010)

Brownlie's Principles of Public International Law, 8th edn (Oxford: Oxford University Press, 2012)

'International law as discipline and profession' (2012) 106 *American Society of International Law Proceedings* 471

'Chance, order, change: the course of international law: general course on public international law' (2013) 365 *Collected Courses of the Hague Academy on International Law* 108

Chance, Order, Change: The Course of International Law: General Course on Public International Law (The Hague: Pocketbooks of the Hague Academy on International Law, 2013)

'The progressive development of international law: history, theory and practice', in D. Alland, V. Chetail, O. de Frouville and J. Vinuales (eds.), *Unity and Diversity of International Law: Essays in Honour of Professor Pierre-Marie Dupuy* (Leiden: Martinus Nijhoff, 2014)

'Kosovo and the criteria for statehood in international law', in M. Milanovic and M. Wood (eds.), *The Law and Politics of the Kosovo Advisory Opinion* (Oxford: Oxford University Press 2015)

Crawford, J. and Grant, T., 'Responsibility of states for injuries to foreigners', in J. P. Grant and J. Craig Barker (eds.), *The Harvard Research in International Law: Contemporary Analysis and Appraisal* (Buffalo, NY: Hein, 2007)

Crawford, J. and Koskenniemi, M., 'Introduction', in J. Crawford and M. Koskenniemi (eds.), *Cambridge Companion to International Law* (Cambridge: Cambridge University Press, 2012)

Crawford, J. and Olleson, S., 'The nature and forms of international responsibility', in M. Evans (eds.), *International Law* (Oxford: Oxford University Press, 2003)

Crawford, J. and Olleson, S., 'The continuing debate on a UN convention on state responsibility' (2005) 54 *International and Comparative Law Quarterly* 959

Crawford, J., Olleson, S. and Peel, J., 'The ILC's articles on responsibility of states for internationally wrongful acts: completion of the second reading' (2001) 12 *European Journal of International Law* 963

Criddle, E. J. and Fox-Decent, E., 'A fiduciary theory of jus cogens' (2009) 34 *Yale Journal of International Law* 331

Culver, K. and Giudice, M., *Legality's Borders: An Essay in General Jurisprudence* (Oxford: Oxford University Press, 2010)

d'Amato, A., 'The concept of special custom in international law' (1969) 63 *American Journal of International Law* 211

The Concept of Custom in International Law (Ithaca, NY: Cornell University Press, 1971)

'What "counts"as law?', in N. Onuf (ed.), *Law-Making in the Global Community* (Durham, NC: Carolina Academic Press, 1982)

'It's a bird, it's a plane, it's jus cogens' (1990) 6 *Connecticut Journal of International Law* 1

Danilenko, G. M., 'The theory of international customary law' (1988) 31 *German Yearbook of International Law* 9

'International jus cogens: issues of law-making' (1990) 2 *European Journal of International Law* 42

Law-Making in the International Community (Leiden: Martinus Nijhoff, 1993)

d'Aspremont, J., 'Abuse of the legal personality of international organizations and the responsibility of member states' (2007) 4 *International Organizations Law Review* 91

'Rebellion and state responsibility' (2009) 58 *International and Comparative Law Quarterly* 427

'Cognitive conflicts and the making of international law: from empirical concord to conceptual discord in legal scholarship' (2009) 46 *Vanderbilt Journal of Transnational Law* 1119

Formalism and the Sources of International Law (Oxford University Press, 2011)

'The politics of deformalization in international law' (2011) 3 *Goettingen Journal of International Law* 503

'Wording in international law' (2012) 25 *Leiden Journal of International Law* 575

'The articles on the responsibility of international organizations: magnifying the fissures in the law of international responsibility' (2012) 9 *International Organizations Law Review* 15

'An autonomous regime of identification of customary international humanitarian law: do not say what you do or do not do what you say?', in R. van Steenberghe (ed.), *Droit International Humanitaire: Un Régime Spécial de Droit International?* (Brussels: Bruylant, 2013)

'The law of international organizations and the art of reconciliation: from dichotomies to dialectics' (2014) 11 *International Organizations Law Review* 428

'The international law of statehood: craftsmanship for the elucidation and regulation of births and deaths in the international society' (2014) 29 *Connecticut Journal of International Law* 201

'The idea of "rules" in the sources of international law' (2014) 84 *British Yearbook of International Law* 103

Epistemic Forces in International Law: Foundational Doctrines and Techniques of International Legal Argumentation (Cheltenham: Elgar, 2015)

'Non-state actors and the social practice of international law', in Math Noortmann, August Reinisch and Cedric Ryngaert (eds.), *Non-State Actors in International Law* (Oxford: Hart, 2015)

'The doctrine of fundamental rights of states and anthropomorphic thinking in international law' (2015) 4 *Cambridge Journal of International and Comparative Law* 501

'The multidimensional process of interpretation: content-determination and law-ascertainment distinguished', in A. Bianchi, D. Peat and M. Windsor (eds.), *Interpretation in International Law* (Oxford: Oxford University Press, 2015)

'The decay of modern customary international law in spite of scholarly heroism', in G. Capaldo (ed.), *Global Community: Yearbook of International Law and Jurisprudence* (Oxford: Oxford University Press, 2015)

'Jus cogens: a social construct without pedigree' (2015) 46 *Netherlands Yearbook of International Law* 85

'The International Court of Justice and the paradox of system-design' (2016) 7 *Journal of International Dispute Settlement* 1

'The professionalization of international law', in J. d'Aspremont, T. Gazzini, A. Nollkaemper and W. Werner (eds.), *International Law as a Profession* (Cambridge: Cambridge University Press, 2016) 19

'Cyber operations and international law: an interventionist legal thought' (2016) 21 *Journal of Conflict & Security Law* 575

'Martti Koskenniemi, the mainstream, and self-reflectivity' (2016) 29 *Leiden Journal of International Law*

d'Aspremont, J. and Besson, S., 'Introduction', in Samantha Besson and Jean d'Aspremont (eds.), *Oxford Handbook on the Sources of International Law* (Oxford: Oxford University Press, 2017) 1

d'Aspremont, J., Gazzini, T., Nollkaemper, A. and Werner, W., *International Law as Profession* (Cambridge: Cambridge University Press, 2016)

d'Aspremont, J., and Singh, S. (eds.), *Concepts for International Law* (Cheltenham: Elgar, 2018) (forthcoming)

Debray, R., *Transmitting Culture*, trans. Eric Rauth (New York: Columbia University Press, 1997)

Degan, V., 'Création et disparition de l'etat (a la lumière du démembrement des trois fédérations multiethniques en europe)' (1999) 279 *Collected Courses of the Hague Academy on International Law* 199

de Hoog, A., *Obligations Erga Omnes and International Crimes* (The Hague: Kluwer, 1996)

Derrida, J., 'Force of law: the "Mystical Foundation of Authority"' in Gil Anidjar (ed.), *Acts of Religion – Jacques Derrida* (New York: Routledge, 2002)

Derrida, J. and Moore, F. T. C., 'Metaphor in the text of philosophy' (1974) 6 *New Literary History* 5

Desautels-Stein, J., 'The judge and the drone' (2014) 56 *Arizona Law Review* 117

'Chiastic law in the crystal ball: exploring legal formalism and its alternative futures' (2014) 2 *London Review of International Law* 263

'Structuralist legal histories' (2015) 78 *Law and Contemporary Problems* 37

'International legal structuralism: a primer' (2016) 8 *International Theory* 201

de Visscher, C., *Théories et Réalités en Droit International Public*, 4th edn (Paris: Pedone, 1970)

de Wet, E., 'The international constitutional order' (2006) 55 *International and Comparative Law Quarterly* 51–76

'The constitutionalisation of public international law', in Michel Rosenfeld and Andras Sajo (eds.), *The Oxford Handbook of Comparative Constitutional Law* (Oxford: Oxford University Press, 2012)

'Jus cogens and obligations erga omnes', in Dinah Shelton (ed.), *Oxford Handbook on Human Rights* (Oxford: Oxford University Press, Oxford, 2013)

de Wilde, M., 'The state of exception: reflections on theologico-political motifs in Benjamin and Schmitt', in Hent de Vries and Lawrence E. Sullivan (eds.), *Political Theologies: Public Religions in a Post-Secular World* (New York: Fordham University Press, 2006)

de Witt Dickinson, E., 'The analogy between natural persons and international persons in the law of nations' (1917) 26 *Yale Law Journal* 564

Dezalay, Y., *Marchands de droit: La restructuration de l'ordre juridique international par les multinationales du droit* (Paris: Fayard, 1992)

Lawyers and the Rule of Law in an Era of Globalization (London: Routledge, 2011)

Dezalay, Y., and Garth, B., 'Merchants of law as moral entrepreneurs: constructing international justice from the competition for transnational business disputes' (1995) 29 *Law and Society Review* 27

Doehring, K., 'States', in R. Bernhardt (ed.), *Encyclopedia of Public International Law*, vol. IV (New York: Elsevier, 2000)

Dos Reis, F. and Kessler, O., 'Constructivism and the politics of international law', in A. Orford and F. Hoffmann (eds.), *The Oxford Handbook of the Theory of International Law* (Oxford: Oxford University Press, 2016)

Dubois, D., 'The authority of peremptory norms in international law: state consent or natural law' (2009) 78 *Nordic Journal of International Law* 133

Dugard, J., 'The future of international law: a human rights perspective – with some comments on the Leiden school of international law' (2007) 20 *Leiden Journal of International Law* 729

Dunoff, J. L. and Pollack, M. A. (eds.), *Interdisciplinary Perspectives on International Law and International Relations: The State of the Art* (Cambridge: Cambridge University Press, 2013)

Dupont, C. and Schultz, T., 'Towards a new heuristic model: investment arbitration as a political system' (2016) 7 *Journal of International Dispute Settlement* 3

Dupuy, P.-.M., 'Dionisio Anzilotti and the law of international responsibility of states' (1992) 3 *European Journal of International Law* 139

'La pratique de l'article 38 du Statut de la Cour internationale de Justice dans le cadre des plaidoiries écrites et orales', in *Collection of Essays by Legal Advisers of States, Legal Advisers of International Organizations and Practitioners in the Field of International Law* (New York: United Nations, 1999)

'L'unité de l'ordre juridique international: cours général de droit international public' (2002) 297 *Collected Courses of the Hague Academy on International Law* 9

Dworkin, R., *Law's Empire* (London: Belknap Press, 1986)

Ely, J. H., 'Constitutional interpretivism: its allure and impossibility' (1978) 53 *Indiana Law Journal* 399

Eagleton, C., *The Responsibility of States in International Law* (New York: New York University Press, 1928)

'Editors' choice 2015' (2016) *European Journal of International Law*

Elias, T. O., 'Problems concerning the validity of treaties' (1971-III) 133 *Collected Courses of the Hague Academy on International Law* 333

Endicott, T., 'Legal Interpretation', in A. Marmor (ed.), *Routledge Companion to Philosophy of Law* (London: Routledge, 2012)

Esquirol, J. L., 'Latin America' in B. Fassbender and A. Peters (eds.), *Oxford Handbook on the History of International Law* (Oxford: Oxford University Press, 2012)

Fabri, H. and Ruiz, 'Enhancing the rhetoric of jus cogens' (2012) 23 *European Journal of International Law* 1049

Feder, E. K., 'Power/knowledge', in D. Taylor (ed.), *Michel Foucault: Key Concepts* (London: Routledge, 2014)

Feichtner, I., 'Critical scholarship and responsible practice of international law: how can the two be reconciled?' (2016) 29 *Leiden Journal of International Law* 4 979

Ferrari, L., Méthodes de recherche de la coutume internationale dans la pratique des etats (1965) 192 *Collected Courses of the Hague Academy on International Law* 243

Fidler, D., 'The return of the standard of civilization' (2001) 2 *Chicago Journal of International Law* 137

Fish, S., *Is There a Text in This Class? The Authority of Interpretive Communities* (Cambridge, MA: Harvard University Press, 1980)

'Fish v. Fiss' (1984) 36 *Stanford Law Review* 1325

Fiss, O., 'Objectivity and interpretation' (1982) 34 *Stanford Law Review* 739

Fitzpatrick, P., *The Mythology of Modern Law* (London: Routledge, 1992)

Focarelli, C., 'Promotional jus cogens: a critical appraisal of jus cogens' legal effects' (2008) 77 *Nordic Journal of International Law* 429

Foucault, M., *Surveiller et Punir* (Paris: Gallimard, 1975)

Frank, J., *Law and the Modern Mind* (Piscataway, NJ: Transaction Publishers, 2009)

Fry, J., 'Attribution of responsibility', in A. Nollkaemper and I. Plakokefalos (eds.), *Principles of Shared Responsibility in International Law* (Cambridge: Cambridge University Press, 2014)

Fuller, L. L., 'Positivism and fidelity to law: a reply to Professor Hart' (1958) 71 *Harvard Law Review* 630

Gaja, G., 'Interpreting articles adopted by the International Law Commission' (2016) 85 *British Yearbook of International Law* 10

Galindo, G., 'Martti Koskenniemi and the historiographical turn in international law' (2005) 16 *European Journal of International Law* 539

'Force field: on history and theory of international law' (2012) 20 *Journal of the Max Planck Institute for European Legal History* 86

García-Salmones Rovira, M., *The Project of Positivism in International Law* (Oxford: Oxford University Press, 2013)

Gardiner, R., *Treaty Interpretation* (Oxford: Oxford University Press, 2008)

Gardner, J., *Law as a Leap of Faith* (Oxford: Oxford University Press, 2012)

Garland, D., 'What is a "history of the present"? On Foucault's genealogies and their critical preconditions' (2014) 16 *Punishment and Society* 365

Gentili, A., *On the Law of War*, trans. J. C. Rolfe (Oxford: Clarendon Press, 1933)

Giddens, A., *Central Problems in Social Theory: Action, Structure and Contradiction in Social Analysis* (Basingstoke: Macmillan, 1979)

Glenn, H. P., *Legal Traditions of the World* (Oxford: Oxford University Press, 2007)

Goldmann, M., 'Inside relative normativity: from sources to standards instruments for the exercise of international public authority' (2008) 9 *German Law Journal* 1865

Gong, G. W., *The Standard of 'Civilisation' in International Society* (Oxford: Clarendon Press, 1984)

Grant, T., 'Defining statehood: the Montevideo Convention and its discontents' (1998–99) 37 *Columbia Journal of Transnational Law* 403

Guggenheim, P., 'What is positive international law?', in G. Lipsky (ed.), *Law and Politics in the World Community: Essays on Hans Kelsen's Pure Theory and Related Problems of International Law* (Berkley: University of California Press, 1953)

Traite de Droit International Public (Paris: Georg & Cie, 1953)

'Les origines de la notion autonome du droit des gens', in J. H. W. Verzijl (ed.), *Symbolae Verzijl: Présentées au Professeur J. H. W. Verzijl a l'occasion de son LXX-ieme anniversaire* (The Hague: Martinus Nijhoff, 1958)

Gur, N., 'Are legal rules content-independent reasons?' (2001) 5 *Problema: Anuario de Filosofia y Teoria del Derecho* 275

Haggenmacher, P., 'La doctrine des deux éléments en droit coutumier dans la pratique de la Cour internationale' (1986) 90 *Revue Générale de Droit International Public* 5

Hall, W. E., *A Treatise on International Law*, 3rd edn (Oxford: Clarendon Press, 1890)

Hameed, A., 'Unravelling the mystery of jus cogens in international law' (2014) 84 *British Yearbook of International Law* 52

Hannikainen, L., *Peremptory Norms (Jus Cogens) in International Law: Historical Development, Criteria, Present Status* (Helsinki: Finnish Lawyers' Publishing Company, 1988)

Harlow, C., 'Global administrative law: the quest for principles and values' (2006) 17 *European Journal of International Law* 1, 187

Harris, D., *Cases and Materials on International Law*, 7th edn (London: Sweet & Maxwell/Thomson Reuters (Legal), 2010)

Hart, H., *Essays on Bentham* (Oxford: Clarendon Press, 1982)
  The Concept of Law (Oxford: Clarendon Press, 1994)

Hathaway, O. A., 'Path dependence in the law: the course and pattern of legal change in a common law system' (2001) 86 *Iowa Law Review* 101

Heffter, A. W., *Le droit international de l'Europe*, trans. Bergson, 4th edn (Paris: Cotillon, 1883)

Henkin, L., 'International law: politics, values and functions: general course on public international law' (1989) 216 *Collected Courses of The Hague Academy on International Law* 9 at 60

Hernandez, G., 'Interpretation', in J. Kammerhofer and J. d'Aspremont (eds.), *International Legal Positivism in a Postmodern World* (Cambridge: Cambridge University Press, 2014)
  The International Court of Justice and the Judicial Function (Oxford: Oxford University Press, 2014)

Higgins, R., *The Development of International Law Through the Political Organs of the United Nations* (Oxford: Oxford University Press, 1963)

Hirsch, M., *Invitation to the Sociology of International Law* (Oxford: Oxford University Press, 2015)

Hobsbawn, E., 'Introduction: inventing traditions', in E. Hobsbawn and T. Ranger (eds.), *The Invention of Tradition* (Cambridge: Cambridge University Press, 1983)

Hoffman, F., 'International legalism and international politics', in A. Orford and F. Hoffmann (eds.), *The Oxford Handbook of the Theory of International Law* (Oxford: Oxford University Press, 2016)

Hollis, D., 'Why state consent still matters – non-state actors, treaties, and the changing sources of international law' (2005) 23 *Berkeley Journal of International Law* 137

Holmes, O. W., 'Natural law' (1918) *Harvard Law Review* 40

Holtermann, J. and Madsen, M., 'Toleration, synthesis or replacement? The "empirical turn" and its consequences for the science of international law' (2016) 29 *Leiden Journal of International Law* 1001

Howse, R., 'Schmitt, Schmitteanism and contemporary international legal theory', in A. Orford and F. Hoffmann (eds.), *The Oxford Handbook of the Theory of International Law* (Oxford: Oxford University Press, 2016)

Hyde, C. C., *International Law Chiefly as Interpreted and Applied by the United States* (Boston: Little, Brown, 1922)

Janis, M., 'The nature of jus cogens' (1988) 3 *Connecticut Journal of International Law* 359

Jansen, N., *The Making of Legal Authority: Non-Legislative Codifications in Historical and Comparative Perspective* (Oxford: Oxford University Press, 2010)

Jellinek, G., *Die rechtliche Natur der Staatenvertrage* (Holder, 1880)
Allgemeine Staatslehre, vol. I: *Das Recht des Modernen Staates* (O. Häring, 1905)

Jennings, R. and Watts, J., *Oppenheim's International Law*, 9th edn, vol. 1 (London: Longmans, 1992)

Jessup, P., *A Modern Law of Nations: An Introduction* (New York: Macmillan, 1956)

Johns, F., *Non-Legality in International Law: Unruly Law* (Cambridge: Cambridge University Press, 2013)

Jouannet, E., *Emer de Vattel et l'émergence doctrinale du droit international classique* (Paris: Pedone, 1998)
'Regards sur un siècle de doctrine française du droit international' (2000) 46 *Annuaire français de droit international* 1
'A critical introduction', in M. Koskenniemi, *The Politics of International Law* (Oxford: Hart, 2011)

Kahn, P. W., *The Cultural Study of Law: Reconstructing Legal Scholarship* (Chicago: University of Chicago Press, 1999)

Kammerhofer, J., *Uncertainty in International Law: A Kelsenian Perspective* (London: Routledge, 2010)
'Uncertainty in the formal sources of international law: customary international law and some of its problems' (2004) 15 *European Journal of International Law* 523

Kanetake, M. and Nollkaemper, A. (eds.), *The Rule of Law at the National and International Levels: Contestations and Deference* (Oxford: Hart, 2016)

Kelly, J. P., 'The twilight of customary international law' (2000) 40 *Virginia Journal of International Law* 449

Kelsen, H., 'Théorie du droit international coutumier' (1939) 1 *Revue Internationale de Théorie du Droit* 253

Kennedy, D., 'Primitive legal scholarship' (1986) 27 *Harvard International Law Journal* 1

International Legal Structures (Baden-Baden: Nomos, 1987)

'A new stream of international legal scholarship' (1988–89) 7 *Wisconsin International Law Journal* 1

'International law and the nineteenth century: history of an illusion' (1997) 17 *Quinnipiac Law Review* 99

'Images of religion in international legal theory', in Mark Janis (ed.), *Religion and International Law* (Dordrecht: Kluwer Academic, 1999)

'The disciplines of international law and policy' (1999) 12 *Leiden Journal of International Law* 9

'When renewal repeats: thinking against the box' (2000) 32 *New York University Journal of International Law and Politics* 2, 335

'Tom Franck and the Manhattan School' (2003) 35 *New York University Journal of International Law and Policy* 397

The Rise and Fall of Classical Legal Thought (New York: Beard Books, 2006)

'The mystery of global governance' (2008) 34 *Ohio Northern University Law Review* 827

'The hermeneutic of suspicion in contemporary American legal thought' (2014) 25 *Law and Critique* 91

A World of Struggle: How Power, Law, and Expertise Shape Global Political Economy (Princeton, NJ: Princeton University Press, 2016)

Kingsbury, B., Krisch, N. and Steward, R., 'The emergence of global administrative law' (2005) 68 *Law and Contemporary Problems* 3

Kingsbury, B. and Straumann, B. (eds.), *The Roman Foundations of the Law of Nations* (Oxford: Oxford University Press, 2011)

Klabbers, J., 'The Curious Condition of Custom' (2002) 8 *International Legal Theory* 29

'Constitutionalism and the making of international law' (2008) 5 *NoFo* 84

'Virtuous interpretation', in Malgosia Fitzmaurice et al. (eds.), *Treaty Interpretation and the Vienna Convention on the Law of Treaties: 30 Years On*, vol. 1 (Leiden: Martinus Nijhoff, 2010)

'The emergence of functionalism in international institutional law: colonial inspirations' (2014) 25 *European Journal of International Law* 645

Knop, K., 'Statehood', in J. Crawford and M. Koskenniemi (eds.), *The Cambridge Companion to International Law* (Cambridge: Cambridge University Press, 2012)

Kolb, R., 'The formal source of ius cogens in public international law' (1998) 53 *Zeitschrift for öffenliches Recht* 69

'Selected problems in the theory of customary international law' (2003) 50 *Netherlands International Law Review* 119

Théorie du jus cogens international (Paris: Publication de IUHEI, 2001)

Notions de Gaetano Morelli (Paris: Pedone, 2013)

Peremptory International Law (Jus Cogens): A General Inventory (Oxford: Hart, 2015)

Koller, D., '... and New York and The Hague and Tokyo and Geneva and Nuremberg and ... : the geographies of international law' (2012) 23 *European Journal of International Law* 97

Koskenniemi, M., 'International legal theory and doctrines', in *Max Planck Encyclopedia of Public International Law*

'The politics of international law (1990) 1 *European Journal of International Law* 4

'Repetition as reform' (1998) 9 *European Journal of International Law* 405

'Letter to the editors of the symposium' (1999) 93 *American Journal of International Law* 351

The Gentle Civilizer of Nations: The Rise and Fall of International Law 1870–1960 (Cambridge: Cambridge University Press, 2001)

'International law and hegemony: a reconfiguration' (2004) 17 *Cambridge Review of International Affairs* 197

From Apology to Utopia: The Structure of International Legal Argument (Cambridge: Cambridge University Press, 2005)

'The fate of public international law: between technique and politics' (2007) *Modern Law Review* 1

'Georg Friedrish von Martens (1756–1821) and the origins of modern international law' (2008) 15 *Constellations* 2

'Miserable comforters: international relations as new natural law' (2009) 15 *European Journal of International Relations* 395

'The politics of international law: 20 years later' (2009) 20 *European Journal of International Law* 7

'Doctrines of state responsibility', in James Crawford, Alain Pellet and Simon Olleson (eds.), *The Law of International Responsibility* (Oxford: Oxford University Press, 2010)

'Between commitment and cynicism: outline for a theory of international law as practice', in *The Politics of International Law* (Cambridge: Cambridge University Press, 2011), pp. 274–75

Kratochwil, F. V., *Rules, Norms, and Decisions: On the Conditions of Practical and Legal Reasoning in International Relations and Domestic Affairs* (Cambridge: Cambridge University Press, 1989)

Krisch, N., *Beyond Constitutionalism: The Pluralistic Structure of Postnational Law* (Oxford: Oxford University Press, 2010)

'Authority, solid and liquid, in postnational governance', in Roger Cotterrell and Maksymilian Del Mar (eds.), *Authority in Transnational Legal Theory: Theorising Across Disciplines* (London: Elgar, 2016)

'Subsidiarity in global governance' (2016) 79 *Law and Contemporary Problems* 1

Kuhn, T., *The Structure of Scientific Revolutions*, 50th anniv. edn. (Chicago: University of Chicago Press, 2012)

Kunz, J. L., 'The nature of customary international law' (1953) 47 *American Journal of International Law* 662

Lachs, M., *Le Monde la Pensée en Droit International* (Paris: Economica, 1989)

Laclau, E., *Emancipation(s)* (London: Verso, 2007)

Lasswell, H. D. and McDougal, M. S., *Jurisprudence for a Free Society* (The Hague: Martinus Nijhoff, 1992)

Lauterpacht, H., *Recognition in International Law* (Cambridge: Cambridge University Press, 1947)

Lawrence, T. J., *The Principles of International Law*, 7th edn (London: Macmillan, 1923)

Leff, A. A., 'Unspeakable ethics, unnatural law' (1979) *Duke Law Journal* 1229

Le Fur, L., *Précis de Droit International Public*, 3rd edn (Paris: Dalloz, 1937)

LePaulle, P., 'Reflections on the sources of law', in Ralph. A. Newman (ed.), *Essays in Jurisprudence in Honor of Roscoe Pound* (Indianapolis: Bobbs-Merrill, 1962), pp. 87, esp. 88–89

Letsas, G., 'Strasbourg's interpretive ethic: lessons for the international lawyer' (2010) 21 *European Journal of International Law* 509

Lévi-Strauss, C., 'The structural study of myth', in 'MYTH, a symposium' (1955) 78 *Journal of American Folklore* 428

'Chapitre XI: La structure des mythes', in *Anthropologie Structural* (Paris: Plon, 1958).

Liebowitz, S. J. and Margolis, S. E., 'Path-dependence, lock-in, and history' (1995) 11 *Journal of Law, Economics, and Organization* 205

Linderfalk, U., 'The effects of jus cogens norms: whoever opened pandora's box, did you ever think about the consequences?' (2008) 5 *European Journal of International Law* 853

'The creation of jus cogens: making sense of article 53 of the Vienna Convention' (2011) 71 *Zeitschrift für ausländisches öffentliches Recht und Völkerrecht* 2, 359

'The source of jus cogens obligations: how legal positivism copes with peremptory international law' (2013) 82 *Nordic Journal of International Law* 369

Lindroos, A. and Mehling, M., 'Dispelling the chimera of "self-contained regimes", international law and the WTO' (2005) 16 *European Journal of International Law* 857

Lorca, B., *Mestizo International Law: A Global Intellectual History 1842–1933* (Cambridge: Cambridge University Press, 2014)

Lorimer, J., *Principes de Droit International*, trans. E. Nys (Brussels: Merzbach & Falk, 1884)

Luhmann, N., *Social Systems*, trans. J. Bednarz, with D. Baecker (Redwood City, CA: Stanford University Press, 1995)

Lusa Bordin, F., 'Reflections on customary international law: the authority of
    codification conventions and ILC draft articles in international law' (2014)
    63 *International and Comparative Law Quarterly* 535

Macdonald, R. St. J., 'Fundamental norms in contemporary international law'
    (1987) 25 *Canadian Yearbook of International Law* 115

MacIntyre, A., *Whose Justice? Which Rationality?* (London: Duckworth, 1988)

Malanczuk, P., *Akehurst's Modern Introduction to International Law*, 7th rev. edn
    (London: Routledge, 1997)

Marmor, A., 'Textualism in context', *USC Gould School of Law Legal Studies
    Research Paper Series*, nos. 12–13, 18 July 2012

Martens, F. F., *Traité de Droit International*, vol. 1, trans. A. Léo (Paris: Librairie
    Maresco Ainé, 1883)

Marks, Susan 'International judicial activism and the commodity-form theory
    of international law' (2007) 18 *European Journal of International
    Law* 199.

McDougal, M., 'Law and power' (1952) 46 *American Journal of International
    Law* 102

McLachlan, C., 'The principle of systemic integration and article 31(3)(c) of the
    Vienna Convention' (2005) 54 *International and Comparative Law
    Quarterly* 279

Meijers, H., 'How is international law made?' (1979) 9 *Netherlands Yearbook of
    International Law* 3

Mendelson, M. H., 'The formation of customary international law' (1998) 272
    Collected Courses of the Hague Academy on International Law 159

Meron, T., 'The Geneva Convention as customary law' (1987) 81 *American Journal
    of International Law* 348
    'International law in the age of human rights: general course on public inter-
    national law' (2003) 301 *Collected Courses of the Hague Academy on
    International Law* 202

Meyer, T., 'Towards a communicative theory of international law' (2012) 13
    Melbourne Journal of International Law 1

Miéville, C., *Between Equal Rights: A Marxist Theory of International Law* (Oxford:
    Pluto Press, 2005)

Mik, C., 'Jus cogens in contemporary law' (2013) 33 *Polish Yearbook of
    International Law* 27

Minton, E. A. and Khale, L. R. (eds.), *Belief Systems, Religion, and Behavioral
    Economics* (New York: Business Expert Press, 2014)

Monaco, R., 'Observations sur la hiérarchie des normes du droit international', in
    Liber Amicorum Hermann Mosler (Berlin: Springer, 1983)

Montaigne, M., *De l'expérience*, essai 3, chap. 13

Moore, R., 'Capital', in Michael Grenfell (ed.), *Pierre Bourdieu: Key Concepts*, 2nd
    edn (London: Routledge, 2012)

Morss, J., 'Structuralism and interpretation in the theory of international law: cracking the code?', available at http://ssrn.com/abstract=2781388

Mouffe, C., *The Return of the Political* (London: Verso, 1993)

Moyn, S., *Christian Human Rights* (Philadelphia: University of Pennsylvania Press, 2015)

Mugerwa, N., 'Subjects of international law', in M. Sørensen (ed.), *Manual of Public International Law* (New York: Macmillan/St Martin's Press, 1968)

Nardin, T., *Law, Morality and the Relations of States* (Princeton, NJ: Princeton University Press, 1983)

Neff, S., *Justice Among Nations* (Cambridge, MA: Harvard University Press, 2014)

Nissel, A., 'The duality of state responsibility' (2013) 44 *Columbia Human Rights Law Review* 793

Nollkaemper, A., *National Courts and the International Rule of Law* (Oxford: Oxford University Press, 2012)

'Constitutionalization and the unity of the law of international responsibility' (2009) 16 *Journal of Global Legal Studies* 535

Nollkaemper, A. and Jacobs, D., 'Shared responsibility in international law: a conceptual framework' (2013) 34 *Michigan Journal of International Law* 408

Nolte, G., 'From Dionisio Anzilotti to Roberto Ago: the classical international law of state responsibility and the traditional primacy of a bilateral conception of inter-state relations' (2002) 13 *European Journal of International Law* 1083

Nutkiewicz, M., 'Samuel Pufendorf: obligation as the basis of the state' (1983) 21 *Journal of the History of Philosophy* 15

O'Connell, D. P., *International Law*, 2nd edn (London: Stevens & Sons, 1970)

International Law for Students (London: Stevens & Sons, 1971)

'Jus cogens, international law's higher ethical norms', in Donald Earl Childress III (ed.), *The Role of Ethics in International Law* (Cambridge: Cambridge University Press, 2012)

O'Hagan, T., *The End of Law?* (Oxford: Blackwell, 1984)

Onuf, G. and Birney, R. K., 'Peremptory norms of international law: their source, function and future' (1974) 4 *Denver Journal of International Law and Policy* 187

Onuf, N., 'Global law-making and legal thought', in N. Onuf (ed.), *Law-Making in the Global Community* (Durham: North Carolina Academic Press, 1982)

'Do rules say what they do? From ordinary language to international law' (1985) 26 *Harvard Journal of International Law* 385

World of Our Making: Rules and Rules in Social Theory and International Relations (Columbia: University of South Carolina Press, 1989)

'The constitution of international society' (1994) 5 *European Journal of International Law* 1

'Constructivism: a user's manual', in V. Kublakova, N. Onuf and P. Kowert (eds.), *International Relations in a Constructed World* (New York: Sharpe, 1998)

Onuma, Y., *Le Droit International et le Japon: Une Vision Trans-Civilisationnelle du Monde* (Paris: Pedone, 2016)

Oppenheim, L., *International Law: A Treatise*, 1st edn (London: Longmans, Green, 1905)

'The science of international law: its task and method' (1908) 2 *American Journal of International Law* 313

Orakhelashvili, A., *Peremptory Norms in International Law* (Oxford: Oxford University Press, 2006)

The Interpretation of Acts and Rules in Public International Law (Oxford: Oxford University Press, 2008)

Research Handbook on the Theory and History of International Law (Cheltenham: Elgar, 2013)

Orford, A., 'The destiny of international law' (2004) 17 *Leiden Journal of International Law* 441

'International law and the limits of history', in W. Werner, A. Galan and M. de Hoon (eds.), *The Law of International Lawyers: Reading Martti Koskenniemi* (Cambridge: Cambridge University Press, 2017) 265

Orford, A. and Hoffmann, F. (eds.), *The Oxford Handbook of the Theory of International Law* (Oxford: Oxford University Press, 2016)

Osiander, A., 'Sovereignty, international relations, and the Westphalian myth' (2001) 55 *International Organization* 251

Ost, F., *Du Sinaï au Champ-de-Mars: L'autre et le même au fondement du droit* (Paris: Lessius, 1999)

(ed.), *Le Temps du Droit* (Paris: Les Éditions Odile Jacob, 1999)

Raconter la loi: aux sources de l'imaginaire juridique (Paris: Les Éditions Odile Jacob, 2004)

Ozsu, U., 'The question of form: methodological notes on dialectics and international law' (2010) 23 *Leiden Journal of International Law* 687

Paddeu, F., 'A genealogy of force majeure in international law' (2013) 82 *British Yearbook of International Law* 381

Pagden, A. and Lawrence, J. (eds.), *Vitoria: Political Writings* (Cambridge: Cambridge University Press, 1991)

Palladini, F., 'Pufendorf disciple of Hobbes: the nature of man and the state of nature: the doctrine of socialitas' (2008) 34 *History of European Ideas* 26

Papstavridis, E., 'Interpretation of security council resolutions under chapter VII in the aftermath of the Iraqi crisis' (2007) *International and Comparative Law Quarterly* 83

Paust, J., 'The reality of jus cogens' (1981) 7 *Connecticut Journal of International Law* 81

Pellet, A., 'The opinions of the Badinter Arbitration Committee. A second breath for the self-determination of peoples' (1992) 3 *European Journal of International Law* 178

'Conclusions', in C. Tomuschat and J.-M. Thouvenin (eds.), *The Fundamental Rules of the International Legal Order: Jus Cogens and Obligations Erga Omnes* (Leiden: Martinus Nijhoff, 2006)

'Cours général: le droit international entre souveraineté et communauté international' (2007) 2 *Anuário Brasileiro de Direito Internacional* 12

'The ILC's Articles on State Responsibility', in James Crawford et al. (eds.), *The Law of International Responsibility* (Oxford: Oxford University Press, 2010)

'Article 38', in A. Zimmermann, C. Tomuschat, K. Oellers-Frahm and C. Tams (eds.), *The Statute of the International Court of Justice: A Commentary*, 2nd edn (Oxford: Oxford University Press, 2012)

Pessôa, E., *Projecto de Codigo de Direito Internacional Publico* (Rio de Janeiro: Imprensa Nacional, 1911)

Peters, A., 'Compensatory constitutionalism: the function and potential of fundamental international norms and structures' (2006) 19 *Leiden Journal of International Law* 579

'The merits of global constitutionalism' (2009) 16 *Indiana Journal of Global Legal Studies* 397

'Does Kosovo Lie in the Lotus-Land of Freedom?' (2011) 24 *Leiden Journal of International Law* 95

'Are we moving towards constitutionalisation of the world community', in A. Cassese (ed.), *Realising Utopia: The Future of International Law* (Oxford: Oxford University Press, 2012)

Piirimäe, P., 'The Westphalian myth and the idea of external sovereignty', in Skinner Kalmo (ed.), *Sovereignty in Fragments: The Past, Present and Future of a Contested Concept* (Cambridge: Cambridge University Press, 2010)

Posner, R. A., 'Path-dependency, pragmatism, and a critique of history in adjudication and legal scholarship' (2000) 67 *University of Chicago Law Review* 573

Postema, G., 'Law's rule, reflexivity, mutual accountability, and the rule of law', in Xiaobo Zhai and Michael Quinn (eds.), *Bentham's Theory of Law and Public Opinion* (Cambridge: Cambridge University Press, 2014)

Pouillon, J., 'L'analyse des myths' (1966) 6 *L'Homme* 100

Prost, M., *The Concept of Unity in Public International Law* (Oxford: Hart, 2012)

Pufendorf, S., *On the Law of Nature and of Nations*, trans C. H. Oldfather and W. A. Oldfather (Oxford: Clarendon Press, 1934, first published 1672)

Purvis, N., 'Critical legal studies in public international law' (1991) 32 *Harvard Journal of International Law* 81

Ragazzi, M., *The Concept of International Obligations Erga Omnes* (Oxford: Clarendon Press, 1997)

Raic, D., *Statehood and the Law of Self-Determination* (Alphen aan den Rijn, Netherlands: Kluwer Law International, 2002)

Rajkovic, N., 'Rules, lawyering, and the politics of legality: critical sociology and international law's rule' (2014) 27 *Leiden Journal of International Law* 331

Rasulov, A., 'The life and times of the modern law of reservations: the doctrinal genealogy of general comment no. 24' (2009) 14 *Austrian Review of International and European Law* 103

'Writing about empire: remarks on the logic of a discourse' (2010) 23 *Leiden Journal of International Law* 449

'The doctrine of sources in the discourses of the Permanent Court of International Justice', in C. Tams and M. Fitzmaurice (eds.), *Legacies of the Permanent Court of International Justice* (Leiden: Martinus Nijhoff, 2013)

Raz, J., *The Morality of Freedom* (Oxford: Clarendon Press, 1986)

Reisman, M., 'International lawmaking: a process of communication' (1981) 75 *American Society of International Law Proceedings* 101

'Lassa Oppenheim's nine lives' (1994) 19 *Yale Journal of International Law* 255

Reisman, M. W., Wiessner, S. and Willard, A. R., 'The New Haven School: a brief introduction' (2007) 32 *Yale Journal of International Law* 575

Reitz, J., 'The importance of and need for legal science', *University of Iowa Legal Studies Research Paper* 2012

Reus-Smit, C., 'Introduction', in Christian Reus-Smit (ed.), *The Politics of International Law* (Cambridge: Cambridge University Press, 2004)

Reuter, P., *Introduction to the Law of Treaties*, 2nd edn (London: Routledge, 1995)

Rivier, A., *Principles du droit des Gens* (1896), p. 35. For a recognition of such paternity, A. Carty, *Philosophy of International Law* (Edinburgh: Edinburgh University Press, 2007)

Robledo, A. and Gomez, 'Le ius cogens international: sa genèse, sa nature, ses fonctions' (1981) 172 *Collected Courses of the Hague Academy on International Law* 9

Rosen, L., *Law as Culture: An Invitation* (Princeton, NJ: Princeton University Press, 2006)

Ryngaert, C. and Sobrie, S., 'Recognition of states: international law or realpolitik? The practice of recognition in the wake of Kosovo, South Ossetia, and Abkhazia' (2011) 24 *Leiden Journal of International Law* 467

Saul, M., 'Identifying jus cogens norms: the interaction of scholars and international judges' (2015) 5 *Asian Journal of International Law* 26

Schachter, O., 'International law in theory and practice: general course in public international law' (1982-V) 178 *Recueil des cours* 1

'Entangled treaty and custom', in Y. Dinstein (ed.), *International Law at a Time of Perplexity: Essays in Honour of Shabtai Rosenne* (Dordrecht: Martinus Nijhoff, 1988)

Schauer, F., *Playing by the Rules* (Oxford: Clarendon Press, 1991)

'Amending the presuppositions of a constitution', in S. Levinson (ed.), *Responding to Imperfection* (Princeton, NJ: Princeton University Press, 1995)

Thinking Like a Lawyer: A New Introduction to Legal Reasoning (Cambridge: Harvard University Press, 2009)

'Is the rule of recognition a rule?' (2012) 3 *Transnational Legal Theory* 2, 173

Schecaira, F. P., *Legal Scholarship as a Source* (New York: Springer, 2013)

Schlag, P., "Le hors de texte, c'est moi': the politics of form and the domestication of deconstruction' (1989–90) 11 *Cardozo Law Review* 1631

'Normative and nowhere to go' (1990) 43 *Stanford Law Review* 167

'Normativity and the politics of form' (1991) 139 *University of Pennsylvania Law Review* 4, 802

Laying Dow the Law: Mysticism, Fetishism, and the American Legal Mind (New York: New York University Press, 1996)

'Law as the continuation of god by other means' (1997) *California Law Review* 85.

'The empty circles of liberal justification' (1997) 96 *Michigan Law Review* 1

'The aesthetics of American law' (2002) 115 *Harvard Law Review* 1047

'A brief survey of deconstruction' (2005) 27 *Cardozo Law Review* 741

Schmitt, C., *Political Theology: Four Chapters on the Concept of Sovereignty*, trans. George Schwab (Chicago: University of Chicago Press, 1985)

Schubert, J. D., 'Suffering/symbolic violence', in Michael Grenfell (ed.), *Pierre Bourdieu: Key Concepts*, 2nd edn (Durham, NC: Acumen Press, 2012)

Schultz, T., *Transnational Legality: Stateless Law and International Arbitration* (Oxford: Oxford University Press, 2014)

Schwarzenberger, G., *International Law*, 3rd edn (London: Stevens & Sons, 1957)

Schwebel, S. M., 'The inter-active influence of the International Court of Justice and the International Law Commission', in A. Calixto et al. (eds.), *Liber Amicorum 'In Memoriam' of José María Ruda* (The Hague: Kluwer, 2000)

Scobbie, I., 'Towards the elimination of international law: some radical scepticism about sceptical radicalism' (1990) 61 *British Yearbook of International Law* 339

'The theorist as judge: Hersch Lauterpacht's concept of the international judicial function' (1997) 2 *European Journal of International Law* 264

Scott, S. V., 'International law as ideology: theorizing the relationship between international law and international politics' (1994) 5 *European Journal of International Law* 313

Shaffer, G. and Ginsburg, T., 'The empirical turn in international legal scholarship' (2012) 106 *American Journal of International Law* 1

Shaw, M., *International Law*, 5th edn (Cambridge: Cambridge University Press, 2003)

International Law, 7th edn (Cambridge: Cambridge University Press, 2014)

Shelton, D., 'Normativity hierarchy in international law' (2006) 100 *American Journal of International Law* 291

Shklar, J. N., *Legalism: Law, Morals, and Political Trials* (Cambridge, MA: Harvard University Press, 1986)

Simma, B., 'Self-contained regimes' (1985) 16 *Netherlands Yearbook of International Law* 112

'The contribution of Alfred Verdross to the theory of international law' (1995) 6 *European Journal of International Law* 33

Simma, B. and Pulkowski, D., 'Of planets and the universe: self-contained regimes and international law' (2006) 17 *European Journal of International Law* 483

Simpson, A. W. B., 'The common law and legal theory' in A. W. B. Simpson (ed.), *Oxford Essays in Jurisprudence*, second series (Oxford: Clarendon Press, 1973)

Simpson, G., 'Book review of *Peremptory Norms (Jus Cogens) in International Law: Historical Developments, Criteria, Present Development* by Lauri Hannikainen' (1991) 13 *Australia Yearbook of International Law* 180

'On the magic mountain: teaching public international law' (1999) 10 *European Journal of International Law* 70

'The sentimental life of international law' (2015) 3 *London Review of International Law* 3

Singh, S., 'International legal positivism and new approaches to international law', in J. Kammerhofer and J. d'Aspremont (eds.), *International Legal Positivism in a Postmodern World* (Cambridge: Cambridge University Press, 2014)

Skouteris, T., *The Notion of Progress in International Law Discourse* (The Hague: TMC Asser Press, 2010)

Somek, A., 'Defective law', *University of Iowa Legal Studies Research Paper Series*, no. 10–33, December 2010

'Legal science as a source of law: a late reply by Puchta to Kantorowicz', *University of Iowa Legal Studies Research Paper Series*, no. 13–7.

Sorel, J. M., 'Article 31', in P. Klein and O. Corten (eds.), *Les Conventions de Vienne sur le Droit des Traités: Commentaire Article par Article* (Brussels: Bruylant, 2006)

Sørensen, M., 'Principes de droit international public' (1960-III) 101 *Collected Courses of the Hague Academy on International Law* 1

Spiermann, O., 'Who attempts too much does nothing well': the 1920 Advisory Committee of Jurists and the Statute of the Permanent Court of International Justice' (2002) 73 *British Yearbook of International Law* 187

International Legal Argument in the Permanent Court of International Justice, The Rise of the International Judiciary (Cambridge: Cambridge University Press, 2005)

Stern, B., 'Et si on utilisait la notion de préjudice juridique? Retour sur une notion délaissée à l'occasion de la fin des travaux de la C.D.I sur la responsabilité des États' (2001) 47 *Annuaire français de droit international* 3

'The elements of an internationally wrongful act', in J. Crawford, A. Pellet and S. Olleson (eds.), *The Law of International Responsibility* (Oxford: Oxford University Press, 2010)

Stone, J., *Legal System and Lawyers' Reasonings* (Redwood City, CA: Stanford University Press, 1968)

Strauss, D. F., *The Life of Jesus Critically Examined*, trans George Eliot, 4th edn (London [1835])

Sunstein, C. R., *Leal Reasoning and Political Conflict* (Oxford: Oxford University Press, 1996)

Sur, S., 'Discussion', in A. Casesse and J. Weiler (eds.), *Change and Stability in International Law-Making* (Berlin: de Gruyter, 1988)

Suy, I. E., 'The concept of jus cogens in public international law', in *Lagonissi Conference: Papers and Proceedings*, vol. II (Geneva: Carnegie Endowment for International Peace, 1967)

Sztucki, J., *Jus Cogens and the Vienna Convention on the Law of Treaties: A Critical Appraisal* (Wien: Springer-Verlag, 1974)

Tamanaha, B., *A General Jurisprudence of Law and Society* (Oxford: Oxford University Press, 2001)

'The history and elements of the rule of law' (2012) *Singapore Journal of Legal Studies* 232

Tams, C., 'Meta-custom and the court: a study in judicial law-making' (2015) 14 *Law and Practice of International Courts and Tribunals* 51

Tams, C. and Tzanakopoulos, A., '*Barcelona Traction* at 40: the ICJ as an agent of legal development' (2010) 23 *Leiden Journal of International Law* 781

Terdiman, R., 'Introduction to Pierre Bourdieu', in 'The force of law: toward a sociology of the juridical field' (1987) 38 *Hastings Law Journal* 805

Teschke, B., *The Myth of 1648: Class, Geopolitics, and the Making of Modern International Relations* (London: Verso, 2009)

Thirlway, H., *The Sources of International Law* (Oxford: Oxford University Press, 2014)

Tomuschat, C., 'International law: ensuring the survival of mankind on the eve of a new century: general course on public international law' (1999) 281 *Collected Courses of the Hague Academy on International Law* 96

'Obligations arising from states without or against their will' (2013) 241 *Collected Courses of the Hague Academy on International Law* 195

Troper, M., 'Les contraintes de l'argumentation juridique dans la production des normes', in O. Pfersmann and G. Timsti (eds.), *Raisonnement Juridique et Interpretation* (Paris: Publication de la Sorbonne, 2001)

Turk, D., 'Recognition of states: a comment' (1993) 4 *European Journal of International Law* 66

Tzevelekos, V., 'The use of article 31(3)(c) of the VCLT in the case law of the ECtHR: an effective anti-fragmentation tool or a selective loophole for the reinforcement of human rights teleology? Between evolution and systemic integration' (2010) 31 *Michigan Journal of International Law* 621

'Juris dicere: custom as matrix, custom as a norm, and the role of judges of (their) ideology in custom making', in N. Rajkovic, T. Aalberts and T. Gammeltoft-Hansen (eds.), *Power of Legality: Practices of International Law and Their Politics* (Cambridge: Cambridge University Press, 2016)

Unger, R. M., *Knowledge and Politics* (New York: Free Press, 1975)

What Should Legal Analysis Become (New York: Verso, 1996)

Vaihinger, H., *La Philosophie du comme si* (1911)

van Aaken, A., 'Behavioral international law and economics' (2014) 55 *Harvard International Law Journal* 421

van Damme, I., 'Some observations about the ILC Study Report on the Fragmentation of International Law: WTO treaty interpretation against the background of other international law' (2006) 17 *Finnish Yearbook of International Law* 21

Treaty Interpretation by the WTO Appellate Body (Oxford: Oxford University Press, 2009)

van de Kerchove, M. and Ost, F., *Legal System Between Order and Disorder*, trans. Iian Stewart (Oxford: Clarendon Press, 1995)

van Hoof, G. J. H. *Rethinking the Sources of International Law* (Deventer: Kluwer Law, 1983)

Venzke, I., 'The role of international courts as interpreters and developers of the law: working out the jurisgenerative practice of interpretation' (2011) 34 *Loyola of Los Angeles International and Comparative Law Review* 99

How Interpretation Makes International Law: On Semantic Change and Normative Twists (Oxford: Oxford University Press, 2012)

'Contemporary theories of international law-making', in C. Brölmann and Y. Radi (eds.), *Research Handbook on the Theory and Practice of International Law-Making* (2014)

'The travails of legal positivism from post-modern perspectives: performativity, deconstructions and governmentality', in J. Kammerhofer and J. d'Aspremont (eds.), *International Legal Positivism in a Postmodern World* (Cambridge: Cambridge University Press, 2014)

'Cracking the frame? On the prospects of change in a world of struggle' (2016) 27 *European Journal of International Law* 831

Verdier, P.-H. and Voeten, E., 'How does customary international law change? The case of state immunity' (2015) 59 *International Studies Quarterly* 209

Verdross, A., 'Forbidden treaties in international law' (1937) 31 *American Journal of International Law* 571

Verdross, A. and Simma, B., *Universelles Völkerrecht: Theorie und Praxis (dritte Auflage)* 3rd edn (London: Duncker & Humblot, 1984)

Verhoeven, J., 'Considérations sur ce qui est commun : cours général de droit international public' (2008) 334 *Collected Courses of the Hague Academy on International Law* 9

'Invalidity of treaties: anything new in/under the Vienna Conventions?', in E. Cannizzaro (ed.) *The Law of Treaties Beyond the Vienna Convention* (Oxford: Oxford University Press, 2011)

Vidmar, J., 'Explaining the legal effects of recognition' (2012) 61 *International and Comparative Law Quarterly* 361

'Norm conflicts and hierarchy in international law: towards a vertical international legal system', in E. De Wet and J. Vidmar (eds.), *Hierarchy in International Law: The Place of Human Rights* (Oxford: Oxford University Press, 2012)

Democratic Statehood in International Law: The Emergence of New States in Post-Cold War Practice (Oxford: Hart, 2013)

'Territorial integrity and the law of statehood' (2013) 44 *George Washington International Law Review* 101

'The concept of the state and its right of existence' (2015) 4 *Cambridge Journal of International and Comparative Law* 547

Villiger, M. E., *Customary International Law and Treaties: A Study of Their Interactions and Interrelations with Special Consideration of the 1969 Vienna Convention on the Law of Treaties* (Dordrecht: Martinus Nijhoff, 1985)

Vinuales, J., 'On legal inquiry', in D. Alland, V. Chetail, O. de Frouville and J. Vinuales (eds.), *Unity and Diversity of International Law: Essays in Honour of Professor Pierre-Marie Dupuy* (Leiden: Martinus Nijhoff, 2014)

Virally, M., 'La notion de fonction dans la théorie de l'organisation internationale', in Charles E. Rousseau (ed.), *Mélanges offerts à Charles Rousseau: La Communauté internationale* (Paris: Pedone, 1974)

von Bernstorff, J., 'International legal scholarship as a cooling medium in international law and politics' (2014) 25 *European Journal of International Law* 977

von Bogdandy, A., Dann, P. and Goldmann, M., 'Developing the publicness of public international law: towards a legal framework for global governance activities' (2008) 9 *German Law Journal* 1375

Waibel, M., 'Demystifying the art of interpretation' (2011) 22 *European Journal of International Law* 571

Walker, N. 'Beyond boundary disputes and basic grids: mapping the global disorder of normative orders' (2008) 6 *I.CONnect* 373

Watson, J., 'State consent and the sources of international obligation jurisprudence of international law: classic and modern views' (1992) 86 *American Society of International Law Proceedings* 108

Weatherall, T., 'Against fragmentation: international common law and the development of jus cogens' (2014), available at SSRN: http://ssrn.com/abstract=2565165.

Jus Cogens: International Law and Social Contract (Cambridge: Cambridge University Press, 2015)

Weckel, P., 'Ouverture de la réflexion sur le droit international à la science des systèmes', in D. Alland, V. Chetail, O. de Frouville and J. Vinuales (eds.), *Unity and Diversity of International Law: Essays in Honour of Professor Pierre-Marie Dupuy* (Leiden: Martinus Nijhoff, 2014)

Weil, P., 'Le droit international en quête de son identité: cours général de droit international public' (1992) 237 *Recueil des cours* 131

Wendel, W. B., *Lawyers and Fidelity to Law* (Princeton, NJ: Princeton University Press, 2010)

Wheaton, H., *Elements of International Law*, vol. 1 (London: B Fellowes, 1836)

Wippman, D., 'The International Criminal Court', in C. Reus-Smit (ed.), *The Politics of International Law* (Cambridge: Cambridge University Press, 2004)

Wolff, C., *Law of Nations Treated According to a Scientific Method*, trans. J. H. Drake (Oxord: Clarendon Press, 1934)

Wood, M., 'What is public international law? The need for clarity about sources' (2011) 1 *Asian Journal of International Law* 205

Woolsey, T. D., *International Law* (New York: Scribner, Armstrong, 1877)

Yee, S., 'Article 38 of the ICJ statute and applicable law: selected issues in recent cases' (2016) 7 *Journal of International Dispute Settlement* 472

Zarbiyev, F., *Le Discours Interprétatif en Droit International Contemporain: Un Essai Critique* (Brussels: Bruylant, 2015)

Zemanek, K., 'The legal foundations of the international system' (1997) 266 *Collected Courses of the Hague Academy on International Law* 9

'The metamorphosis of jus cogens: from an institution of treaty law to the bedrock of the international legal order?', in E. Cannizzaro (ed.), *The Law of Treaties Beyond the Vienna Convention* (Oxford: Oxford University Press, 2011)

INDEX

CAMBRIDGE STUDIES IN INTERNATIONAL
AND COMPARATIVE LAW

Books in the Series